Overview-Map Key

Five-Star Trails

Louisville
& Southern Indiana

Your Guide to the Area's Most Beautiful Hikes

Valerie Askren

 MENASHA RIDGE PRESS
menasharidge.com

Five-Star Trails: Louisville and Southern Indiana

All rights reserved
Published by Menasha Ridge Press
Distributed by Publishers Group West
Printed in the United States of America
First edition, first printing

Editors: Larry Bleiberg and Susan Haynes
Project editor: Ritchey Halphen
Cover design and cartography: Scott McGrew
Text design: Annie Long
Cover and interior photos: Valerie Askren except where noted
Proofreader: Holly Cross
Indexer: Ann Cassar / Cassar Technical Services

Frontispiece: Whether covered with ice in late winter or gushing with warm spring rains, waterfalls delight the soul. *(See Hike 17, Fairmount Falls, page 124.)*

Library of Congress Cataloging-in-Publication Data

Askren, Valerie.
 Five-star trails: Louisville and southern Indiana : your guide to the area's most beautiful hikes / Valerie Askren.
   p. cm.
 Includes index.
 ISBN 13: 978-0-89732-625-4 — ISBN 10: 0-89732-625-3
 eISBN: 978-0-89732-626-1
 1. Hiking—Kentucky—Louisville Region—Guidebooks.
 2. Hiking—Indiana—Guidebooks. 3. Trails—Kentucky—
Louisville Region—Guidebooks. 4. Trails—Indiana—
Guidebooks. 5. Louisville Region (Ky.)—Guidebooks.
 6. Indiana—Guidebooks. I. Title.
 GV199.42.K42.L683 2013
 796.5209772--dc23
                2012047135

Menasha Ridge Press
P.O. Box 43673
Birmingham, AL 35243
menasharidgepress.com

Disclaimer

This book is meant only as a guide to select trails in and around Louisville, Kentucky, and does not guarantee hiker safety in any way—you hike at your own risk. Neither Menasha Ridge Press nor Valerie Askren is liable for property loss or damage, personal injury, or death that may result from accessing or hiking the trails described in this guide. Be especially cautious when walking in potentially hazardous terrains with, for example, steep inclines or drop-offs. Do not attempt to explore terrain that may be beyond your abilities. Please read carefully the introduction to this book, as well as safety information from other sources. Familiarize yourself with current weather reports and maps of the area you plan to visit (in addition to the maps provided in this guidebook). Be cognizant of park regulations, and always follow them. *Do not take chances.*

Contents

Indiana: North of Louisville and West of I-65 155

Indiana: North of Louisville and East of I-65 225

Appendixes & Index 255

Dedication

To my parents, who first shared with me their love of the outdoors; to my husband, who understands my need to be immersed in nature; and to my children, who have inherited the joy of frolicking with Mother Earth.

Acknowledgments

Hiking and walking opportunities abound in the Greater Louisville area, thanks in part to those 19th-century visionaries who believed that communing with nature was essential in order for urban dwellers to thrive. With the establishment of the city's first park, Baxter Square Park, in 1880 and the purchase of a 313-acre tract of land called Burnt Knob (which later became Iroquois Park) by Mayor Charles Jacob in 1888, Louisville laid the foundation for a metropolitan area laced with urban forests, walking trails, picnic areas, and other forms of outdoor recreation.

Louisville established the Board of Parks Commissioners in 1890 with the intent of developing a park in each section of the city: east, west, and south, with the north bounded by the Ohio River. A year later the city hired Frederick Law Olmsted, the father of American landscape architecture, to design seven parks plus several interconnecting parkways. Olmsted was already well known for designing such notable spaces as Central Park in New York; the Niagara Reservation, adjoining Niagara Falls; George Vanderbilt's Biltmore Estate, in North Carolina; Chicago's "Emerald Necklace" of parks and boulevards; and the grounds surrounding the U.S. Capitol. Clearly, the city of Louisville was aiming high in its desire to build a world-class park system.

Throughout the 20th century, Louisville continued investing in that system by acquiring land to establish the Jefferson Memorial Forest—now the nation's largest urban forest—in 1946 and the "Rainbow Chain of County Parks" in the 1950s, as well as creating a unified city–county Metropolitan Park and Recreation Board in 1968.

And Louisville hasn't even begun to slow down. The 21st century has brought a host of new land acquisitions, including the Louisville Extreme Park and several historic properties; the latest addition, the nearly 4,000-acre Parklands of Floyds Fork, is still under development. To preserve and expand the city's park system in perpetuity, Louisville works with several nonprofit organizations such as 21st Century Parks, the Olmsted Park Conservancy, the Future Fund Land Trust, The Trust for Public Land, and the Louisville and Jefferson County Environmental Trust.

Outside Louisville, many other entities work diligently to protect our natural areas while providing additional opportunities for outdoor recreation. Private endowments (such as Bernheim Arboretum and Research Forest and Creasey Mahan Nature Preserve), nonprofit organizations (including The Nature Conservancy), state agencies (both Kentucky's and Indiana's state parks and nature preserves), and national forests and wildlife refuges all provide an endless array of hiking opportunities.

It is these partners and others whom we should acknowledge and thank for their vision and perseverance.

—*Valerie Askren*

Preface

Despite the myriad hiking possibilities in the Greater Louisville area, many people are familiar with only a few of the better-known outdoor locales. While these might be terrific choices, the most popular places tend to be packed to the gills on beautiful weekends and holidays. Further, hiking the same places again and again can become a bit tedious.

Wouldn't it be cool to find some new ones?

Hiking is enjoying an explosion in popularity, as more people are turning to walking for its health and relaxation benefits. And now that the baby-boom generation is beginning to retire, more people are looking for recreational opportunities. Simultaneously, Generations X and Y are increasingly strapped with children and demanding careers that compete for their free time, yet they're not ready to give up their outdoor pursuits.

But how many of us have the time to hike the Appalachian Trail? And who wants to spend more time driving to a day hike than actually being out on the trail? I say, *think global, hike local*.

Happily, Louisville and the surrounding countryside brim with hiking opportunities off the beaten path. Nearly everyone will discover a trail in this book that's just right for them—from a half-mile stroll on a level trail to a 12.5-mile hike across rugged terrain. Family visiting from out of town? Try a paved path on the riverfront. Kids out of school for the day? Check out one of the many hiking areas with a nature center. Looking for a romantic but cheap date? Explore one of the region's many waterfalls. History buff? Geology nerd? There's a trail for that, too!

Situated along the Ohio River, the Louisville area is chock-full of stunning wildflower displays, towering forests, fascinating caves, quiet trails, and friendly naturalists. Stroll a paved riverfront trail during lunch to clear your head or burn off some steam. After work, you're just minutes away from a heart-pumping power walk through a forest or a slice of solitude overlooking a peaceful stream. On half- or full-day trips, you can explore a multitude of small, narrow gorges; steep ravines; tumbling creeks; and dazzling overlooks.

Five-Star Trails: Louisville and Southern Indiana lets you experience all this and more.

Recommended Hikes

Best for Geology

Best for History

Best for Kids

Best for Lake Views

Best for Ohio River Views

THE WEB OF LIFE. *(See Hike 13, Otter Creek Loop, page 97.)*

Best Paved Trails

Best for Rigor

Best for Solitude

Best for Waterfalls

Best for Waterfowl

Best for Wildflowers

ART IS WHERE YOU ARE. *(See Hike 6, Iroquois Park Summit, page 52.)*

Introduction

About This Book

Five-Star Trails: Louisville and Southern Indiana covers 37 hikes in the city and surrounding area. Given that Louisville is situated on the Ohio River, about half of the hikes are south of the river, in north-central Kentucky, and about half are north of the river, in southern Indiana.

Geologically speaking, Louisville sits on the far western fringe of the Outer Bluegrass, characterized by rolling hills and narrow ridgetops. Deciduous-hardwood forests dominated by oak, maple, beech, and hickory cover most of this area, except for the occasional meadow, a leftover remnant of land that was cleared for farming. Just south of Louisville lies the Knobs, a region distinguished by distinctive steep-sloping, often cone-shaped hills capped with limestone and sandstone, rendering their peaks more erosion-resistant compared with the rock beneath. Southwest of Louisville lie the Mississippian Plateau and the far-eastern edge of the Muldraugh Hills. Unlike the isolated hills of the Knobs, the Muldraughs are an escarpment, or ring of continuous hills, that divides the Plateau from the Bluegrass.

North of Louisville, in southern Indiana, the terrain is also quite hilly and in geological terms is referred to as the Southern Hills and Lowlands. This part of the Hoosier State was largely untouched by encroaching glaciers, preserving a rich ecosystem of plants and animals that thrive on the steeper topography found closer to the river.

The hikes in this book are divided into five geographic regions:

LOUISVILLE: INSIDE I-265 This section comprises hikes close to the heart of the city, bounded by Interstate 265 to both the south (in Kentucky, where it's known as the Gene Snyder Freeway) and the north (in Indiana). Most of these hikes are lightly wooded trails traversing a gently rolling landscape in urban parks, or they consist of level paved walkways adjacent to the Ohio River. (The exception is the trail at Iroquois Park, which ascends a 260-foot knob.) Several of the hikes begin at nature centers, making them perfect for cold or rainy days.

KENTUCKY: SOUTH OF LOUISVILLE AND WEST OF I-65 The trails southwest of Louisville generally travel through moderately hilly woods, including the Jefferson Memorial Forest. Two hikes lie just south of the Ohio River. (Fort Knox, a U.S. Army base southwest of Louisville, limits additional hiking opportunities.)

KENTUCKY: SOUTH OF LOUISVILLE AND EAST OF I-65 Most of the terrain in this region encompasses gently rolling hills, with the exception of the Knobs due south of Louisville. Adding to the diversity of trails in this region are Fairmount Falls, Taylorsville Lake, and Salato Wildlife Education Center.

INDIANA: NORTH OF LOUISVILLE AND WEST OF I-65 Hiking areas in the northwest quadrant can vary from rolling hills to steep ravines and cliffs, the latter being representative of the karst geology of southern Indiana. The Hoosier National Forest dominates much of this region. Also found here are the remnants of an old-growth forest.

INDIANA: NORTH OF LOUISVILLE AND EAST OF I-65 The terrain in this section varies tremendously, from small, intimate gorges (which escaped the leveling glacial flows that transformed other parts of Indiana) to the shallow lakes and waterfowl-breeding grounds of the Muscatatuck Plateau.

How to Use This Guidebook

The following section walks you through this guidebook's organization, making it easy and convenient to plan great hikes.

Overview Map, Map Key, & Map Legend

The overview map on the inside front cover shows the primary trailheads for all 37 hikes. The numbers on the overview map pair with the map key on the facing page. A legend explaining the map symbols used throughout the book appears on the inside back cover.

Trail Maps

In addition to the overview map on the inside cover, a detailed map of each hike's route appears with its profile. On each of these maps, symbols indicate the trailhead, the complete route, significant features, facilities, and topographic landmarks such as creeks, overlooks, and peaks.

To produce the highly accurate maps in this book, I used a handheld GPS unit to gather data while hiking each route, then sent that data to Menasha Ridge Press's expert cartographers. Be aware, though, that your GPS device is no substitute for sound, sensible navigation that takes into account the conditions that you observe while hiking.

Further, despite the high quality of the maps in this guidebook, the publisher and myself strongly recommend that you always carry an additional map, such as the ones noted in each profile opener's "Maps" listing.

Elevation Profile (Diagram)

For trails with significant changes in elevation, the hike descriptions include this graphical element. Entries for fairly flat routes, such as a lake loop, do *not* display an elevation profile. Also, each entry's key information lists the elevation at the start of that specific route to its highest point.

For hike descriptions that include an elevation profile, this diagram represents the rises and falls of the trail as viewed from the side, over the complete distance (in miles) of that trail. On the diagram's vertical axis, or height scale, the number of feet indicated between each tick mark lets you visualize the climb. To avoid making flat hikes look steep and steep hikes appear flat, varying height scales provide an accurate image of each hike's climbing challenge.

The Hike Profile

Each profile opens with the hike's star ratings, GPS trailhead coordinates, and other key at-a-glance information—from the trail's distance and configuration to contacts for local information. Each profile also includes a map (see "Trail Maps," page 3). The main text for each profile includes four sections: Overview, Route Details, Nearby Attractions, and Directions (for driving to the trailhead area).

STAR RATINGS

The hikes in *Five-Star Trails: Louisville and Southern Indiana* have been carefully chosen to give the hiker an overall five-star experience and represent the diversity of trails found in the region. Each hike is assigned a one- to five-star rating in each of the following categories: scenery, trail condition, suitability for children, level of difficulty, and degree of solitude. While one hike may receive a five-star rating for its stunning scenery, that same trail may rank as a two-star trail for children. Similarly, another hike might receive two stars for difficulty but earn five stars for solitude. While it's unlikely that any one trail could receive a five-star rating in all five categories, each trail offers excellence in at least one category, if not others.

Here's how the star ratings for each of the five categories break down:

FOR SCENERY:

★ ★ ★ ★ ★   Unique, picturesque panoramas

★ ★ ★ ★   Diverse vistas

★ ★ ★   Pleasant views

★ ★   Unchanging landscape

★   Not selected for scenery

FOR TRAIL CONDITION:

★ ★ ★ ★ ★   Consistently well maintained

★ ★ ★ ★   Stable, with no surprises

★ ★ ★   Average terrain to negotiate

★ ★   Inconsistent, with good and poor areas

★   Rocky, overgrown, or often muddy

FOR CHILDREN:

★ ★ ★ ★ ★   Babes in strollers are welcome

★ ★ ★ ★   Fun for any kid past the toddler stage

★ ★ ★   Good for young hikers with proven stamina

★ ★   Not enjoyable for children

★   Not advisable for children

FOR DIFFICULTY:

★ ★ ★ ★ ★   Grueling

★ ★ ★ ★   Strenuous

★ ★ ★   Moderate—won't beat you up, but you'll know you've been hiking

★ ★   Easy, with patches of moderate

★   Good for a relaxing stroll

FOR SOLITUDE:

★ ★ ★ ★ ★   Positively tranquil

★ ★ ★ ★   Spurts of isolation

★ ★ ★   Moderately secluded

★ ★   Crowded on weekends and holidays

★   Steady stream of individuals and/or groups

GPS TRAILHEAD COORDINATES

As noted in "Trail Maps," page 3, I used a handheld GPS unit to obtain geographic data and sent the information to the cartographers at Menasha Ridge. In the opener for each hike profile, the coordinates— the intersection of latitude (north) and longitude (west)—will orient you from the trailhead. In some cases, you can drive within viewing distance of a trailhead. Other hiking routes require a short walk to the trailhead from a parking area.

This guidebook uses the degree–decimal minute format for expressing GPS coordinates. The latitude–longitude grid system is likely quite familiar to you, but here's a refresher, pertinent to visualizing the coordinates:

Imaginary lines of latitude—called *parallels* and approximately 69 miles apart from each other—run horizontally around the globe. The equator is established to be 0°, and each parallel is indicated by degrees from the equator: up to 90°N at the North Pole and down to 90°S at the South Pole.

Imaginary lines of longitude—called *meridians*—run perpendicular to lines of latitude and are likewise indicated by degrees. Starting from 0° at the Prime Meridian in Greenwich, England, they continue to the east and west until they meet 180° later at the International Date Line in the Pacific Ocean. At the equator, longitude lines also are approximately 69 miles apart, but that distance narrows as the meridians converge toward the North and South Poles.

To convert GPS coordinates given in degrees, minutes, and seconds to degrees–decimal minutes, the seconds are divided by 60. For more on GPS technology, visit **usgs.gov.**

DISTANCE & CONFIGURATION

Distance indicates the length of the hike from start to finish, either round-trip or one-way depending on the trail configuration. If the hike description includes options to shorten or extend the hike, those distances will also be factored here. *Configuration* defines the type of route—for example, an out-and-back (which takes you in and out the same way), a point-to-point (or one-way route), a loop, a figure-eight, or a balloon.

HIKING TIME

Two to three miles per hour is a general rule of thumb for hiking the trails in this book, depending on the terrain and whether you have children with you. That pace typically allows time for taking photos, for dawdling and admiring views, and for alternating stretches of hills and descents. When deciding whether or not to follow a particular trail in this guidebook, consider your own pace, the weather, your general physical condition, and your energy level on a given day.

HIGHLIGHTS

This section lists features that draw hikers to the trail: waterfalls, historic sites, and the like.

ELEVATION

In each hikes's key information, you will see the elevation (in feet) at the trailhead and another figure for the peak height you will reach on the trail. For routes that involve significant ascents and descents, the hike profile also includes an elevation diagram (see page 3).

ACCESS

Fees or permits required to hike the trail are detailed here—and noted if there are none. Trail-access hours are also listed here.

MAPS

Resources for maps, in addition to those in this guidebook, are listed here. As noted earlier, we recommend that you carry more than one map—and that you consult those maps before heading out on the trail in order to resolve any confusion or discrepancy.

FACILITIES

Includes restrooms, phones, water, picnic tables, and other basics at or near the trailhead.

WHEELCHAIR ACCESS

Notes paved sections or other areas where persons with disabilities can safely use a wheelchair.

COMMENTS

Here you'll find assorted nuggets of information, such as whether or not dogs are allowed on the trails.

CONTACTS

Listed here are phone numbers and websites for checking trail conditions and gleaning other day-to-day information.

Overview, Route Details, Nearby Attractions, & Directions

These four elements compose the heart of the hike. "Overview" gives you a quick summary of what to expect on that trail; the "Route Details" guide you on the hike, from start to finish; and "Nearby

Attractions" suggests appealing adjacent sites, such as restaurants, museums, and other trails (note that not every hike profile has these). "Directions" will get you to the trailhead from a well-known road or highway.

Weather

As a river city, Louisville can get quite hot and humid during the summer. For that reason alone, hiking during June, July, and August can be less than ideal. During this time of year, you may want to consider a shorter trail or one with a reprieve from the heat, such as a nature center. Fall and spring are by far the most popular times of the year for hiking. Colorful leaf and wildflower displays always draw crowds. During these months, try to avoid hiking the more popular spots on holidays and beautiful weekends. If possible, hike during the week, after work when the days get longer, or on a less-well-known trail.

For many hikers, wintertime presents an excellent opportunity to get out on the trails. Crowds (and bugs) disappear, cliffs and rocky outcroppings are easier to see, and the contours of the earth become more apparent. And if we get a good snow, animal tracks along the trails, birds at their feeders, and ice formations on the waterways make for wonderful sights along the way.

The following chart provides a month-by-month snapshot of the weather in the Louisville area. For each month, "Hi Temp" shows the average daytime high, "Lo Temp" gives the average nighttime low, and "Rain" lists the average precipitation.

MONTH	HI TEMP	LO TEMP	RAIN
January	43°F	27°F	3.24"
February	48°F	30°F	3.29"
March	58°F	38°F	4.17"
April	69°F	47°F	4.01"
May	77°F	57°F	5.27"
June	85°F	66°F	3.79"

MONTH	HI TEMP	LO TEMP	RAIN
July	89°F	70°F	4.23"
August	88°F	69°F	3.33"
September	82°F	61°F	3.05"
October	70°F	49°F	3.22"
November	58°F	40°F	3.59"
December	46°F	30°F	3.83"

Water

How much is enough? Well, one simple physiological fact should convince you to err on the side of excess when deciding how much water to pack: a hiker walking steadily in 90° heat needs about 10 quarts of fluid per day—that's 2.5 gallons. A good rule of thumb is to hydrate prior to your hike, carry (and drink) 6 ounces of water for every mile you plan to hike, and hydrate again after the hike. For most people, the pleasures of hiking make carrying water a relatively minor price to pay to remain safe and healthy, so pack more water than you anticipate needing, even for short hikes.

If you find yourself tempted to drink "found water," proceed with extreme caution. Many ponds and lakes you'll encounter are fairly stagnant, and the water tastes terrible. Drinking such water presents inherent risks for thirsty trekkers. Giardia parasites contaminate many water sources and cause the dreaded intestinal ailment giardiasis, which can last for weeks after onset. For more information, visit the Centers for Disease Control and Prevention website: **cdc.gov/parasites/giardia.**

In any case, effective treatment is essential before you drink from any water source along the trail. Boiling water for 2–3 minutes is always a safe measure for camping, but day hikers can consider iodine tablets, approved chemical mixes, filtration units rated for giardia, and ultraviolet filtration. Some of these methods (for example, filtration with an added carbon filter) remove bad tastes typical in stagnant water, while others add their own taste. As a precaution, carry a means of water purification in case you've underestimated your consumption needs.

Clothing

Weather, unexpected trail conditions, fatigue, extended hiking duration, and wrong turns can individually or collectively turn a great outing into a very uncomfortable one at best—and a life-threatening one at worst. Thus, proper attire plays a key role in staying comfortable and, sometimes, in staying alive. Some helpful guidelines:

★ Choose silk, wool, or synthetics for maximum comfort in all of your hiking attire—from hats to socks and in between. Cotton is fine if the weather remains dry and stable, but you won't be happy if that material gets wet.

★ Always wear a hat, or at least tuck one into your day pack or hitch it to your belt. Hats offer all-weather sun and wind protection as well as warmth if it turns cold.

★ Be ready to layer up or down as the day progresses and the mercury rises or falls. Today's outdoor wear makes layering easy, with such designs as jackets that convert to vests and zip-off or button-up legs.

★ Mosquitoes, poison ivy, and thorny bushes found along many trails can generate short-term discomfort and long-term agony. A lightweight pair of pants and a long-sleeved shirt can go a long way toward protecting you from these pests.

★ Wear hiking boots or sturdy hiking sandals with toe protection. Flip-flopping along a paved urban greenway is one thing, but you should never hike a trail in open sandals or casual sneakers. Your bones and arches need support, and your skin needs protection.

★ Pair that footwear with good socks! If you prefer not to sheathe your feet when wearing hiking sandals, tuck the socks into your day pack—you may need them if temperatures plummet or if you hit rocky turf and pebbles begin to irritate your feet. And if it's cold and you've lost your gloves, you can adapt the socks into mittens.

★ Don't leave rainwear behind, even if the day dawns clear and sunny. Tuck into your day pack, or tie around your waist, a jacket that's breathable and either water-resistant or waterproof. Investigate different choices at your local outdoors retailer. If you are a frequent hiker, ideally you'll have more than one rainwear weight, material, and style in your closet to protect you in all seasons in your regional climate and hiking microclimates.

Essential Gear

Today you can buy outdoor vests that have up to 20 pockets shaped and sized to carry everything from toothpicks to binoculars. Or, if you don't aspire to feel like a burro, you can neatly stow all of these items in your day pack or backpack. The following list showcases never-hike-without-them items—in alphabetical order, as all are important:

★ *Extra food:* trail mix, granola bars, or other high-energy snacks.

★ *Extra clothes:* raingear, a change of socks, and depending on the season, a warm hat and gloves.

★ *Flashlight or headlamp* with extra bulb and batteries.

★ *Insect repellent.* For some areas and seasons, this is vital.

★ *Maps and a high-quality compass.* Even if you know the terrain from previous hikes, don't leave home without these tools. And, as previously noted, bring maps in addition to those in this guidebook, and consult your maps prior to the hike. If you're GPS-savvy, bring that device, too, but don't rely on it as your sole navigational tool—battery life is limited, after all—and be sure to check its accuracy against that of your maps and compass.

★ *Pocketknife and/or multitool.*

★ *Sunscreen.* Check the expiration date on the tube or bottle.

★ *Water.* As we've emphasized more than once, bring more than you think you'll drink. Depending on your destination, you may want to bring a container and iodine or a filter for purifying water in case you run out.

★ *Whistle.* It could become your best friend in an emergency.

★ *Windproof matches and/or a lighter,* as well as a fire starter.

★ Finally, don't forget your sense of adventure!

First-Aid Kit

In addition to the preceding items, those that follow may seem daunting to carry along for a day hike. But any paramedic will tell you that the products listed here—again, in alphabetical order, because all are important—are just the basics. The reality of hiking is that you can be out for a week of backpacking and acquire only a mosquito bite. Or you can hike for an hour, slip, and suffer a bleeding abrasion or broken bone. Fortunately, the items listed pack into a very small space. You may also purchase convenient prepackaged kits at your local outdoor retailer or pharmacy, or online.

* ★ Ace bandages or Spenco joint wraps

* ★ Adhesive bandages

* ★ Antibiotic ointment (Neosporin or the generic equivalent)

* ★ Athletic tape

* ★ Benadryl or the generic equivalent, diphenhydramine
  (in case of allergic reactions)

* ★ Blister kit (such as Moleskin or Spenco 2nd Skin)

* ★ Butterfly-closure bandages

* ★ Epinephrine in a prefilled syringe (typically by prescription only, and
  for people known to have severe allergic reactions to hiking mishaps
  such as bee stings; check the expiration date)

* ★ Gauze (one roll and a half-dozen 4-by-4-inch pads)

* ★ Hydrogen peroxide or iodine

Note: Consider your intended terrain and the number of hikers in your party before you exclude any article listed above. A botanical-garden stroll may not inspire you to carry a complete kit, but anything beyond that warrants precaution. When hiking alone, you should always be prepared for a medical need. And if you're a twosome or with a group, one or more people in your party should be equipped with first-aid material.

General Safety

The following tips may have the familiar ring of Mom's voice as you take note of them.

★ *Always let someone know where you'll be hiking and how long you expect to be gone.* It's a good idea to give that person a copy of your route, particularly if you're headed into any isolated area. Let him or her know when you return.

★ *Always sign in and out of any trail registers provided.* Don't hesitate to comment on the trail condition if space is provided; that's your opportunity to alert others to any problems you encounter.

★ *Don't count on a cell phone for your safety.* Reception may be spotty or nonexistent on the trail, even on an urban walk—especially one embraced by towering trees or buildings.

★ *Always carry food and water, even for a short hike.* And bring more water than you think you'll need. (We can't emphasize this enough!)

★ *Ask questions.* Public-land employees are on hand to help. It's a lot easier to solicit advice before a problem occurs, and it will help you avoid a mishap away from civilization when it's too late to amend an error.

★ *Stay on designated trails.* Even on the most clearly marked trails, you usually reach a point where you have to stop and consider in which direction to head. If you become disoriented, don't panic. As soon as you think you may be off-track, stop, assess your current direction, and then retrace your steps to the point where you went astray. Using a map, a compass, and this book, and keeping in mind what you've passed thus far, reorient yourself, and trust your judgment on which way to continue. If you become absolutely unsure of how to continue, return to your vehicle the way you came in. Should you become completely lost and have no idea how to find the trailhead, remaining in place along the trail and waiting for help is most often the best option for adults, and always the best option for children.

★ *Always carry a whistle,* another precaution that we can't overemphasize. It may become a lifesaver if you get lost or hurt.

★ *Be especially careful when crossing streams.* Whether you're fording the stream or crossing on a log, make every step count. If you have any doubt about maintaining your balance on a log, ford the stream instead: use a trekking pole or stout stick for balance and *face upstream as you cross.* If a stream seems too deep to ford, turn back. Whatever is on the other side isn't worth risking your life for.

★ *Be careful at overlooks.* While these areas may provide spectacular views, they are potentially hazardous. Stay back from the edge of outcrops, and make absolutely sure of your footing—a misstep can mean a nasty and possibly fatal fall.

★ *Standing dead trees and storm-damaged living trees pose a significant hazard to hikers.* These trees may have loose or broken limbs that could fall at any time. While walking beneath trees, and when choosing a spot to rest or enjoy your snack, look up!

★ *Know the symptoms of subnormal body temperature, or hypothermia.* Shivering and forgetfulness are the two most common indicators of this stealthy killer. Hypothermia can occur at any elevation, even in the summer, especially when the hiker is wearing lightweight cotton clothing. If symptoms develop, get to shelter, hot liquids, and dry clothes ASAP.

★ *Likewise, know the symptoms of heat exhaustion, or hyperthermia.* Lightheadedness and loss of energy are the first two indicators. If you feel these symptoms, find some shade, drink your water, remove as many layers of clothing as practical, and stay put until you cool down. Marching through heat exhaustion leads to heatstroke—which can be deadly. If you should be sweating and you're not, that's the signature warning sign. Your hike is over at that point: heatstroke is a life-threatening condition that can cause seizures, convulsions, and eventually death. If you or a companion reaches that point, do whatever you can to cool down, and seek medical attention immediately.

★ *Most importantly, take along your brain.* A cool, calculating mind is the single most important asset on the trail. Think before you act. Watch your step. Plan ahead. Avoiding accidents before they happen is the best way to ensure a rewarding and relaxing hike.

Watchwords for Flora & Fauna

Hikers should remain aware of the following concerns regarding plant life and wildlife, described in alphabetical order.

MOSQUITOES Ward off these pests with insect repellent and/or repellent-impregnated clothing. Long pants and a long-sleeved shirt may offer your best protection. In general, mosquitoes are at their worst during spring and early summer. In warm weather, mosquitoes typically hatch four to six days after significant rainfall. However, recent mild winters in the Louisville area have extended the mosquito season to basically whenever nighttime temperatures don't dip below freezing for a prolonged period of time. When examining your hiking options, consider the presence of low-lying areas (including wetlands) and bodies of water such as lakes and ponds, which may provide a breeding ground for those little minions of evil. In some areas, mosquitoes are known to carry the West Nile virus, so take extra care to avoid their bites. Several cases of West Nile are reported in Jefferson and surrounding counties each year.

POISON IVY, OAK, & SUMAC Recognizing and avoiding poison ivy, oak, and sumac are the most effective ways to prevent the painful, itchy rashes associated with these plants. Poison ivy occurs as a vine or groundcover, three leaflets to a leaf; poison oak occurs as either a vine or shrub, also with three leaflets; and poison sumac flourishes in swampland, each leaf having 7–13 leaflets. Urushiol, the oil in the sap of these plants, is responsible for the rash. Within 14 hours of exposure, raised lines and/or blisters will appear on your skin, accompanied by a terrible itch. Try to refrain from scratching, though, because bacteria under your fingernails can cause an infection.

Wash and dry the affected area thoroughly, applying calamine lotion to help dry out the rash. If the itching or blistering is severe, seek medical attention. To keep from spreading the misery to someone else, wash not only any exposed parts of your body but also any oil-contaminated clothes, hiking gear, and pets. Again, long pants and a long-sleeved shirt may offer the best protection.

SNAKES Rattlesnakes, cottonmouths, copperheads, and corals are among the most common venomous snakes in the United States, and their hibernation season is typically October–April. But despite their fearsome reputation, rattlesnakes like to bask in the sun and won't bite unless threatened.

You will possibly encounter the copperhead while hiking in the Louisville area. The snakes you'll most likely see, however, are non-venomous species and subspecies, particularly Eastern garter and rough green snakes. The best rule is to leave all snakes alone, give them a wide berth as you trek past, and make sure your hiking companions (including dogs) do the same.

When hiking, stick to well-used trails, and wear over-the-ankle boots and loose-fitting long pants. Don't step or put your hands beyond your range of detailed visibility, and avoid wandering around in the dark. Step *onto* logs and rocks, never *over* them, and be especially careful when climbing rocks. Always avoid walking through dense brush or willow thickets.

TICKS These arachnids are often found on brush and tall grass, where they seem to be waiting to hitch a ride on warm-blooded passersby. Adult ticks are most active April–May and again October–November, but Louisville's recent mild winters have greatly extended the tick season, from March through November. The black-legged (deer) tick is the primary carrier of Lyme disease.

A few precautions: Wear light-colored clothing, which will make it easy for you to spot ticks before they migrate to your skin. After hiking, inspect your hair, the back of your neck, your armpits, and your socks. During your posthike shower, take a moment to do a more complete body check. To remove a tick that is already embedded, use tweezers made just for this purpose. Treat the bite with disinfectant solution.

Hunting

A number of rules, regulations, and licenses govern the various hunting types and their related seasons. In Kentucky and Indiana, hunting seasons vary each year by animal, county, location, and type of weapon. Though no problems generally arise, hikers may wish to forgo their trips during these times, when the woods suddenly seem filled with orange and camouflage. For more information, visit the websites of the Kentucky Department of Fish and Wildlife Resources **(fw.ky.gov)** and the Indiana Department of Natural Resources **(in.gov/dnr).**

Trail Etiquette

Always treat trails, wildlife, and fellow hikers with respect. Here are some reminders.

★ Plan ahead in order to be self-sufficient at all times. For example, carry necessary supplies for changes in weather or other conditions. A well-planned trip brings satisfaction to you and to others.

★ Hike on open trails only.

★ In seasons or construction areas where road or trail closures may be a possibility, use the websites or phone numbers listed in the "Contacts" section at the beginning of each hike profile to check conditions before you head out for your hike. And don't try to circumvent such closures.

★ Avoid trespassing on private land, and obtain all permits and authorizations as required. Also, leave gates as you found them or as directed by signage.

★ Be courteous to other hikers, bikers, equestrians, and others you encounter on the trails.

★ Never spook wild animals or pets. An unannounced approach, a sudden movement, or a loud noise startles most critters, and a surprised animal can be dangerous to you, to others, and to itself. Give animals plenty of space.

★ Observe the YIELD signs around the region's trailheads and backcountry. Typically they advise hikers to yield to horses, and bikers to yield to both horses and hikers. Observing common courtesy on hills, hikers and bikers yield to any uphill traffic. When encountering mounted riders or horsepackers, hikers can courteously step off the trail, on the downhill side if possible. So that horses can see and hear you, calmly greet their riders before they reach you, and do not dart behind trees. Also resist the urge to pet horses unless you are invited to do so.

★ Stay on the existing trail, and do not blaze any new trails.

★ Pack out what you pack in, leaving only your footprints. No one likes to see the trash someone else has left behind. The Leave No Trace Center for Outdoor Ethics is an excellent resource (visit **lnt.org** for more information).

Think Global, Hike Local: Tips for Enjoying Hiking in Greater Louisville

Think inside the circle. Hiking opportunities abound inside both I-265 and I-264 (also known as the Henry Watterson Expressway). For quick lunchtime power-walks, consider the Olmsted Parks, such as Cherokee and Iroquois, as well as the paved multiuse trails along the riverfront. The other urban trails listed in this book are within easy reach of most Louisville residents, so they're good for parents when the kids are in school or for family outings after school.

Think outside the circle. Just outside I-265 are a handful of trails perfect for after work, particularly when the days are a bit longer. Creasey Mahan Nature Preserve, Blackacre State Nature Preserve, Fairmount Falls, and all of the Jefferson Memorial Forest are just minutes outside the beltway. Even Mount St. Francis, in southern Indiana, is just 20 minutes from downtown Louisville.

Think social. Friends in town for the weekend? Family coming to visit? Not everyone wants to sit on the living-room couch all afternoon. Looking for an inventive (and cheap) date idea? A first-run movie and popcorn may set you back more than you care to spend. So head out to an urban trail or catch a cascading waterfall. Enjoy the natural beauty around you, pack a picnic or maybe a kite, and you've got instant fun.

Think indoors. Weather too cold or wet to hit the trail? Are the kids driving you absolutely crazy? Check out one of the many free nature centers around Louisville. Blackacre State Nature Preserve, Creasey Mahan Nature Preserve, and Salato Wildlife Education Center are free to enter, although donations are always appreciated. Spring Mill State Park, Patoka Lake Nature Center, and Falls of the Ohio State Park charge nominal admission fees.

If you're feeling brave, bring boots and a raincoat and let the rugrats stomp every puddle from one end of the trail to the other. Tuck in a change of shoes and maybe some clothes for the ride home, and everyone will sleep well tonight.

Think winter. During the cold months, bugs and crowds vanish and nonstop views take their place. Cliffs and waterfalls become a winter wonderland as icicles sparkle like stalactites in the sun. Even a light snowfall can turn a simple walk in the woods into a gorgeous adventure.

Think intellectual. If asked "Hey! Wanna trudge 3 miles, swat mosquitoes, and get sore feet?," how many people would say yes? Only the hardcore among us exercise purely for fun. But each trail on this hike can offer an exploration into history, geology, biology, photography, art, and more. Once you're mentally engaged, the miles can fly by.

Think adventure. To keep your hikes fresh, try new trails, new hiking partners, new seasons for discovering the natural world around you. Bring your maps, your raingear, even the entire contents of your favorite local outdoors store. But don't forget to bring your sense of adventure and your smile. You'll be sure to come back for more.

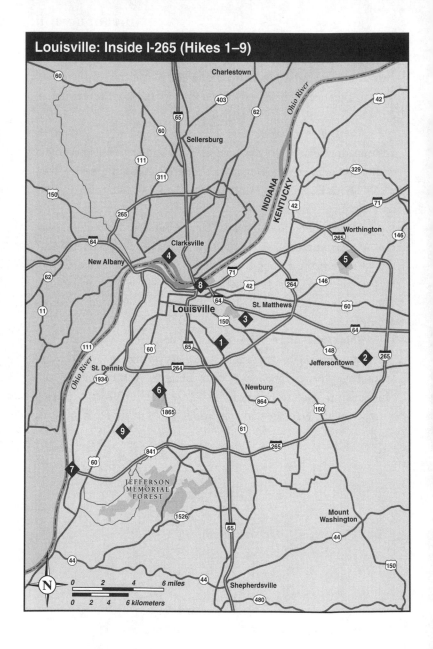

Louisville: Inside I-265 (Hikes 1–9)

Louisville:
Inside I-265

BEARGRASS CREEK BUBBLES MIRTHFULLY AS IT FLOWS DOWNSTREAM TO THE OHIO RIVER. *(See Hike 3, Cherokee Park Loop, page 34.)*

Beargrass Creek State Nature Preserve:
White Oak Nature Trail

SCENERY: ★ ★ ★
TRAIL CONDITION: ★ ★ ★ ★
CHILDREN: ★ ★ ★ ★
DIFFICULTY: ★
SOLITUDE: ★ ★

THE WATER FEATURE AND NATIVE PLANTINGS AT THE EDUCATION CENTER OFFER VISITORS AN INVITING RECEPTION.

GPS TRAILHEAD COORDINATES: N38° 12.594' W85° 42.669'

DISTANCE & CONFIGURATION: 1.5-mile loop

HIKING TIME: 1 hour

HIGHLIGHTS: Nature center and bird blind

ELEVATION: 533' at trailhead, descending to 453' at low point

ACCESS: Trails are open daily, sunrise–sunset. The nature center is open Monday–Saturday, 9 a.m.–4 p.m.; closed Sundays and holidays. Free admission; donations welcome.

MAPS: Available on-site and at the first website below

FACILITIES: Restrooms and picnic tables

WHEELCHAIR ACCESS: Only at the nature center

COMMENTS: No pets

CONTACTS: Louisville Nature Center, 502-458-1328; **louisvillenaturecenter.org/bcsnp.htm** or **tinyurl.com/beargrasscreek**

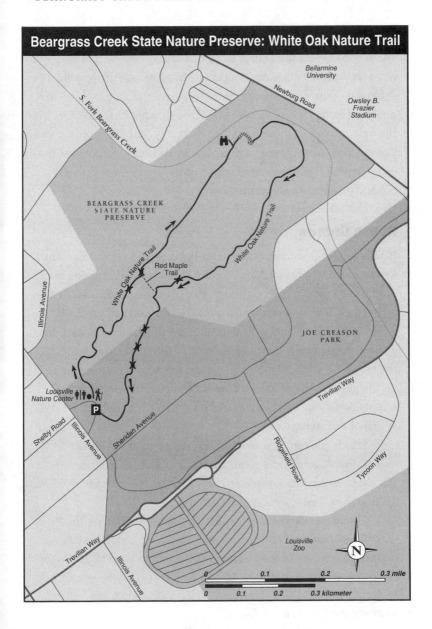

Beargrass Creek State Nature Preserve: White Oak Nature Trail

Overview

The White Oak Nature Trail at Beargrass Creek State Nature Preserve lies near the heart of Louisville and within easy reach of every child in Jefferson County. Take your kids (or someone else's) to explore every nook and cranny of this 41-acre woodland wonder. Beargrass Creek is the only urban forest owned by the Kentucky State Nature Preserve Commission. Comanaged with the Louisville Nature Center, the preserve provides four seasons of opportunity to tire those little rascals out and get them to bed early.

Route Details

If this is your first visit, you should begin at the Louisville Nature Center. As you approach, you'll notice small signs identifying many of the trees and native plantings that dot the landscape. A new sensory garden has been installed in front of a small pond, with a raised "table" for planting flowers and vegetables. Rain chains dangle as downspouts on both sides of the front entrance to the center, designed to catch both your eye and the surplus water that runs off the gutters. Operated as a nonprofit, the nature center gratefully accepts donations for the upkeep of its facilities and sells rain barrels as one of its fundraisers.

Inside the center you'll find several hands-on exhibits for the kids to investigate and a room that serves as both a library and a gift shop. Be sure to say hello to Amie the stuffed armadillo, who's visiting from Texas.

The nature center also has an informative display on the Beargrass Creek watershed, which drains 61 square miles of Jefferson County. Every drop of metro-Louisville runoff ends up in this watershed—encompassing Muddy, Middle, and South Forks—on its way to the Ohio River. Think about that impact while you try to keep your lawn and garden chemical-free.

The Louisville Nature Center takes its educational outreach programs seriously, offering a preschool program for the little tykes, hosting school groups throughout the year, and operating youth camps in the summer. Scout troops frequently roam the area dressed in those adorable blue and brown outfits, complete with neckerchiefs. The facility is also available for rent (think birthday parties), and the Jefferson County Master Gardener Association uses it for luncheons and meeting space.

A large bird blind lies just out the back door of the nature center, overlooking several feeders. Frequent avian visitors include dark-eyed (or slate-colored) juncos, cardinals, white-breasted nuthatches, tufted titmice, and downy woodpeckers. Walk about the blind slowly and quietly—although the exterior wall has tinted one-way glass, the birds are very aware of shadows and noise as you move about the room.

The White Oak Nature Trail starts just to the left of the bird blind. The nature center provides a small brochure that fits easily in your back pocket and describes the 20 information markers posted along the way. To follow the guided trail sequentially, start your hike here, looping clockwise to return to the parking lot on the front side of the nature center. Highlights include several small wooden bridges and walkways, the sycamore "hugging tree," and some of the largest poison ivy vines you've ever seen. Known in scientific circles as *Toxicodendron radicans*, poison ivy produces an irritating oil called urushiol. Curiously, wildlife is immune to this irritant: a variety of birds, deer, rabbits, and other small mammals eat the grayish-white berries throughout the fall and winter. Adhere to the old adage "leaves of three, let it be," and maybe you won't wake up itching. (For more on the subject, see page 15.)

If you want to shorten your hike to less than 0.7 mile, take the shortcut across the Red Maple Trail to the other side of the White Oak Nature Trail. But if one of your objectives is to wear out the kids, don't even mention that as an option.

Shortly after you pass the Red Maple Trail, about 0.3 mile into the hike, you'll notice an increasing number of old bricks embedded within the dirt path. This section of the White Oak Nature Trail was an old paved roadbed that led to Basil Prather's homestead. Prather, a Revolutionary War captain, bought this property in 1789. The roadbed is elevated above the surrounding wetlands—a.k.a. mosquito-breeding grounds. Hikers may want to avoid this section during late spring and early summer.

At the far northeastern end of the trail, about 0.7 mile from the trailhead, the path traverses a wooden walkway before ascending gently and eventually returning to the nature center. Along the second half of the trail, you may see two or three paths veering left (southeast); these lead to Joe Creason Park, just south and east of the preserve.

To keep kids interested as they walk along the trail, try a photo scavenger hunt. Provide an inexpensive digital camera and a list of sights to find and record photographically. Hunt items could include a left- or right-hand mitten hidden in one of the many old sassafras trees that line the trail; white blooms or red berries on an invasive honeysuckle; sightings of snakeroot, witch hazel, or poplar (Kentucky's state tree); a photo op with Amie . . . you get the idea.

And don't forget about Beargrass Creek on inclement-weather days. Load up with raincoats and boots or a warm winter coat with hat and mittens, and look for animal tracks. It's always surprising how many mammals frequent our urban backyard. And on cold days, the bird blind will be chattering with activity.

Nearby Attractions

Both **Joe Creason Park** and the **Louisville Zoo** are just south of the preserve. All three parks share adjacent borders, with Creason in the middle and Beargrass and the zoo serving as bookends. A 1.5-mile multiuse trail encircles Joe Creason Park; the 3.1- and 6.2-mile loops are popular with cross-country runners. Ambitious hikers can use one of the connector paths between Beargrass Creek and Creason Park to hike both trail systems. Joe Creason Park also has nine clay tennis courts, soccer fields, and two pedestrian bridges that cross

Beargrass Creek. In winter, the large hill in front of the Metro Parks Administrative Office is great for snow-sledding.

Directions

From I-264 (Henry Watterson Expressway), take Exit 14 (Poplar Level Road/KY 864), head north on Poplar Level Road, and drive 0.7 mile. Turn right (east) at Trevilian Way, and in 0.1 mile turn left (north) on Illinois Avenue. The park is 0.2 mile ahead, on your right.

Blackacre Waterfall Trail

SCENERY: ★ ★ ★
TRAIL CONDITION: ★ ★ ★
CHILDREN: ★ ★ ★ ★
DIFFICULTY: ★
SOLITUDE: ★ ★ ★ ★

MULTIPLE SPRINGS ON THE PROPERTY PROMISE YEAR-ROUND WATER.

GPS TRAILHEAD COORDINATES: N38° 11.788' W85° 31.979'

DISTANCE & CONFIGURATION: 1.1-mile loop

HIKING TIME: 1 hour

HIGHLIGHTS: Historic home, working farm

ELEVATION: 682' at trailhead, ascending to 713' at high point

ACCESS: Trails and grounds are open daily. Hours are sunrise–sunset on weekends, holidays, and non–school days; 3 p.m.–sunset on school days. The Presley Tyler House is open Sunday, 1–5 p.m., April–December. Free admission; donations welcome (some special events incur a small fee).

MAPS: Blackacre State Nature Preserve, USGS *Jeffersontown*

FACILITIES: Nature center, house and farm tours, picnic tables, restrooms

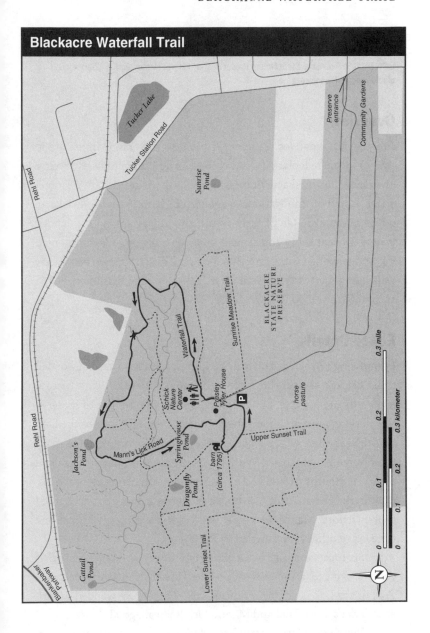

Blackacre Waterfall Trail

WHEELCHAIR ACCESS: None on trails; first floor of house during tour is accessible.

COMMENTS: No dogs or smoking

CONTACTS: Blackacre State Nature Preserve and Historic Homestead, 502-266-9802; blackacreconservancy.org

Overview

Are your little natives restless? Or perhaps the grandparents are in town and you're looking for a way to entertain them for a few hours? Then consider Blackacre State Nature Preserve and Historic Homestead. Listed on the National Register of Historic Places, Blackacre offers a fine example of farm life in the 1800s among the landed gentry. Docent tours and several miles of trails provide an interesting and relaxing visit for all. The loop trail described here is an easy walk along the Waterfall Trail, past Jackson's Pond, then back to the springhouse and double-crib barn.

Route Details

Comprising 170 acres of historic buildings, open pasture, and wooded trails, Blackacre Nature Preserve was created in 1979 by Judge Macauley Smith and his wife, Emilie Strong Smith, who sought to preserve the working farm and homestead. Moses Tyler first settled the land in 1795, and later Tyler's son, Presley, and his wife, Phoebe, built their home here in 1844. With 10 children, the younger Tylers had plenty of mouths to feed and a built-in labor force to work the fields. Built in the Federal style, the house is open seasonally for docent-led tours. Historic Mann's Lick Road traverses the property and at one time led to other farms owned by the Tylers.

Six trails are available for hiking anytime the preserve is open. If you're looking for an open-meadow hike, consider the Sunrise Meadow Trail or the Lower or Upper Sunset Trail. For a more wooded experience, Tyler's Trace Trail and Mann's Lick Road are good choices.

But if water attracts you like a divining rod, consider the Waterfall Trail, which includes several creek crossings, meanders through lightly wooded areas before reaching Jackson's Pond, and returns to the homestead via historic Mann's Lick Road. To reach the trailhead, begin at the large kiosk at the far northeastern edge of the primary parking lot. Head north toward the Tyler House, then bear right (east) to get to the Schick Nature Center.

Before you start your hike, it's worth spending a little time at Schick. To the left of the nature center's front door hangs an unusual map of the homestead, fashioned from metal and stamped with Braille lettering. To the right of the front door hangs an old farm gate painted with a picture of the homestead in *American Gothic* style.

Feel free to go inside and explore the nature center. Despite several preserve signs admonishing NO STICKS, RUNNING, OR SHOUTING. QUIET VOICES ONLY, the nature center is all about kids. The exterior of the quaint yet rustic wooden building has a 1970s contemporary look, yet inside is set up like an old one-room schoolhouse. From the plastic snake dangling from the deer antlers to the extensive collection of children's nature books, the atmosphere will make kids feel immediately at home.

The nature center hosts many programs throughout the year, with topics ranging from owls and tree frogs to planets and stars to heirloom tomatoes and canning. Special summer programs include Pioneer Day and camps for the kids. More information, including farm-animal feeding schedules, is available at **blackacreconservancy.org.**

Out the back door of the Schick Nature Center stands a separate building housing the bathrooms, fully outfitted with Clivus Multrum composting toilets long before such facilities were fashionable. The preserve notes that the compost is indeed used on the farm to fertilize the crops.

Behind the nature center and next to the bathrooms you'll see the sign for the Waterfall Trail. The first creek crossing is a scant 0.1 mile from the trailhead. The trail along this section can be quite muddy in the spring; well-worn alternative trails circumvent the wet spots. Several small waterfalls form where various drainages tumble down the hillsides. At the third creek crossing, about 0.3 mile from the trailhead, a small footbridge takes hikers across to the other side. Cedar, redbud, and dogwood provide plenty of seasonal interest along the way.

About 0.5 mile from the trailhead, the path splits into a Y. The left branch heads southwest toward Mann's Lick Road, while the right branch heads northwest toward Jackson's Pond. Take a right here and walk 5 minutes (about 0.2 mile) more to reach the pond. An old beaver lodge is embedded within the earthen berm containing the pond, close to the outtake pipe. Other evidence of beaver activity includes nibbled tree branches and stumps lining the pond.

The trail loops left (south), crosses a small bridge, and rejoins Mann's Lick Road. Just don't expect a paved thoroughfare with yellow painted lines and rumble strips. This road was built long before Henry Ford was knee-high to a grasshopper, and it's easy to see why wagon wheels broke down so often.

Turning left (south) on Mann's Lick and walking another 5 minutes (0.2 mile) bring you to the back side of the circa-1795 springhouse. A small spring in front of the stone building flows under the structure and enters a small pond. Food was kept cool in the springhouse during warm summer days, and the pond provided swimmers a welcome relief from the heat.

The trail continues behind the springhouse, between the smokehouse and the weaving shed. Bear right (west) down the gravel road 20 yards or so until you reach the Appalachian-style barn, also built in 1795. The barn is a rare double-crib style, with an enclosed dogtrot down the middle. Here the rough-hewn walls are hung with old farm equipment, including harnesses, yokes, pitchforks, scythes, cross draw saws, plows, barrel hoops, reaping hooks, hay crooks, corn knives, and the like. A corn sheller and cider press sit opposite the wall, where several old horseshoes hang open-side up to catch all the luck before it falls out. Note the magnet used by veterinarians to remove wire from cows' stomachs. Stored on the other side of the barn are several old horse-drawn vehicles, including buggies, farm wagons, and an old sleigh.

Just outside the barn, several fields house the resident horses, goats, and cattle. The horses and goats love your attention, while the cows couldn't care less. The parking lot and your horseless carriage will be sitting just north of the pastures.

Nearby Attractions

If you enjoy old homes, public gardens, and early-American history, **Historic Locust Grove** is another great place to spend the day. The restored Georgian house was home to Revolutionary War hero General George Rogers Clark during his later years. Locust Grove sits on 55 acres of woods and meadows, sprinkled with period-style gardens featuring rare and historic plants. For more information, call 502-897-9845 or go to **locustgrove.org.**

Directions

From I-265 (KY 841/Gene Snyder Freeway), head west off Exit 23 (Taylorsville Road) and drive 0.8 mile. Turn right (north) on Tucker Station Road, drive 0.3 mile, and turn left (west) at the sign for Blackacre State Nature Preserve. Pass through the old green metal farm gate, and follow the gravel road around to the Tyler House. Park in the large lot to your left. Parking for the disabled is available near the house.

Cherokee Park Loop

SCENERY: ★ ★ ★ ★
TRAIL CONDITION: ★ ★ ★
CHILDREN: ★ ★ ★
DIFFICULTY: ★ ★ ★
SOLITUDE: ★

THEY JUST DON'T BUILD BRIDGES LIKE THIS ANYMORE.

GPS TRAILHEAD COORDINATES: N38° 14.010' W85° 40.919'

DISTANCE & CONFIGURATION: 4.2-mile balloon

HIKING TIME: 1.5 hours

HIGHLIGHTS: Beargrass Creek, Hogan's Fountain, stone bridges

ELEVATION: 466' at trailhead, ascending to 579' at high point

ACCESS: Daily, sunrise–sunset; free admission

MAPS: Louisville Metro Parks, USGS *Louisville*

FACILITIES: Picnic tables and shelters, restrooms, playground

WHEELCHAIR ACCESS: None on this trail, although the park offers several miles of paved trails.

COMMENTS: Pets must be leashed. Hiking is prohibited in wet conditions and during freeze–thaw cycles.

CONTACTS: Louisville Metro Parks, 502-456-8100; **louisvilleky.gov/metroparks**

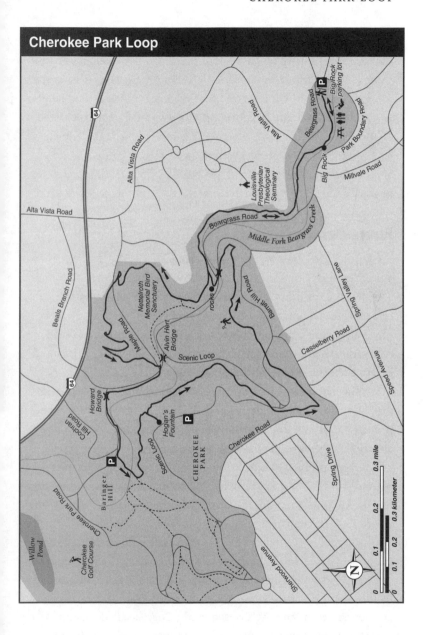

Cherokee Park Loop

Overview

Cherokee Park—part of one of only four city-park systems in the United States created by Frederick Law Olmsted—is a jewel in the rough. Designed by Olmsted and his firm in 1891, it's among Louisville's 18 parks and 6 interconnecting parkways attributed to the father of American landscape architecture. Cherokee Park is undergoing a lengthy revitalization process to reclaim its former glory as a sanctuary for outdoor recreation. The Cherokee Park Loop takes hikers along Beargrass Creek and through much of the heart of this 409-acre park.

Route Details

Frederick Law Olmsted, who also designed Central Park in New York City, the Biltmore Estate outside of Asheville, North Carolina, and the grounds of the U.S. Capitol, believed that city parks were an essential element of healthy urban communities. His design philosophy encompassed three elements: recreative use (such as walking or relaxing), gregarious use (picnicking and other social activities), and exertive use (including ball fields and courts).

The main artery for travel in Cherokee Park is the 2.4-mile Scenic Loop, a one-way paved road divided evenly between vehicular and pedestrian use. On almost any day of the week, and on most evenings as well, the pedestrian lane is filled with walkers, joggers, cyclists, and parents pushing strollers. The Scenic Loop combines manicured plantings with a pastoral backdrop of natural forests and tumbling creeks. Multiple stone bridges and two large fountains provide the hardscape that completes the look.

Originally Cherokee Park was surrounded by beautiful homes to the north and south and Seneca Park (another Olmsted park) to the west. Today the Louisville Presbyterian Theological Seminary lies to the east, I-64 crosses the northern tip of Cherokee Park, and a golf course lies to the west. Consequently, Cherokee Park has suffered from the growing pains of overuse due to increased urban density. In addition, a 1974 tornado—part of that year's devastating multistate "super outbreak"—destroyed many of the large, mature trees that dominated the landscape. The loss of canopy has resulted in less-desirable and more-invasive plant species taking root in the park.

Admittedly, Cherokee Park can be quite crowded, and solitude is hard to find. Litter is a constant eyesore, and Beargrass Creek (which runs through the middle of the park) is polluted with urban runoff. Nevertheless, the "bones" of Cherokee Park remain sound, and Louisvillians continue to be drawn to its natural beauty. The last several years have seen a tremendous push to revitalize all the Olmsted parks. Several nonprofits and foundations are working together with the city to bring the Louisville park system back its glory days.

The 4.2-mile Cherokee Park Loop gives hikers a broad overview of the space's beauty and diversity. Highlights include a hike along Beargrass Creek, the Nettelroth Memorial Bird Sanctuary, Hogan's Fountain, and numerous limestone cliffs. An incredible maze of trails includes paved, multiuse, mixed-use, and just-plain-rogue paths that can confuse the first-time or casual hiker. The trail described here, in contrast, prepares you for repeat visits by sharpening your sense of bearing and navigational skills.

At the far end of the parking lot described in the Directions, the trail begins behind the kiosk. Follow the dirt path along Beargrass Creek (creek-right as the current flows downstream). Here the creek flows over small rocks, creating a soothing, musical sound before falling into a deeper pool that surrounds "Big Rock," at the base of a limestone cliff. A tattered hanging rope provides evidence of summer swims for those daring to brave the water quality. Debris piles near the shoreline demonstrate how high water levels can rise after heavy spring rains.

The trail brings you to the corner of Beargrass and Alta Vista Roads, and a set of large millstones hand-hewn from conglomerate rock. Each stone is more than 5 feet around and 12 inches thick—much too heavy for pranksters to carry off.

A little more than 0.2 mile from the parking lot, the trail joins the road. Keep left and walk in the pedestrian lane facing the traffic. This is a good place to spot mallard ducks near the old stone retaining wall. The birds feed off the insects and young plants along the creek bottom, their rear tail feathers standing vertical off the surface of the water as their heads dive deep below.

At 0.34 mile, carefully cross the road at the sign for the multiuse trail. Bernard and Rosa Bernheim, who with Bernard's brother, Isaac Wolfe Bernheim, helped establish Bernheim Arboretum and Research Forest (see Hikes 14 and 15), donated the bridge on the west side of the road in 1928. The stonework on the bridge is simply magnificent.

From here the trail follows the park's boundary with the Presbyterian Theological Seminary. Here volunteers have worked hard to remove much of the invasive honeysuckle that plagues the park. Naturalized hollies and native wild cherries thrive in the newly opened canopy. In early spring, yellow trout lilies, as well as the slightly invasive small blue periwinkle, bloom here. Unfortunately, the sweet yellow flowers of lesser celandine—named Kentucky's Least Wanted Plant of 2011 by the Kentucky State Nature Preserves Commission—are pervasive here as well.

The trail then rejoins the creek, crosses an old abandoned road, and continues up a small hill on a mixed-use trail. (I told you the trail system at Cherokee can be confusing!) About 0.8 mile from the trailhead, bear right (northeast) at the Y in the path, toward the house atop the hill with the French mansard roof and the naturalized meadow as a backyard.

The trail now begins to skirt the bird sanctuary, which has been fenced off to protect reforestation efforts under way here. Woodcocks, colloquially known as timberdoodles, have been known to frequent this area. With long, slender bills and 360-degree vision, these birds tend to feed in the early evening by probing the soil for invertebrates. Woodcocks are also known for their elaborate mating rituals. Given that the females are much larger than the males, we can only guess who wins.

While the trail is lined with cedars and pine, in the middle of the meadow stands a stately walnut tree, generously studded with mistletoe. Stay on the path as it follows a series of switchbacks and crosses a narrow road. The Kentucky Mountain Bike Association has put in hundreds of hours renovating these and other switchbacks in the park, and its efforts show.

The trail then descends toward the Scenic Loop and Maple Road, to bring you about 1.55 miles from the trailhead. Don't cross the Alvin Hert Bridge—instead, follow the Scenic Loop right (north) by staying in the pedestrian lane. Walk another 0.6 mile and then turn left (south) on the paved Baringer Hill path, just past the intersection with Cochran Hill Road. After the trail crosses Beargrass Creek, take a sharp left up the hill on the dirt trail to head east back along the creek. Several other trails will come in to your right, but keep bearing left to stay high above Beargrass Creek. The cliffs below are home to several varieties of sedum and wild columbine, and pileated woodpeckers like to haunt this area.

At the top of the hill, look right and you'll see Hogan's Fountain, a gift from Mr. and Mrs. W. J. Hogan to the city in 1904. The fountain features the Greek nature god Pan and served as a watering spot for horses and dogs. Make a quick detour to see the fountain, then return to the trail to continue your journey.

The trail crosses the Scenic Loop once again, traverses a small wooded area, goes past the tennis courts, and then traverses more woods before descending to Barrett Hill Road. Turn left (north) and cross the stone bridge (passing Beargrass Road on your right). A final right-hand turn takes you back to walking along the creek (now upstream, but still creek-right). Retrace your steps back to the parking lot.

Nearby Attractions

Louisville Metro Parks opens several hills for sled riding, including Baringer Hill at Cherokee Park, at the corner of Alexander Road and the Scenic Loop. In the winter, signs are posted indicating when snows are sufficient and sledding is permitted, provided proper equipment (that is, no old-car hoods or garbage-can lids) is used. Park staff will even light and maintain bonfires, supply first-aid kits, and call emergency services if necessary. What more could you ask for your tax dollar? Grab a thermos of hot chocolate, and you're ready for some wintertime fun.

Directions

From I-264 (Henry Watterson Expressway), take Exit 17 and head west on Taylorsville Road, toward downtown Louisville. After 1 mile, turn right (north) on Pee Wee Reese Road (just west of Bowman Field Airport). After 1.5 miles, turn left (west) on Seneca Park Road and drive 0.3 mile to the intersection with Park Boundary Road. The parking lot will be straight ahead, on the northeast side of the bridge over Beargrass Creek (across the creek from the Big Rock parking lot and playground). The trailhead begins from this small parking lot.

Falls of the Ohio Levee Trail

SCENERY: ★ ★ ★
TRAIL CONDITION: ★ ★ ★ ★ ★
CHILDREN: ★ ★ ★ ★ ★
DIFFICULTY: ★ ★
SOLITUDE: ★

THE DOWNTOWN LOUISVILLE SKYLINE, IMPRESSIVE DURING THE DAY, ONLY GETS BETTER AT NIGHT.

GPS TRAILHEAD COORDINATES: N38° 17.268' W85° 46.535'

DISTANCE & CONFIGURATION: 4-mile out-and-back

HIKING TIME: 1.5 hours

HIGHLIGHTS: Ohio River, Louisville skyline, historic-home site

ELEVATION: 451' at trailhead, with no significant elevation change

ACCESS: Trails are open daily, 7 a.m.–11 p.m. Falls of the Ohio Interpretive Center open Monday–Saturday, 9 a.m.–5 p.m.; Sunday, 1–5 p.m. Free to hike; see Directions for fees to enter the interpretive center.

MAPS: Available at the first website below and at the interpretive center

FACILITIES: Nature center, restrooms, playground

WHEELCHAIR ACCESS: Yes

COMMENTS: The paved trail is for pedestrians and bikers only.

CONTACTS: Falls of the Ohio State Park, 812-280-9970; **tinyurl.com/fotosp** or **fallsoftheohio.org**

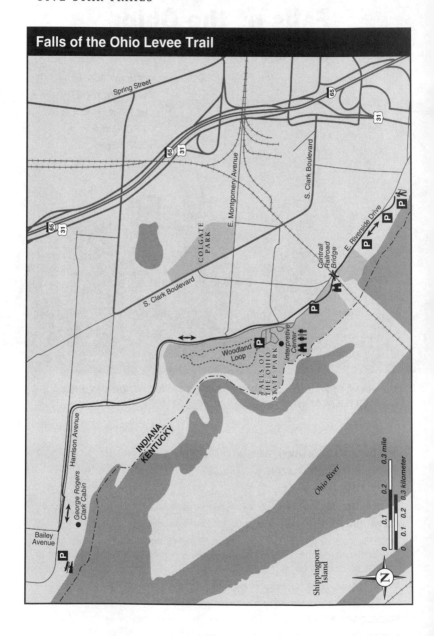

Falls of the Ohio Levee Trail

Overview

The paved Levee Trail is perfect for an after-work power walk, a sprint with the jogging stroller, or a leisurely saunter on a Sunday afternoon. The 2-mile (one-way) trail connects East Riverside Drive with Falls of the Ohio State Park and Lewis and Clark Park. Just across the river from downtown Louisville, in southern Indiana, most of the trail runs atop the earthen-berm floodwall that protects the city of Clarksville from the mighty Ohio River.

Route Details

The Falls of the Ohio Levee Trail can be accessed from either end, and at a variety of points along the way. Following the driving directions provided later, the route assumes you've parked at the far eastern trailhead along East Riverside Drive. Regardless, your chances of getting lost in the Mall St. Matthews are much greater than getting lost here.

Beginning from the far eastern trailhead, the paved trail threads a line between the northern bank of the Ohio River and a popular playground area. The downtown Louisville skyline is clearly in view looking across the river. Ten minutes (less than 0.4 mile) of walking will bring you to the underpass of the Contrail Railroad Bridge, and a small overlook of the lowhead dam (also known as a fixed-weir dam) that forms the large pool of water just above the Falls of the Ohio. They're difficult to see from the overlook, but the shipping locks are behind the far island, on the Kentucky side of the river.

At this point, two islands divide the Ohio River into three distinct chutes of water. Nearest you, on the Indiana side of the river, is the Indian Chute (the "hero" route for early canoeists); on the far side, the Kentucky Chute holds the locks; and between the two is the Middle Chute. Goose Island, between the Indian and Middle Chutes, is protected as part of Falls of the Ohio State Park. The island contains several fossil beds and plays host to various habitats dominated by willow and cottonwood trees, and prairie grass. Access to the island is by private boat only.

Another 10 minutes (about 0.4 mile) of walking brings you to the Falls of the Ohio Interpretive Center and better views of the river below the dam. The pool of water formed by the dam obscures the falls, but the water spewing from the release valves provides for plenty of action as the river races along the bumpy riverbed. Occasionally you might see whitewater kayakers working on their eddy turns and peelouts in the swift current, or oar rigs practicing for a trip on the Colorado River. But be forewarned—this place is not safe for swimming, for man or beast. Keep Fido on a short leash, and restrain yourself from lobbing that limb into the strong current.

Continue walking downstream along the paved Levee Trail, which now moves northwest and slightly away from the river. The sounds of the falls begin to fade as the wooded area insulates you from the riverbank. The trail takes on a comfortable pace as the trees continue to block the river views. Your eye may become slightly more voyeuristic as tidy backyards on the opposite side of the trail come into view.

Traffic on the paved trail follows the normal rules of the road: stay right, except when you want to pass, and watch for oncoming traffic, which could include cyclists, inline skaters, and runners pushing jogging strollers. Local neighborhood kids love to race their Big Wheels along the levee, and many a child has learned to ride a two-wheeler on the smooth paved surface.

As the trail begins to parallel Harrison Avenue (about 1.8 miles from the trailhead), views of the river appear once more. The trail officially ends at the old road that leads to the George Rogers Clark cabin, near the entrance to the Lewis and Clark Park, and where Bailey Avenue dead-ends into Harrison. Known as Clarks Point, this land was given to George Rogers Clark (an older brother of William Clark, of Lewis and Clark fame) as part of a Revolutionary War land grant. In 1803 Clark built a small cabin here, which was later torn down; a replica was built in 2001. Call 812-280-9970 for a schedule of free cabin tours.

From the porch of the cabin, take in the skyline of downtown Louisville and try to imagine what Clark saw from this vantage point. As you walk the 2 miles back to your vehicle, imagine running the falls in a dugout canoe while trying to keep your moccasins dry.

Nearby Attractions

If all this water has you waxing nostalgic, make time for the **Howard Steamboat Museum.** Just a 2-mile (5-minute) drive from the Levee Trail, the museum is housed in a beautiful Victorian mansion built by the Howard family in 1894. The Howards were among the major steamboat builders of their time, and the master craftsmen who worked for the shipyard helped construct the house.

The museum is located at 1101 E. Market St. in Jeffersonville, Indiana; hours are Tuesday–Saturday, 10 a.m.–4 p.m., and Sunday, 1–4 p.m. For more information, call 812-283-3728 or visit **steam boatmuseum.org.**

Directions

From downtown Louisville, drive north on I-65 across the Ohio River and take Exit 0 toward Jeffersonville and Falls of the Ohio State Park. At the bottom of the exit ramp, turn left (west) on West Court Avenue. West Court will take you back under I-65; immediately turn left (south) on Broadway Street, then very quickly take another left on South Indiana Avenue. Drive 0.3 mile; parking and the eastern trailhead will be on your left, just above the riverbank. Additional free parking is plentiful in the lots across from The Widow's Walk Ice Creamery, at 415 East Riverside Drive.

Parking is also free and plentiful at the opposite (far western) end of the trail at Lewis and Clark Park, near the end of Harrison Avenue. To reach this lot from downtown Louisville, take I-65 North across the Ohio River into Indiana. Take Exit 1 north toward Jeffersonville/Clarksville, immediately merge onto US 31 North, and drive

0.8 mile. Bear slightly right (still traveling north) on IN 62 and drive 0.7 mile. Take the first left (south) on Randolph Avenue and continue 0.4 mile. Finally, turn right (west) on Harrison Avenue and drive 0.8 mile to the parking lot.

Parking at the Falls of the Ohio Interpretive Center costs $2 if you don't pay the entrance fee for the center ($5 for age 19 and older, $2 for age 18 and younger, free under age 2). This parking lot is about one-third of the distance from the eastern trailhead of the Levee Trail to the far western trailhead at Lewis and Clark Park (see **fallsofthe ohio.org/map.html** for detailed directions).

5 Goose Creek Loop at Tom Sawyer Park

SCENERY: ★ ★ ★ ★
TRAIL CONDITION: ★ ★ ★
CHILDREN: ★ ★ ★
DIFFICULTY: ★ ★
SOLITUDE: ★ ★

HOW GLORIOUS GROW THE PLATINUM THREADS OF THE MILKWEED.

GPS TRAILHEAD COORDINATES: N38° 17.130' W85° 33.430'

DISTANCE & CONFIGURATION: 2.2-mile loop

HIKING TIME: 1 hour

HIGHLIGHTS: Diverse scenery, many special events

ELEVATION: 697' at trailhead, with no significant change in elevation

ACCESS: Daily, sunrise–sunset; free admission

MAPS: None except for a sign posted at the trailhead kiosk

FACILITIES: Restrooms, picnic tables, soccer fields, archery range, outdoor swimming pool, tennis and basketball courts, BMX track, and softball fields

WHEELCHAIR ACCESS: None

COMMENTS: Pets must be leashed.

CONTACTS: E. P. "Tom" Sawyer State Park, 502-429-7270; **tinyurl.com/tomsawyerpark**

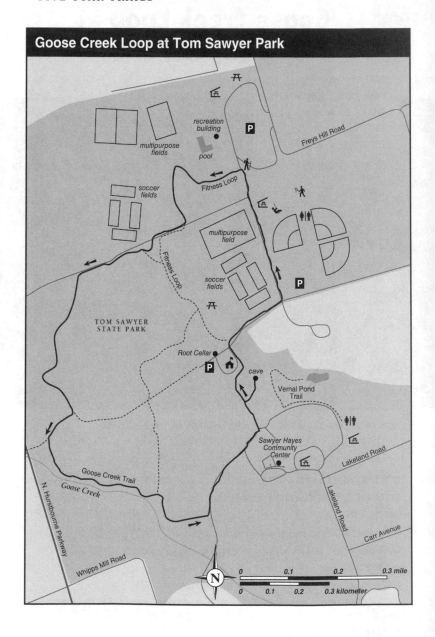

Goose Creek Loop at Tom Sawyer Park

Overview

The Goose Creek Loop lies within the well-loved E. P. "Tom" Sawyer State Park, in northeastern Jefferson County. The trail winds around much of the 550-acre park, across open fields, and through lightly wooded areas along Goose Creek. Other trails traverse the park and are frequently utilized for cross-country practice and meets. The suburban park is extremely popular after work and on weekends, and offers an excellent array of educational programs focusing on the great outdoors.

The park was named after Erbon Powers Sawyer (1915–1969), a well-respected Jefferson County judge and the father of newscaster Diane Sawyer. The state bought the land from the Kentucky Department of Mental Health in 1969. Much of the property had been used as a farming operation for the mental hospital on the premises. Consequently, several outbuildings still stand on the property and many old farm roads crisscross the park.

Route Details

The Goose Creek Loop takes advantage of the small amount of wooded area within the park. The trailhead is just south of the large brown activity building, near the southwestern edge of the parking lot. This route combines portions of the 1-mile finely graveled Fitness Trail with the 1.25-mile Goose Creek Trail to create a 2.2-mile loop. The park website offers neither trail nor park maps, and none are available at the trailhead kiosk; however, a large map posted at the kiosk can give you a general feel for the layout of the park. You'll quickly notice that the multitude of cross-country trails, the Fitness Trail, and the profusion of gravel and paved farm roads create a spaghetti junction rivaling that found in downtown Louisville.

From the trailhead, walk almost due west from the kiosk to follow the 1-mile Fitness Trail counterclockwise. This portion of the trail follows the edge of several large open fields, with a pleasant array of trees and picnic tables providing some visual interest. The trail then veers left (south), and you'll come to an intersection with a gravel road, which leads west to the model-airplane field. Leave the Fitness Trail by turning right (west) on the gravel road, and walk a short distance until you see a small dirt path on your left. This is the start of the Goose Creek Trail. The trail is not marked, although an old wooden post stands silent sentry.

The Goose Creek Trail continues west, paralleling the gravel road for a short distance and meandering through some small patches of open fields. The path then turns left (south) and follows the far western edge of the park boundary. You may hear some road noise from Hurstbourne Parkway. A few smaller trails will come in on your right, leading to a small parking lot just off Hurstbourne.

As the trail goes progressively deeper into the lightly wooded area, Goose Creek will appear on your right, just south of the trail and a little less than a mile from the trailhead. The narrow, intimate creek is downright pretty in spots, with small fish darting amid the shadows. The trail continues creekside for several hundred yards. At one point you'll see a rogue trail cross the creek. Don't follow this path—instead, bear left (east), staying on the same side of the creek you started on.

Soon you will come to an intersection with a fine gravel trail. Turn right (south) and follow this path a short distance. The trail then intersects an abandoned paved road. Turn left (north) at this junction, then left again (now heading northwest) on another gravel road. Confused? You're not alone. As mentioned, the trails here twist, turn, cross, and intersect again and again. But stick with my directions and you'll be fine.

In about 30 yards you'll see a grassy path duck under some trees just to the right (east) of the trail. This short trail leads to an old cave, shored up with brick. While it's interesting to explore, you can't see much unless you've packed a flashlight.

Back on the gravel road, you'll see some buildings straight ahead and the archery range on your right. Follow the trail around the "Root Cellar" and rejoin the Fitness Trail. Head right (east) on the trail and you'll return to the parking lot.

Before you get back in your vehicle, note the array of classes and programs listed on the trailhead kiosk. The park offers an Outdoor Skills Series that includes classes on orienteering, knot tying and uses, and shelter and fire building. Other programs range from Leave No Trace principles to park geology, and how to play pickleball. The annual "In the Park After Dark" is "geocaching with a ghoulish twist"; using a GPS device, participants navigate the park from 8 p.m. to midnight. That might be easier than the trail gyrations I've described above.

Nearby Attractions

On the eastern side of Freys Hill Road, the park has established a community garden. It leases 85 plots for $25 each. Further information is available on-site.

The **Louisville Astronomical Society** hosts free monthly "star parties" at the park. Although you probably won't see Lady Gaga here, the parties are fun (and they make for a cheap date). You can use their telescopes or bring your own. See **louisville-astro.org** for more information.

Directions

From I-265 (KY 841/Gene Snyder Freeway), take Exit 32 and head west on Westport Road (KY 1447). Drive 0.5 mile and, at the second light, turn left (south) on Freys Hill Road. Drive another 0.4 mile. The dog park and community garden will be on your left; immediately following, the main park entrance will be on your right.

Iroquois Park Summit

SCENERY: ★ ★ ★ ★
TRAIL CONDITION: ★ ★ ★ ★ ★
CHILDREN: ★ ★ ★
DIFFICULTY: ★ ★ ★
SOLITUDE: ★ ★

IROQUOIS PARK IS PERFECT FOR HIKING YEAR-ROUND.

GPS TRAILHEAD COORDINATES: N38° 10.113' W85° 47.140'

DISTANCE & CONFIGURATION: 4.4-mile balloon

HIKING TIME: 1.5 hours

HIGHLIGHTS: Paved path, views of downtown Louisville and Jefferson County

ELEVATION: 556' at trailhead, ascending to 746' at high point

ACCESS: Daily, 6 a.m.–11 p.m.; free admission. This is a gated paved road. Pedestrians and cyclists may use the road to the top of the summit daily throughout the year. Motorized-vehicle access is available Wednesday, Saturday, and Sunday, 8 a.m.–8 p.m., April 1–October 28.

MAPS: Louisville Metro Parks, USGS *Louisville West*. Most online navigation tools (including MapQuest and Google Maps) also include street maps of the park.

FACILITIES: Picnic tables and shelters, playground

WHEELCHAIR ACCESS: Yes, but not for the faint of heart. A granny gear and really good brakes are required.

COMMENTS: Pets must be leashed. Hiking is prohibited in wet conditions and during freeze–thaw cycles.

CONTACTS: Louisville Metro Parks, 502-456-8100; **louisvilleky.gov/metroparks**

Overview

Iroquois Park is truly urban, completely surrounded by residential and commercial districts in southwest Louisville. Designed by Frederick Law Olmsted, it's among the 18 parks and 6 interconnecting parkways in Louisville attributed to him and his firm. Perched atop a heavily forested knob, the park offers commanding views of downtown Louisville and much of the surrounding countryside. The trail reaches the park summit by way of a paved road that is open to vehicular traffic only on certain days and during certain times of year.

Route Details

Iroquois Park is extremely popular with walkers, joggers, and cyclists throughout the year. The east side of the park is home to the Sunnyhill Pavilion, the Iroquois Amphitheater, playgrounds, tennis courts, and a disc-golf course. The Iroquois Golf Course is on the northern side of the park, and the southwestern corner is where Louisville Mounted Police horses are boarded and train. All of these activities are connected by Rundill Road, which circles the perimeter of the park and is open for pedestrian and cyclists to use. Only a portion of Rundill Road allows vehicular traffic.

The heart of Iroquois Park can be reached via Uppill Road, as it winds around and up a large knob—a steeply sloping, often-cone-shaped hill common across much of central Kentucky. The top of the knob affords views in all directions, including the downtown Louisville skyline. Myriad dirt trails, the result of hikers, mountain bikers, and the resident deer population, crisscross the park. Unfortunately, these trails bear little resemblance to any published maps of the park and can be quite convoluted.

For the first-time summit hiker, walking Uppill Road to the top of the knob is the best assurance that you'll arrive where you want to be—and that you know how to get back down. As noted, the road to the summit is open seasonally on certain days of the week. I suggest that you avoid walking this paved trail when motorized

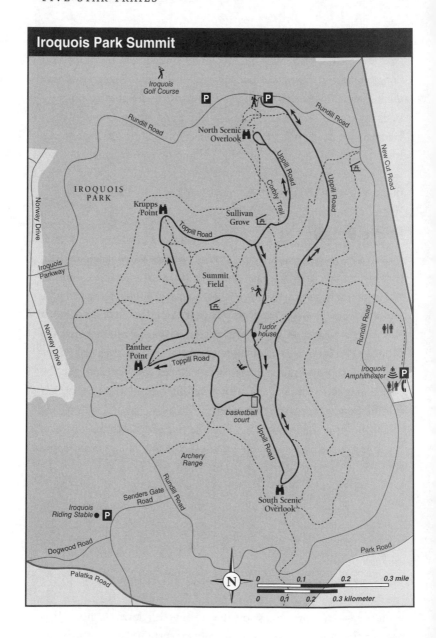

Iroquois Park Summit

Iroquois
Golf Course

Rundill Road

North Scenic
Overlook

Uppill Road

Corby Trail

New Cut Road

IROQUOIS
PARK

Krupps
Point

Toppill Road

Sullivan
Grove

Uppill Road

Norway Drive

Iroquois
Parkway

Summit
Field

Norway Drive

Tudor
house

Rundill Road

Iroquois
Amphitheater

Panther
Point

Toppill Road

basketball
court

Uppill Road

Archery
Range

Senders Gate
Road

Rundill Road

South Scenic
Overlook

Iroquois
Riding Stable

Dogwood Road

Park Road

Palatka Road

N

0   0.1   0.2   0.3 mile

0   0.1   0.2   0.3 kilometer

traffic is present. Instead, choose a day in the off-season or during the week (with the exception of Wednesday), and you'll have the road to yourself.

Uppill Road will be gated and locked on the days it's closed. Simply walk to either side of the gate and continue up the road. Immediately you'll find yourself immersed in mature hardwood forests, with three or four robins to keep you company (since they all look the same, who knows if it's the same one?). The road is rather steep for a jogging stroller, but if you have the fortitude (and the calf muscles), it's not unheard of to see little tykes at the top. Cyclists and runners also use the ascent for training purposes.

The climb to the first overlook is 0.95 mile from the parking lot and leads you to the South Scenic Overlook, which faces, well, south. Enjoy the view while you catch your breath and snap a few pictures.

Continue up the road another 0.2 mile and congratulate yourself on reaching the top of the knob. A lonely basketball court stands to your left, torn nets twirling in the breeze. Any loose balls would surely plummet off the knob at breakneck speeds, only to wind up in Rupp Arena amid a sea of blue.

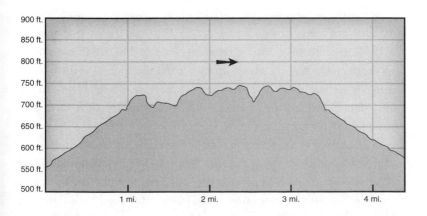

Just past the basketball court, turn left (west) and continue walking the road past the South and North Shelters (both are beautiful 1920s stone structures) to Panther Point, which is 1.55 miles from the parking lot below. You're now on Toppill Road. On this side of the knob you'll be facing due west, with views of rural Jefferson County (or what's left of it). Continue on Toppill Road as you circle the top of the knob and what is primarily an open meadow, referred to as Summit Field.

The Metro Park service periodically mows paths across these open fields. Here the bird populations, including meadowlarks, Eastern kingbirds, and even woodcocks, are always bustling. The small spring-fed ponds atop the knob provide fresh water for the wildlife that frequents these meadows.

Toppill Road continues circling the open fields until it reaches the next overlook, Krupps Point, which faces north toward the downtown Louisville skyline. Take time to notice the engraved stone set in the retaining wall. In the springtime, this side of the summit is a symphony of spring peepers, the latest generation living in the ponds atop the knob. Another 5 minutes (about 0.2 mile) of walking on Toppill Road will bring you back to Uppill Road. Bear left (north) here.

This dead-end section of Uppill Road (labeled as Downill Road on the park map and Iroquois Park Road on Google Maps) leads you to the North Scenic Overlook, about 2.5 miles from the parking area. A 1970s face-lift to the stone retaining walls and overlook has not aged gracefully, but the views up here continue to be worthwhile, with 270-degree vistas of the city and countryside. Spend a few minutes enjoying the scenery before heading back on Uppill Road the same way you came.

Just west of the road you may notice a dirt path marked COR-BLY TRAIL, which was built after the Switchback Trail was closed and serves as a shortcut to the parking lot. Some hikers prefer to take this route to the parking area rather than walking the road back down. However, the Corbly Trail can be muddy, and the park forbids hiking on wet trails and during freeze–thaw cycles.

Taking the road back, you'll pass Toppill Road once more. Stay straight here, along Uphill Road. Shortly you will pass a historic stone structure with English Tudor architectural elements. At one time this building housed restrooms and a large open-air covered pavilion, replete with stone fireplace and limestone mantel. Sadly, persistent vandalism led to the permanent closing of the restrooms.

Continue straight on Uppill Road, backtracking your steps when you get to the basketball courts. It's all downhill from here. Slowly work your way back down from the top of the knob, thinking about what these woods must have looked like when Frederick Law Olmsted first trekked up here.

Nearby Attractions

A unique Louisville landmark, the **Little Loomhouse** is just a few blocks from Iroquois Park, at 328 Kenwood Hill Road. On the National Register of Historic Places, the site consists of three wood cabins built in the 1860s and is dedicated to celebrating the life of Lou Tate and her passion for textiles and weaving. Lou inherited the property in the early 1900s and immediately began offering weaving classes to the women of Louisville and selling textiles to the public—including Eleanor Roosevelt, who placed an order for linens for the White House. Mrs. Roosevelt visited the Little Loomhouse several times in support of Lou's commitment to textile arts.

Open Tuesday, Wednesday, Thursday, and the third Saturday of each month, the Loomhouse relies totally on volunteer staffing, so call ahead to be sure the cabins are available for touring. It's also available for private parties and classes. Admission is $3.50; for more information, call 502-367-4792 or visit **littleloomhouse.org.**

Directions

From I-264 (Henry Watterson Expressway), take Exit 9, head south on Taylor Boulevard, and drive 1.3 miles. To reach the trailhead parking lot, use the far northern entrance to Iroquois Park, where Taylor

Boulevard turns into New Cut Road and Southern Parkway intersects from the northeast. Turn right (west) into the park and drive 0.2 mile. Turn right (north) on Rundill Road, toward the golf course, and drive another 0.3 mile. Before you reach the golf clubhouse, you'll see a small parking lot to your left, south of where Rundill and Uppill Roads intersect. Park here and get ready to hike up.

7 # Ohio River Levee Trail

SCENERY: ★ ★ ★
TRAIL CONDITION: ★ ★ ★ ★ ★
CHILDREN: ★ ★ ★
DIFFICULTY: ★ ★
SOLITUDE: ★ ★ ★

WALKING ATOP THE LEVEE AFFORDS COMMANDING VIEWS OF THE OHIO RIVER VALLEY.

GPS TRAILHEAD COORDINATES: N38° 5.793' W85° 53.661'

DISTANCE & CONFIGURATION: 7.4-mile out-and-back

HIKING TIME: 3 hours

HIGHLIGHTS: Pastoral views of the Ohio River, historic home

ELEVATION: 477' at trailhead, with no significant elevation change

ACCESS: Daily, 6 a.m.–11 p.m. Free to hike; see **riverside-landing.org** for fees to tour historic Riiverside, The Farnsley-Moreman Landing.

MAPS: Available at the website below

FACILITIES: Visitor center, restrooms, picnic area, historic-home tour

WHEELCHAIR ACCESS: Both the trail and the buildings are accessible.

COMMENTS: Drinking-water access is extremely limited along the trail.

CONTACTS: Louisville Metro Parks, 502-456-8100; **tinyurl.com/metroloop**

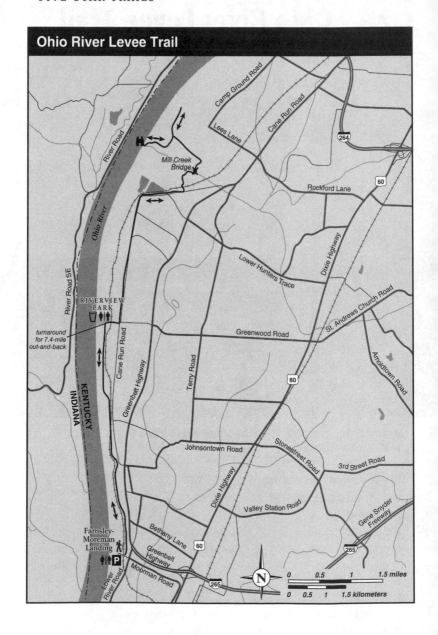

Ohio River Levee Trail

Camp Ground Road

Cane Run Road

Lees Lane

264

Mill Creek Bridge

Rockford Lane

60

River Road

Ohio River

Lower Hunters Trace

Dixie Highway

River Road SE

RIVERVIEW PARK

St. Andrews Church Road

Greenwood Road

turnaround for 7.4-mile out-and-back

Cane Run Road

Greenbelt Highway

Terry Road

60

Arnoldtown Road

KENTUCKY
INDIANA

Johnsontown Road

Stonestreet Road

3rd Street Road

Dixie Highway

Valley Station Road

Gene Snyder Freeway

Farnsley-Moreman Landing

Bethany Lane

60

265

Greenbelt Highway

Moorman Road

Lower River Road

265

N

0   0.5   1   1.5 miles

0   0.5   1   1.5 kilometers

Overview

The Ohio River Levee Trail is part of Louisville's ambitious plan to create 100 miles of multiuse paths around the city. The suggested out-and-back hike begins at the Farnsley-Moremen Landing, travels 3.7 miles to Riverview Park, then returns on the same paved trail. The level multiuse path lies atop the levee and provides pastoral views of the Ohio River Valley. The trail is open to walkers, joggers, and cyclists.

Route Details

Our apologies to Don McLean if we're out of tune, but this hike will have you humming "Bye, bye, Miss American Pie / Drove my Chevy to the levee / But the levee was dry" the entire way. But what a great earworm to have as you walk atop the levee, with intermittent views of the Ohio River, tall grass wavering in the breeze, and butterflies fluttering back and forth.

The paved Ohio River Levee Trail begins at the Farnsley-Moremen Landing and runs north for 9.5 miles before joining several miles of bike lanes, which connect it to the 6.9-mile paved Riverwalk Trail. While cyclists can easily make the 19-mile round-trip ride on the Levee Trail, the average hiker wouldn't be interested in pounding his or her feet for that many miles. But shorter sections of the trail are popular with hikers and joggers. And it's not unusual to see parents walking the path pushing jogging strollers or strolling along as their kids ride their first two-wheelers.

When is a good time to hike the Ohio River Levee Trail? For most walkers, spring and fall are ideal when temperatures are well within reasonable ranges and breezes are gentle. The mixture of hardwoods along the river and the small knobs on the Indiana side provide nice fall color. In the peak of summer, however, the trail becomes less than ideal as the humidity climbs and the pavement reflects all that heat back onto you. Wintertime hiking is also a challenge here, as the winds can be quite cold and biting; on the upside, you're guaranteed to have the place to yourself.

This hike runs between the Farnsley-Moremen Landing and Riverview Park, then back again. Walkers can begin at either endpoint, but parking at the landing is a little more relaxing because more people use the parking lot at Riverview. So follow the directions on the next page and park at Farnsley-Moremen. Take a quick tour of the visitor center, hit the restrooms, and top off that water bottle or hydration pack—there's only one water fountain (open seasonally) between Farnsley-Moremen and Riverview, and no other facilities.

Just north of the visitor center lies a historic home built in 1837 by Gabriel Farnsley. Alanson and Rachel Moremen bought the house and surrounding farmland in 1862, naming the site Riverside. Descendants of the Moremens sold the property to Jefferson County in 1988. Riverside is available for tours year-round (see **riverside-landing.org** for admission fees and hours). "A Family Exploration Guide of the Riverside Landing" is available free at the visitor center.

To reach the trailhead, walk to the northern end of the parking area, then turn right (east) and backtrack the way you drove into the park. At the top of the hill you'll see the trailhead sign and the paved path heading north from Moorman Road. You may have noticed the sign when you first entered the park off Lower River Road.

The Ohio River Levee Trail runs north atop the levee, parallel to the river and above Cane Run Road. In about 0.5 mile you'll see the historic Moremen Family Chapel (circa 1888), which originally stood at the corner of Bethany Lane and Dixie Highway. The chapel was moved to the new site and is currently being renovated.

The next 3 miles along the Ohio River Levee Trail consist of a peaceful walk with occasional views of the river to your left (west) and private homes to your right (east). The scenery is pleasant enough but changes only with the pace of your walk. Deer, rabbits, and turkey can be seen. On weekends, particularly during the summer, a golf cart carrying members of the Jefferson County Sheriff's Department may pass, ready to lend a hand to those in need.

About 3.7 miles from the trailhead, you'll see Riverview Park, also known as Greenwood Boat Ramp because of the facilities here.

The park has picnic tables, both a traditional playground and a "spray ground" in the summer, and restrooms. Riverview is extremely popular with families, boaters, and fishermen. Enjoy the lively activity here and the bucolic scenes of the riverfront. Take a last glance before retracing your steps south, back to the Farnsley-Moremen Landing.

Take heart and turn that hum into a whistle. Or, if no one else is within earshot, belt out a full-blown melody: "Them good ol' boys were drinkin' whiskey and rye. . . ." Try to remember as many verses as you can before thanking Don for his "American Pie" and for a wonderful day on the levee.

Nearby Attractions

A 4.8-mile round-trip section of the Ohio River Levee Trail of interest to hikers starts at 5300 Cane Run Road, near the corner of Cane Run Road and Lower Hunters Trace, just north of Riverview Park. The Ohio River Levee Trail continues north of this intersection, travels through a small wooded area before crossing Mill Creek Bridge, and goes on to the Ohio River Overlook, which is just north of the LGE Cane Run Generating Station. The one-way distance from the Cane Run Road–Lower Hunters Trace intersection to the overlook is 2.4 miles.

This portion of the Ohio River Levee Trail briefly borders a light industrial area, but the rest of the hike is rather scenic, passing over Mill Creek before leading to the overlook at the river's edge. Again, bring plenty of water—there are no facilities on the trail.

Directions

Take I-65 South from downtown Louisville and turn right (west) on I-265 (KY 841/Gene Snyder Freeway). After about 9 miles, I-265 West becomes the Greenbelt Highway (KY 1934)—watch for a RIVERPORT sign. Drive 1.2 additional miles after the road changes; then, at the stoplight, turn left (south) on Lower River Road and drive 0.2 mile. Turn right (west) on Moorman Road, which ends in 0.2 mile at the Farnsley-Moremen Landing and the trailhead parking.

8

Waterfront Park

SCENERY: ★ ★ ★ ★
TRAIL CONDITION: ★ ★ ★ ★
CHILDREN: ★ ★ ★ ★
DIFFICULTY: ★
SOLITUDE: ★ ★

WATERFRONT PARK CAN PROVIDE A BRIEF RESPITE FROM A HARRIED URBAN EXISTENCE.

GPS TRAILHEAD COORDINATES: N38° 15.765' W85° 44.264'

DISTANCE & CONFIGURATION: 2.7-mile loop

HIKING TIME: 1.2 hours

HIGHLIGHTS: Panoramic views of the Ohio River, fountains, sculptures, Lincoln Memorial

ELEVATION: 444' at trailhead, with no significant elevation change

ACCESS: Daily, 6 a.m.–11 p.m.; free admission

MAPS: Available at the website below

FACILITIES: Restrooms, picnic tables, drinking fountains (in season), playgrounds, "splashground" (water-play area)

WHEELCHAIR ACCESS: Yes

COMMENTS: Parking is free and plentiful.

CONTACTS: Louisville Metro Parks, 502-456-8100; **louisvillewaterfront.com**

Waterfront Park

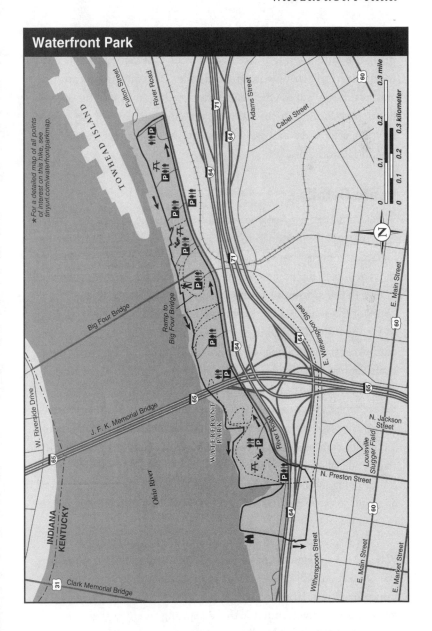

★ For a detailed map of all points of interest on this hike, see tinyurl.com/waterfrontparkmap.

Overview

Bring the family. Bring a date. Bring your walking shoes and head to the riverfront of downtown Louisville. The Waterfront Park trail starts at the base of the Big Four Bridge and loops around this 85-acre linear park located in the heart of the city. The paved path passes multiple sculptures and water features, urban gardens, the Lincoln Memorial, and more.

Route Details

Waterfront Park has become such a fixture in the River City that it's hard to imagine what downtown Louisville was like before it was created. Groundbreaking for Phase I of the park started in 1994, and most of Phase III is complete. The city continues to dream big with its efforts to transform this former industrial riverfront into an integral spoke of the social hub of downtown Louisville.

The Falls of the Ohio, just downstream of the park, is the only natural obstruction along the nearly 1,000-mile Ohio River as it flows from Pennsylvania before joining the Mississippi River in Cairo, Illinois. For thousands of years, migrating buffalo crossed the Ohio here to reach the salt licks and cane that grew along the riverbanks. Various Indian tribes followed these migrations, and the crossing soon became a point of commerce. As development occurred on both sides of the river, Louisville quickly grew as a point of warehousing and support for the shipping industries. Eventually the Louisville and Portland Canal was built to move boat traffic through the locks and avoid the portaging that was necessary to bypass the falls.

The transformation of the transportation industry post–World War II led to a significant decline in commercial boat traffic along the Ohio. Louisville's waterfront fell into neglect until a revitalization project was launched in the late 1980s. What had become an eyesore is now eye candy for those wanting to enjoy the amenities a park can bring: paved walkways, water features, gardens, benches, and artwork—all in an outdoor urban environment.

The 2.7-mile Waterfront Park loop trail begins in the parking lot adjacent to the ramp of the Big Four Bridge (more about that later). Our route runs counterclockwise along the riverfront and circles back around, following Witherspoon Street and River Road before completing the loop back along the river.

From the parking lot, walk north toward the riverfront. Turn left (west) and head downstream along the promenade toward the I-65 bridge over the Ohio. The first thing you'll pass on your left is the Swing Garden, a wide, grassy knoll scattered with bench-style swings facing the water. The Lincoln Memorial is just past the swings. The paved path continues along the waterfront, past the Fred Wiche Grove (named after a beloved local gardening expert who had his own radio show) and then past the Upland Meadows. Feel free to wander off the path at any point to explore the inner workings of this linear park.

Past the meadows (about 0.4 mile from the trailhead), the trail takes a left turn away from the river as it bears south along the Harbor (a.k.a. the Great Lawn Docks). Just past this small harbor, the path makes a hard right-hand turn to head back toward the riverfront. You'll now be skirting the North Great Lawn and *Gracehoper*, a black painted-steel abstract sculpture designed by the late Tony Smith.

Once again the trail turns left (south) away from the river as it follows the canal leading to the Dancing Waters and the *Tetra* sculpture, created by Charles Perry. At Witherspoon Street, turn left (east)—yes, lots of left-hand turns to complete this loop!—and continue along the edge of the Great South Lawn. *Flock of Finns*, a group of sculptures created by the late folk artist Marvin Finn, sits at the corner of Witherspoon Street and River Road.

Turn left on River Road and follow the paved path east. You'll now be on the southern side of the Upland Meadows, Fred Wiche Grove, and the Lincoln Memorial. Continue past the Big Four Bridge lot (where you parked) along River Road, and past the Brown-Forman Amphitheater until you see the building that houses the Louisville Rowing Club. Take a left here and head back toward the riverfront.

Once on the back side of the club, turn left at the waterfront and head west past the Amphitheater Docks, Tumbleweed Tex Mex Grill, and Adventure Playground. In minutes you'll be back at the parking lot adjacent to the Big Four Bridge ramp.

Nearby Attractions

While you're at the waterfront, you may want to walk across the **Big Four Bridge,** a trail for pedestrians and cyclists that connects Waterfront Park with Jeffersonville, Indiana. The bridge, named after the Cleveland, Cincinnati, Chicago, and St. Louis Railway, is a little more than 1 mile long one-way, including the entrance ramps on either side, making for a 2-mile round-trip.

The construction of the six-span railroad-truss bridge, which began in 1888, ultimately claimed the lives of 37 workers. Twelve men drowned after the collapse of a caisson that was suppose to hold the water back when they were building the pier foundation, and another four men died when a wooden beam broke while they were working on another caisson. The worst disaster occurred in December 1893, when heavy winds knocked over a crane, which in turn caused a truss to fall into the river, bringing with it 41 men and killing 21 of them.

The Big Four Bridge was closed in 1969, and both approach ramps were removed and sold for scrap. The railroad span stood abandoned—earning the moniker "The Bridge That Goes Nowhere"—until 2009, when construction began to convert the span to a paved pedestrian walkway. Opened in 2013, the walkway offers spectacular views of the Ohio River and downtown Louisville.

Directions

Waterfront Park is between River Road and the Ohio River, just north of the spaghetti junction where I-64, I-65, and I-71 intersect in downtown Louisville; see **louisvillewaterfront.com/park/directions** for detailed directions from these interstates. Louisville Slugger Field is immediately south of the park.

9

Waverly Park Loops

SCENERY: ★ ★ ★ ★
TRAIL CONDITION: ★ ★ ★ ★
CHILDREN: ★ ★
DIFFICULTY: ★ ★ ★
SOLITUDE: ★ ★

CUTLEAF TOOTHWORT, ALSO KNOWN AS CROW'S TOES OR PEPPER ROOT, GROWS ALL OVER EASTERN NORTH AMERICA.

GPS TRAILHEAD COORDINATES: N38° 7.786' W85° 49.924'

DISTANCE & CONFIGURATION: 4.7-mile pair of adjoining loops

HIKING TIME: 1.8 hours

HIGHLIGHTS: Classic hardwood forest in suburban Louisville

ELEVATION: 547' at trailhead, ascending to 727' at high point

ACCESS: Daily, 8 a.m.–sunset; free admission

MAPS: Louisville Metro Parks, USGS *Louisville West*

FACILITIES: Picnic tables, grills, small fishing lake, playground, portable toilet

WHEELCHAIR ACCESS: None

COMMENTS: Pets must be leashed.

CONTACTS: Louisville Metro Parks, 502-456-8100; **louisvilleky.gov/metroparks**

Waverly Park Loops

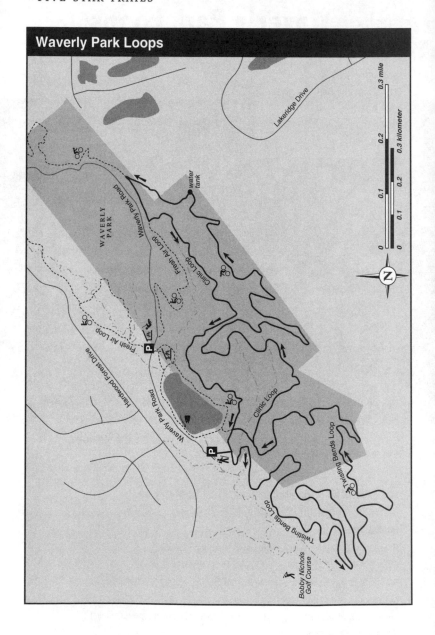

Overview

For many Louisville residents, Waverly Park, in southwestern Jefferson County, means two things: fishing and mountain biking. But the hiking here is top-notch, and peaceful trails can be found during the week and off-season. The perfect after-work or weekend getaway, Waverly has four distinct trail loops, two of which can be combined to make a 4.7-mile hike. These amoeba-shaped trails run through hardwood forests, winding their way over creeks, up ridges, and down moguls, and are well maintained, thanks in large part to the Kentucky Mountain Bike Association.

Route Details

The road through 300-acre Waverly Park ends at a small fishing lake and three distinct parking areas. The trailhead for both of these loops has recently been relocated to the parking lot west of the lake, where the park road dead-ends. A short connector trail leads you on a 5-minute walk to the junction of the 2.2-mile Twisting Bends Loop and the 2.4-mile Clinic Loop.

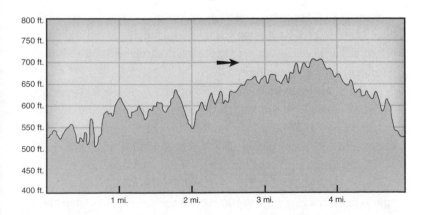

Long a haven for the mountain-biking community, these trails have been faithfully maintained for years by the Kentucky Mountain Bike Association (KyMBA). The loops are tight and slightly technical singletrack, with the occasional wooden bridge traversing small creeks where needed. The Twisting Bends Loop earned its moniker honestly. In the spirit of sustainability, it packs a lot of trail into a small amount of acreage. For the most part, the trail is well drained despite the heavy clay content of the soil. The nine-hole Bobby Nichols Golf Course encircles much of the loop, buffering hikers from the suburban neighborhoods that surround the park.

Bear right (west) at the junction of the two trails to begin the Twisting Bends Loop through a beautiful hardwood forest of mature oaks, sweetgums, and beeches. The trail immediately takes on the graceful rhythm of a firefly on the wing. Ferns dot much of the forest floor, providing splashes of green year-round. Spring hikers will be greeted with an array of wildflowers, including cut-leaf toothwort and bluets. Early-blooming cornelian cherry dogwood (*Cornus mas*), a small multitrunked tree, is also plentiful along the hillsides. In July, the small, dainty yellow blooms of this dogwood mature into bright-cherry-red fruits that are quickly gobbled up by the resident squirrels and birds. In the summer there is enough shade and shadows at Waverly that the moss doesn't grow just on the north side of the huge white and red oaks along the trail. And fall hikers will enjoy the bright-yellow beech leaves as they contrast sharply with the reds and purples of the sweetgum trees.

After a little more than 2 miles of hiking, you'll find yourself back at the main junction, with the short trail to the parking lot straight ahead. Bear right (east) and follow the Clinic Loop uphill if you're ready for more hiking. The trail then follows a narrow ridge as it gains elevation. The Clinic Loop is considerably more strenuous than the Twisting Bends; the downhills are much faster and the uphills more challenging. KyMBA has built several moguls (short but steep hills), creating a roller-coaster effect along parts of the trail. One long downhill is affectionately referred to as The Luge.

About 3.5 miles from the trailhead (or 1.5 miles from where the Clinic Loop begins), the trail joins the Fresh Air Loop, a 2.9-mile trail that runs on either side of the main park road. To stay on the Clinic Loop, bear left (south) and make a hairpin turn away from the Fresh Air Loop. At the 4-mile point, the trail is at its highest elevation and offers views of the small fishing lake below. From here the trail travels southwest before dropping toward the lake and back to the junction with the Twisting Bends Loop. Bear right (north) at this junction to return to the parking area.

At Waverly Park, bikers must give way to hikers, but sometimes practicality trumps courtesy. And given how much effort the biking community has put into trail building and trail maintenance, hikers should keep that in mind. In addition, mountain bikers typically ride the trails clockwise. The hiking directions given here suggest a counterclockwise rotation so hikers are "facing traffic," so to speak.

At the time that Waverly was developing into a cycling Mecca, few other alternatives existed. Now there is a multitude of good mountain biking trails in central Kentucky and southern Indiana. That has relieved some of the crowding at Waverly, as cyclists have more options, particularly on weekends. On the other hand, recent trail improvements have attracted more riders to Waverly from outside the state, so before you hike, you may want to check **kymba.org** to see if a race has been scheduled on a given day.

Nearby Attractions

Waverly's wide, flat **Lake Loop** runs 0.4 mile on a mostly gravel surface. This is a great hike for young kids, who can race around the lake in no time.

The 2.9-mile **Fresh Air Loop,** at the park's northeastern end, covers a wooded terrain very similar to the two loops featured here. But because the Fresh Air Loop is much straighter than the Twisting Bends Loop and generally has fewer steep hills than the Clinic Loop, cyclists can build up a lot of speed. The Fresh Air Loop can be accessed from either side of the park road, near the playground, and from the Clinic Loop.

Directions

From the intersection of I-264 (Henry Watterson Expressway) and Dixie Highway (US 31W/US 60), travel southwest out of Louisville on Dixie Highway for 3.2 miles. Turn left (east) on St. Andrews Church Road (KY 1931). After 1 mile, turn right (south) on Arnold-town Road. Drive 1 mile and turn left (west) on Waverly Park Road. In 1.2 miles, the park road dead-ends at a small parking lot, just west of the fishing lake.

Opposite: **WAVERLY FOREST CAN BE A WINTER WONDERLAND.**

Kentucky: South of Louisville and West of I-65 (Hikes 10–13)

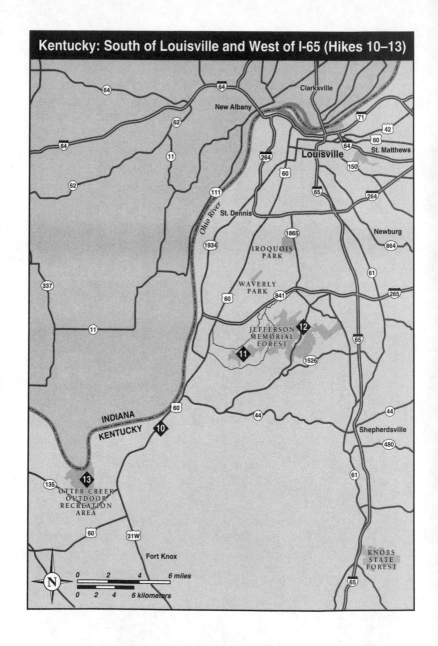

WERE THOSE BULLET HOLES THERE BEFORE OR AFTER THIS CAR SETTLED HERE?
(See Hike 11, Jefferson Memorial Forest: Scott's Gap Trail, page 85.)

10

Fort Duffield

SCENERY: ★ ★ ★ ★ ★
TRAIL CONDITION: ★ ★ ★ ★
CHILDREN: ★ ★ ★
DIFFICULTY: ★ ★ ★
SOLITUDE: ★ ★ ★

THIS SWEET LITTLE PIECE OF REAL ESTATE CAN BE YOURS FOR THE ASKING.

GPS TRAILHEAD COORDINATES: N37° 59.505' W85° 56.734'

DISTANCE & CONFIGURATION: 2.4-mile loop; more mileage readily available

HIKING TIME: 1.5 hours

HIGHLIGHTS: Kentucky's largest earthen fortification, panoramic views, creekside trails

ELEVATION: 458' at trailhead, ascending to 696' at high point

ACCESS: Daily, 8 a.m.–sunset; free admission

MAPS: Available at park trailhead kiosk; USGS *Vine Grove*

FACILITIES: Restrooms, picnic tables and shelters

WHEELCHAIR ACCESS: A gated road leads to the top of the fort. Access to this road is limited to times when park volunteers are present.

COMMENTS: Dogs on leashes welcome

CONTACTS: Fort Duffield Park and Historic Site, 502-922-4574; **fortduffield.com**

Overview

Fort Duffield offers panoramic views of the Ohio River Valley, the best-preserved earthen fortification in Kentucky, and 10 miles of nationally renowned mountain-biking trails. On reenactment weekends, the noise of cannon fire and musket balls can be heard over the sounds of derailleurs shifting and chain rings spinning. Consequently, the park attracts one of the more interesting combinations of outdoor aficionados. But on most days, hikers are left with tumbling creeks and quiet woods to roam and explore.

Route Details

Fort Duffield is the perfect place if you like your hiking served with a generous side-helping of history. As you approach the park, you cross the Louisville, Henderson, and St. Louis Bridge, a relic from the days when steamboats navigated the Salt River on their way to the Ohio River. Fort Duffield, authorized by General William Tecumseh Sherman and built at the mouth of the Salt River, sits atop a 300-foot bluff overlooking the Ohio River Valley. The fort was designed to protect both the Union's supply base at West Point, Kentucky, and the city of Louisville by monitoring activity along the surrounding waterways and railways.

After parking in the trailhead lot, stop at the kiosk and pick up a green trail map and tan fort brochure if you haven't visited before. The trail map shows a winding set of hiking and mountain-biking trails. In reality, if you hike beyond the fort the trails are even more convoluted than shown. But take a close look at the map and you'll see some good boundary markers that can help guide your hike. The western park boundary is constrained by a steep bluff that parallels Dixie Highway and overlooks the Ohio River and the town of West Point. The northern park boundary is constrained by another bluff, this one towering above the Salt River. Finally, the eastern boundary is defined by a set of power lines, the southern boundary by an old roadbed.

Fort Duffield

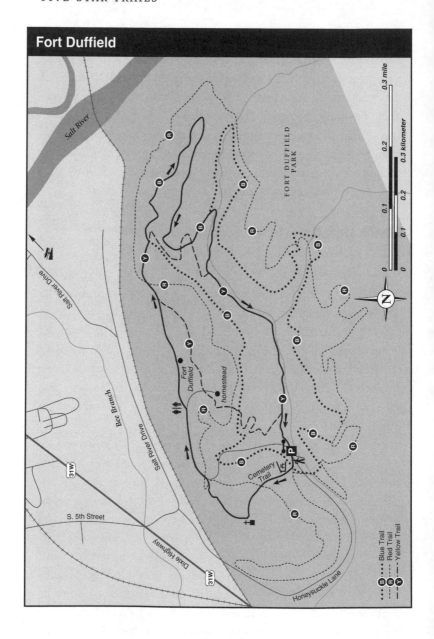

As you face the kiosk, a paved road climbs steeply in front of you, to the north; the Duffield Memorial Cemetery Trail begins to your left (west); and the Fort Trail begins to your right (east). The quickest way to the fort is straight up the paved road; this may also be the best option for stroller access and those with disabilities. However, volunteers staff the park, and the gate blocking motorized access to this road may or may not be locked depending on who's working at the time.

To walk the 2.4-mile loop clockwise, and to mix your history with your hiking, bear west out of the parking lot to begin the Cemetery Trail, just on the other side of the picnic shelter. This short but steep 0.25-mile climb leads you to the memorial grounds honoring 36 soldiers who died at Fort Duffield between 1861 and 1862, all members of the Ninth Michigan Infantry Regiment that served here.

Ionia Sweet. Miles Woods. Lafayette Porter. Isaac Columbus Tower. Philetus Bacon. Take time to read the names on the memorial markers and feel the gentle breeze blowing up the Ohio Valley. The views here are beautiful and the ambiance serene, belying the skirmishes that took place nearby.

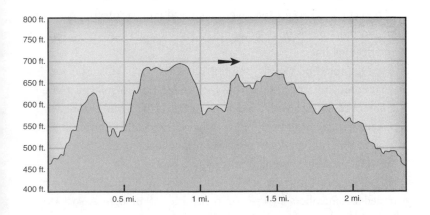

The Cemetery Trail continues on the other side of the flagpole hoisting Old Glory, leading you along a wide gravel trail that descends back to the paved road leading to Fort Duffield. Continue walking straight on the merged road/trail another few minutes (about 50 yards). The fort sits just ahead, on the highest point of the bluff overlooking the Ohio River and the town of West Point. The earthen fortification took one and a half months to build and provided camping for 1,000 men. Rarely do today's defense contractors work that fast.

Several small wood cabins and a few other structures built more recently are used by the reenactment crowd and during living-history events. Likewise, young hikers with a need to play make-believe can use the cabins and lean-tos to battle Lord Voldemort or Darth Vader.

The hiking trail continues on the northern side of the earthen fortification and under several large walnut trees that grace the center of the fort, playing host to the mistletoe that thrives here. The trail then merges with what is known alternately as the Down Hill Course Trail and the Red Loop Trail. Walk northeast for a few minutes along the bluff overlooking the Salt River, and the Blue Loop Trail will soon come in on your right, to the south of the bluff. Follow the Blue Loop Trail as it winds downhill, before meeting up with one of two creek drainages that eventually lead you back to the parking lot. Both drainages offer an abundance of spring wildflowers, ferns, and deer habitat.

As noted previously, the trails at Fort Duffield can be somewhat confusing. It's not unusual for the red trail to split into three different trails, each with a red blaze, or for the blue trail to fork, with one blazed trail heading uphill and the other winding downhill. Just keep in mind the park boundaries outlined earlier, and the parking lot will always be downhill from there.

Many of the trails at Fort Duffield were built and are maintained by members of the Kentucky Mountain Bike Association (KyMBA). Ranked as one of the top mountain-biking destinations in the United States, these trails are primarily singletrack, technical, and fun. KyMBA has built several ramps, moguls, and jumps for those wanting more than just creek crossing and log hopping. Although bikers must always give way to hikers, one way to show our appreciation for the efforts of the biking community is to share the trail.

Nearby Attractions

Founded in 1796, the small town of **West Point, Kentucky,** can provide an interesting diversion for those with a little extra time. Located where the Salt River flows into the Ohio River, West Point earned its moniker for at one time being the westernmost outpost for those traveling down the Ohio River. West Point also proudly notes that it lies on the 38th parallel—the same dividing line between North and South Korea. (Someone in the chamber of commerce has been quite busy.)

Your first stop might be the **Star Café,** in the old West Point Hotel at the intersection of South Fourth Street and South Street, behind the little red caboose. The café serves huge helpings of beans and cornbread and a constellation of homemade pies. According to its website (**wpstarcafe.com**), even Robert Plant of Led Zeppelin fame has proclaimed the food "excellent." Maybe he'll be there the next time you visit.

On the front porch of the café, you'll find a box of tourist literature, including a brochure on historic homes and sites in West Point. Nearly all of these are just a few blocks from the café on Elm Street, which borders the Ohio River. West Point was the location of a pre–Civil War stagecoach stop, riverfront inn, and boat ramp, or embarcadero (Spanish for "embarking place"). It was at this embarcadero in 1806, that Thomas Lincoln loaded a flatboat of produce for his 60-day journey to New Orleans. The story goes that the trip was profitable enough that he was able to finalize his marriage plans to Nancy Hanks.

If the concept of a Sears and Roebuck house is new to you, be sure to visit the one built in 1899 across from the river landing. These "kit" houses were purchased from catalogs, shipped by rail, and assembled by local craftsmen. This particular house, at **201 Elm St.,** is in the "Three I" style, named for its popularity in Indiana, Illinois, and Iowa.

Directions

Fort Duffield is southwest of Louisville and just south of West Point, Kentucky. From the intersection of Dixie Highway (US 31W/US 60) and I-265 (KY 841/Gene Snyder Freeway), drive west on Dixie Highway for 7.5 miles. Just south of West Point, you'll see a sign for Fort Duffield on your right and the park entrance on your left. After you turn left (south) on Salt River Drive, the road immediately Ts, with the boat ramp to your left and the fort to your right. Turn right (southwest) on Honeysuckle Lane and drive 0.25 mile, being careful when crossing the railroad tracks. The road dead-ends into the trailhead parking lot.

11

Jefferson Memorial Forest: Scott's Gap Trail

SCENERY: ★ ★ ★ ★ ★
TRAIL CONDITION: ★ ★ ★ ★ ★
CHILDREN: ★ ★ ★
DIFFICULTY: ★ ★ ★
SOLITUDE: ★ ★ ★ ★

WHILE YOU'RE HIKING, LOOK UP AS WELL AS AHEAD.

GPS TRAILHEAD COORDINATES: N38° 3.526' W85° 50.540'

DISTANCE & CONFIGURATION: 3.3-mile balloon (on a short string). An additional 0.6-mile prairie hike lies adjacent to the trailhead.

HIKING TIME: 1.5 hours

HIGHLIGHTS: Classic Kentucky hardwoods, a bounty of spring wildflowers, pastoral views

ELEVATION: 522' at trailhead, ascending to 802' at high point

ACCESS: Daily, 8 a.m.–sunset; free admission

MAPS: Louisville Metro Parks, Jefferson Memorial Forest Welcome Center and website, USGS *Valley Station*

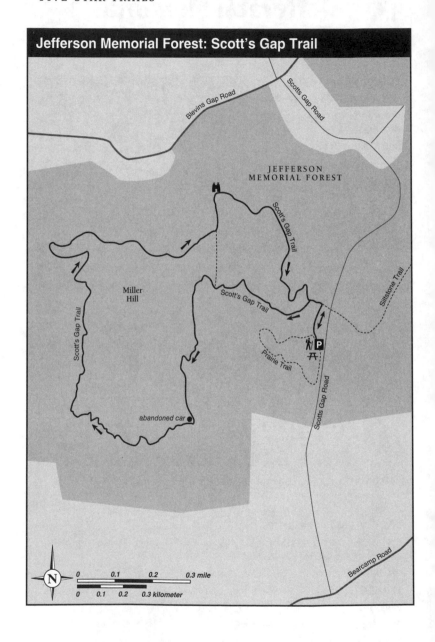

Jefferson Memorial Forest: Scott's Gap Trail

FACILITIES: Picnic tables

WHEELCHAIR ACCESS: None

COMMENTS: Dogs on leashes welcome

CONTACTS: Jefferson Memorial Forest, 502-368-5404; **memorialforest.com**

Overview

In less time than it takes to drive the Henry Watterson Expressway, you could be hiking a beautiful trail in southern Jefferson County, complete with scenic overlooks, native hardwoods, and meandering creeks. And best of all, there's a good chance you won't have any company. This trail is rated as strenuous by the staff of Jefferson Memorial Forest, but many hikers (including myself) find it a bit easier.

Route Details

Scott's Gap Trail lies in the far southwestern reaches of Jefferson Memorial Forest (JMF), away from the more well-known (and crowded) Tom Wallace, Horine, and Paul Yost sections of the park. Louisville Metro Parks obtained the Scott Tract in 1982, and in contrast to some of the

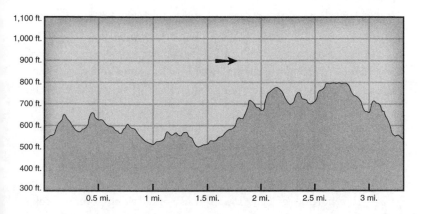

other trails in the JMF, horses are not permitted in this area. Consequently, trails tend to be in much better condition for hiking.

To begin the hike, walk north of the parking lot to the trailhead kiosk. The Scott's Gap Trail begins behind the kiosk on a finely graveled path. A quick 30 yards of walking brings you to the intersection with the Siltstone Trail. Bear left (west) at this crossroad to keep on Scott's Gap Trail.

You'll soon come to another T-intersection, where the loop trail itself begins. Bear left (south) to hike the trail clockwise, steeply up and around a small balding knob before going up to the ridgetop and then back again. The ups, downs, twists, and turns of this trail will challenge your sense of direction, but the trail is easy to follow and occasionally blazed with bright-red paint.

Less than 0.5 mile from the trailhead, you'll see a sign indicating the shortcut loop, blazed in red and white, which reduces the total length of the loop trail to 1.5 miles. But to go the full 3.3 miles, bear left (west) here to stay on the main trail.

The surrounding forest is classic Kentucky hardwood, including black cherry, oak, sweetgum, hickory, and ash. Elusive wild turkeys like to haunt this area, and hopeful hikers wanting to catch a glimpse of Benjamin Franklin's choice for the national bird are cautioned to walk as lightly as possible and to talk even less—the quiet of the forest amplifies any noise. While not the smartest creatures, wild turkeys are extremely shy, albeit talkative.

About 1 mile from the trailhead you'll come to an old car lying in the middle of a small stream, slowly washing farther down the creek bed with each heavy rain. The passenger door has been left open, perhaps as an escape for the driver, who endured a spray of bullets that peppered the door on his side. It's easy to sit on the adjacent log and imagine all the scenarios that brought this twisted pile of metal to rest before your eyes.

This portion of Scott's Gap Trail winds along several creek drainages, promising a riot of wildflowers for spring hikers. A careful eye might detect jack-in-the-pulpit, trillium, toothwort, anemone, pussy toes, or dwarf crested iris. Cold-weather hikers will be greeted with Christmas fern and winter creeper.

About halfway around the loop, the trail ascends the ridgetop once again as it circles the base of Miller Hill. Lower-elevation syca- more and beech trees give way to the cedar and walnut that thrives above. As you walk this narrow ridge, notice the mature oak trees with their deeply crevassed bark and thick, stubby arms. These oaks have survived many a fire, ice storm, and strong wind. The oldest trees in the forest are not always those with the largest girth, as the thin topsoil found here has restricted their trunk diameter.

While the fall colors are spectacular atop the ridge, the pasto- ral views are equally beautiful after the leaves have dropped. At 2.5 miles, the trail once again intersects the shortcut loop—bear left (north) at this junction to continue on Scott's Gap Trail. Another 0.5 mile of walking will bring you to the top of the small bald knob you first viewed from below. A short descent completes the loop, as you continue right (south) to return to the parking lot.

Nearby Attractions

The 0.6-mile **Prairie Trail** leaves due west from the same parking lot as Scott's Gap Trail. This loop circles a small open meadow that's home to many birds. A bat house and several birdhouses have been erected along the perimeter. The trail can be wet and spongy during the spring and after a heavy rain, but the soft ground makes it easy to identify the deer and other animal tracks imprinted before you arrived. A small pond, a drinking source for the local critters, is host to many a spring peeper and summer mosquito.

If you're interested in a longer hike, the **Siltstone Trail** is 6.7 miles one-way and leads to Tom Wallace Lake and the JMF Welcome Center. From the Scott's Gap Trailhead, follow the finely graveled path just behind the kiosk to the first trail intersection. Bear right (east) at this intersection, and you'll soon cross a small bridge and the road you drove in on. The Siltstone Trail is quite popular with local hikers and can be accessed from a variety of trailheads. Unfortunately, a loop configuration is not available, forcing hikers to do either an out-and-back or set up a shuttle. Maps for the Siltstone can be obtained from Louisville Metro Parks (see "Contacts"), or you can use the USGS *Valley Station* map.

Directions

Scott's Gap Trail is southwest of Louisville, in the Jefferson Memorial Forest. Travel west on I-265 (KY 841/Gene Snyder Freeway). At Exit 3, turn left (south) on Stonestreet Road, which becomes Blevins Gap Road. After 2.7 miles, turn left (south) on Scotts Gap Road. Trailhead parking will be less than 1 mile ahead, on your right.

12

Jefferson Memorial Forest:
Yost Ridge to Mitchell Hill Lake

SCENERY: ★ ★ ★ ★
TRAIL CONDITION: ★ ★ ★ ★ ★
CHILDREN: ★ ★ ★
DIFFICULTY: ★ ★ ★
SOLITUDE: ★ ★ ★

CAN YOU IMAGINE A MORE TRANQUIL LOCATION THIS CLOSE TO DOWNTOWN LOUISVILLE?

GPS TRAILHEAD COORDINATES: N38° 5.083' W85° 46.032'

DISTANCE & CONFIGURATION: 3.3-mile balloon

HIKING TIME: 1.2 hours

HIGHLIGHTS: Ridgetop trail descending to Mitchell Hill Lake

ELEVATION: 593' at trailhead, ascending to 868' at high point

ACCESS: Daily, 8 a.m.–sunset; free admission

MAPS: Louisville Metro Parks, Jefferson Memorial Forest Welcome Center and website, USGS *Valley Station*

FACILITIES: Restrooms at Welcome Center, open Monday–Saturday, 8:30 a.m.–4:30 p.m.; Sunday, 10 a.m.–3 p.m.

WHEELCHAIR ACCESS: None

COMMENTS: Pets must be leashed.

CONTACTS: Jefferson Memorial Forest, 502-368-5404; **memorialforest.com**

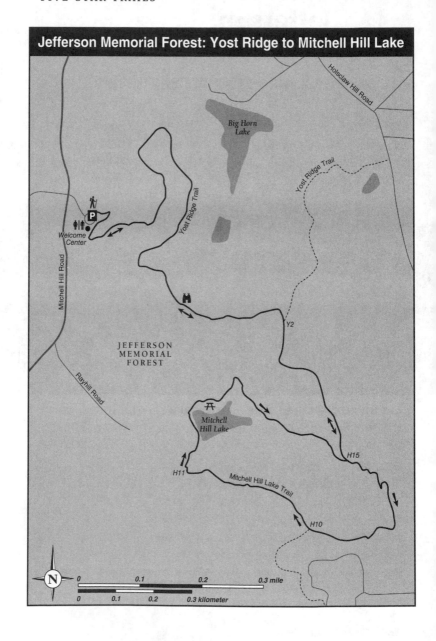

Jefferson Memorial Forest: Yost Ridge to Mitchell Hill Lake

Holsclaw Hill Road

Big Horn Lake

Yost Ridge Trail

Yost Ridge Trail

Welcome Center

P

Mitchell Hill Road

Y2

JEFFERSON MEMORIAL FOREST

Rayhill Road

Mitchell Hill Lake

H15

H11

Mitchell Hill Lake Trail

H10

N

| 0 | 0.1 | 0.2 | 0.3 mile |

| 0 | 0.1 | 0.2 | 0.3 kilometer |

Overview

Yost Ridge and Mitchell Hill Lake lie within the Paul Yost Recreation Area and the adjacent Horine Reservation, both part of the Jefferson Memorial Forest, just southwest of Louisville. The trail leaves from the Welcome Center, climbs Yost Ridge, and then descends to Mitchell Hill Lake. This hike is popular on weekends during late spring and early fall, and after work when the days get long. Otherwise, you may find you have the trail to yourself for relaxing and enjoying the beauty of a hardwood forest.

Route Details

After parking, meander around the Jefferson Memorial Forest Welcome Center and grab a hiking stick before you hit the trail. The Welcome Center offers a variety of maps, a small selection of gifts, and a few activities for the kids.

To reach the trailhead, circle to the back of the center to find the trail marked YOST RIDGE TRAIL (Y1). (A handy tip: trails in the Yost Recreation Area begin with Y, and those in the Horine

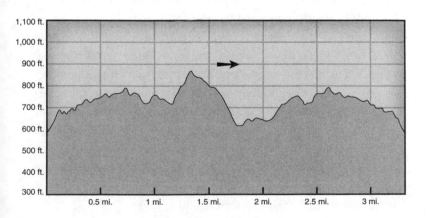

Reservation begin with *H*.) As you walk around the center, you'll see evidence of a previous Boy Scout project to name many of the native shrubs and trees planted here, including fringetree, serviceberry, buttonbush, bottlebrush buckeye, witch hazel, and various species of winterberry.

Adjacent to the trailhead, you'll see a rather short and spindly tree with sharp thorns protruding from the slender trunk in all directions—the devil's walking stick. While it's bereft of any leaves in winter, in late spring small panicles of creamy-white flowers appear. In the fall, the long, narrow leaves turn an attractive bronze-red with a yellow tinge on the outer edges. If you keep a sharp eye out, you'll find more devil's walking sticks all along the trail as you climb Yost Ridge.

And climb you will. From the Welcome Center, the trail ascends 200 feet in a little more than 0.5 mile. About 0.7 mile from the trailhead, the trail begins to flatten and you get great views of the downtown Louisville skyline—about 13 miles away as the crow flies.

A little less than 0.9 mile from the Welcome Center, the trail intersects the Mitchell Hill Lake Trail, marked as Y2 on park maps. To reach the lake, bear right (south) and follow the trail to the ridgetop. Although the path may not be wide enough for Dorothy and her three buddies, you can easily lock arms with your BFF as you walk under a canopy of hardwood trees and the occasional cedar.

The trail then begins a small descent to the Mitchell Hill Lake Trail, which makes a loop about 1.15 miles from the trailhead, at trail marker H15. From here you can hike either way on the loop, but clockwise is the preferred route, so bear left (southeast) at this intersection. The next 0.2 mile involves a strong vertical ascent. If you find yourself getting short of breath, you can always stop after about 100 yards and admire the large oak. Or stop in another 100 yards to look at the large woodpecker holes. Or stop in the last 100 yards to inspect the three large shagbark hickories growing magnificently along the path. And voilà! You're at the top of another ridge.

Over the next 0.4 mile, the trail descends once more among clouds of white dogwoods and pink redbuds rising off the forest floor in the spring, or the spectacular fall colors of the oaks, sugar maples, and pawpaws in midautumn. At trail marker H10, continue right (northwest) on the trail to reach the lake, at marker H11.

The trail then proceeds atop a small earthen berm that forms Mitchell Hill Lake. A creek serves as overflow for the lake—you can either slog across it or walk around. On the far northern side of the lake, two wooden benches and two picnic tables offer a respite at the water's edge. You're now about 1.85 miles from the trailhead, and many leagues from civilization. An old bat house stands as testimony to the mosquito populations that thrive here in the summer.

Once you've soaked up the peaceful sights, follow the trail to the north side of the small lake and along the drainage that feeds the bottomlands. In the spring, blooming cutleaf toothwort, rue anemone, and bluets will be scattered across the forest floor.

The trail then heads south, past several small waterholes and the delightful cacophony of spring peepers that inhabit these overgrown puddles. In no time, you'll have completed the loop and be back to marker H15. Head left (north) and hike back up to Yost Ridge, bearing left (east) at marker Y2. The ridgetop breezes here are quite welcome after you've ascended past the rocky, scruffy scree along the trail. Finally, make your way back down the ridge to the Welcome Center.

Nearby Attractions

If this type of hiking appeals to you, you can choose from a number of other trails in the immediate vicinity. The Horine Reservation is also home to the **Red Trail** (a 4.8-mile mostly loop trail) and the shorter **Orange Trail** (a 2-mile loop). While the Paul Yost Recreation Area serves equestrian riders, the **McConnell Trail** (a strenuous 5.3-mile loop) is for hikers only. Finally, the Tom Wallace Recreation Area hosts both the 6.7-mile (one-way) **Siltstone Trail** and a variety of shorter hikes.

How lucky we are to have so many fine hiking choices. Please support Louisville's City of Parks Initiative, including The Parklands of Floyds Fork (see Hike 18, page 129), the paved Louisville Loop (a shared-use path of more than 100 miles), the Olmsted Parks Conservancy, and a host of other park projects. *Think global, hike local.*

Directions

From I-265 (KY 841/Gene Snyder Freeway), take Exit 6 and turn south on New Cut Road (KY 1865), which becomes West Manslick Road. After 1.4 miles, turn right (west) on Mitchell Hill Road. Drive 1.5 miles to the Jefferson Memorial Forest Welcome Center, on your left.

13 **Otter Creek Loop**

SCENERY: ★ ★ ★ ★ ★
TRAIL CONDITION: ★ ★ ★ ★
CHILDREN: ★ ★
DIFFICULTY: ★ ★ ★
SOLITUDE: ★ ★ ★

TAKE OFF THOSE BOOTS AND RUN YOUR TOES THROUGH THE SAND WHERE OTTER CREEK MEETS THE OHIO.

GPS TRAILHEAD COORDINATES: N37° 56.602' W86° 2.087'

DISTANCE & CONFIGURATION: 4.9-mile loop

HIKING TIME: 2.5 hours

HIGHLIGHTS: Creekside hiking, panoramic views of the Ohio River, wildlife

ELEVATION: 477' at trailhead, ascending to 658' at high point

ACCESS: Wednesday–Saturday, sunrise–sunset; closed Monday and Tuesday, except for holidays. Daily entry fee, $3; free for children age 11 and younger. See website below for additional fees.

MAPS: Available at the park entrance gate or from the website below; USGS *Ekron*

FACILITIES: Portable toilets, picnic shelters, campground

WHEELCHAIR ACCESS: None

COMMENTS: Trails are closed in wet or muddy conditions (call 502-942-5052 to check trail status). The recreation area is closed during firearms deer-hunting season (check website below for a full list of hunting seasons).

CONTACTS: Otter Creek Outdoor Recreation Area, 502-942-9171; **tinyurl.com/ottercreek**

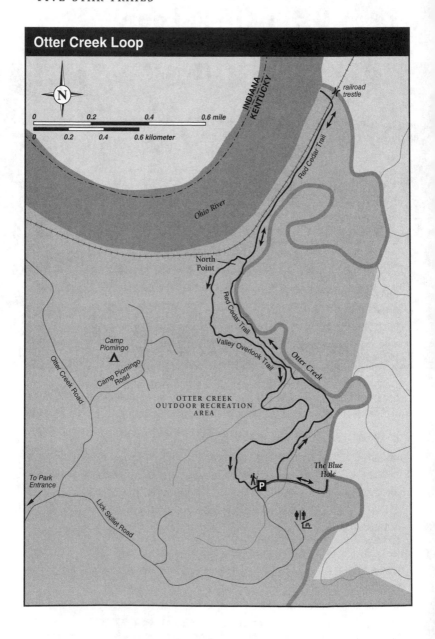

Otter Creek Loop

INDIANA
KENTUCKY

railroad
trestle

Red Cedar Trail

Ohio River

North
Point

Red Cedar Trail

Valley Overlook Trail

Otter Creek

Camp
Piomingo

Camp Piomingo Road

Otter Creek Road

OTTER CREEK
OUTDOOR RECREATION
AREA

The Blue
Hole

To Park
Entrance

Lick Skillet Road

P

0   0.2   0.4   0.6 mile

0   0.2   0.4   0.6 kilometer

Overview

This loop trail begins at the Blue Hole parking lot and travels along Otter Creek until it reaches the sandy banks of the Ohio River. Views here are panoramic, and wildlife is plentiful. The return hike ascends to North Point and follows the ridgetop Valley Overlook Trail back to the parking lot.

Route Details

The history of Otter Creek Outdoor Recreation Area is an interesting one. In 1934 the National Park Service bought 3,000 acres of land in Meade County, southwest of Louisville, to provide outdoor recreational opportunities for residents of the city and the surrounding towns. The park was opened in 1937, and a year later property was leased to the YMCA to form Camp Piomingo. In 1947 the federal government gave the park to Louisville in recognition of the city's service during World War II.

In 2008, however, Louisville closed the park as part of city-wide budget cuts. Otter Creek was essentially abandoned until the

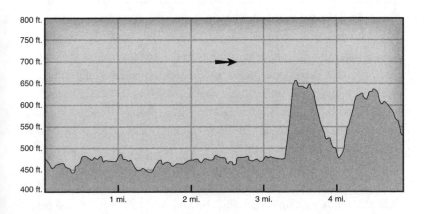

Kentucky Department of Fish and Wildlife reopened it in 2011. After land swaps with Fort Knox (which lies east of the park), the Otter Creek Outdoor Recreation Area now covers about 2,600 acres. Camp Piomingo continues to operate on the premises.

The transition from park to outdoor recreation area resulted in a more elaborate land-use management plan. Otter Creek is stocked with trout and is open for hunting. Horseback riding is permitted, and the mountain-biking community spins its gears on many of the trails. Daily fees vary by type of activity; annual-use permits are available.

Many hikers are hesitant to share horse paths, but the trails at Otter Creek are in excellent condition. The park has very strict rules on use during wet or muddy conditions, and most of the trails are covered with fine gravel or a mixture of sand and clay soil. There is very little evidence of damage to the trails by hikers, horses, or mountain bikers.

The Otter Creek Loop begins at the Blue Hole parking lot and combines parts of the Red Cedar and Valley Overlook Trails. From the eastern edge of the parking lot, take the old gravel road next to the sign proclaiming BLUE HOLE 0.5 MI VIA OTTER CREEK TRAIL. If you're looking at the park map, this is the small blue connector line marked "Blue Hole, Hiking Trail." But according to the map, the Otter Creek Trail is nowhere close. *Hmmm.*

A word of warning: although the trails are marked, they don't always jibe with the park map. For example, the legend on the map indicates that you're now on the *red-dashed* Red Cedar Trail (RCT), a biking/hiking/horse path, but *not* the Otter Creek Trail (OCT), which is signified by the solid black line on the park map. To muddy the waters further, *RCT* can also indicate the *solid-red* Red Cedar Trail for hikers and horses (but not bikers). If you're OCD, the OCT and the solid-red RCT merge on this section of the red-dashed RCT.

Yes, this does sound confusing, but if you follow my directions, you should be just fine. Basically, the loop will take you on a short spur to Blue Hole, then head north and downstream along Otter Creek until you reach the river. The return trail, Valley Overlook, climbs to a small ridge and then travels back south to the parking lot, roughly paralleling the creek route you just took.

The old road leading from the parking lot quickly comes to a Y. Bear right (east) on the OCT/RCT. Walk about 0.3 mile until the trail Ys for a second time. Keep straight at this junction to continue east, then bear left (north) at the BLUE HOLE 0.1 MILE sign (another blue connector trail on the park map). This short spur takes you to a sand-and-gravel bar that borders Otter Creek. Although the name suggests a refreshing swimming hole, the creek is not overly deep, particularly from midsummer to late fall.

To resume the hike, retrace your steps and, at the first Y, go right (north) on the dotted Red Cedar Trail, then right again at the second Y (marked OCT/RCT on the park map). The trail continues to follow an old fine-gravel road through deep woods and past large areas of flattened grass where deer have bedded down for the night. The path becomes singletrack and passes through a small valley with the creek on your right and a line of intimate rocky bluffs on your left. Otter Creek is a migratory path for songbirds, including warblers, and their voices frequently fill the air. Turkeys and a variety of woodpeckers also haunt these woods.

After a short distance, OCT/RCT intersects a yellow connector trail. Bear right at the OCT O-8 sign to stay along the creek. You'll soon pass a nice place to sit on the rocks by the water's edge to have lunch or a snack. Soon the creek quiets as the banks narrow and the water deepens. Move quietly to spot herons, kingfishers, and cobalt-blue dragonflies.

About 1.7 miles from the trailhead, go straight (north) on RCT O-7, as OCT bears left (west). The path is soon sandwiched between a set of railroad tracks and the creek. The trail narrows as filtered sun encourages grass to grow on either side, brushing your legs with wet dew on a summer morning or dry wisps in the fall. A grove of massive Eastern cottonwoods greets passersby.

At 2.4 miles, the trail passes under an old railroad trestle, which crosses Otter Creek. Shortly you will be standing on the sandy banks of the Ohio River, gazing at the fields far on the other side. The views here are grand and serene.

If you have time, take a few minutes and sit on one of the logs that adorn the riverbank. Great blue heron footprints the size of a man's hand can be found along the water's edge, while the sound of a bobwhite carries across the water. A pair of eagles have taken up nesting just across the river, feeding off many of the fish that come to feed where the creek joins the main waterway.

When you're ready to leave, retrace your steps back to RCT 0-7, but this time bear right (west) on OCT. The trail makes a very sharp ascent to North Point, which offers views of the Ohio River Valley. Atop the rocky outcropping, turn left (south) onto yellow connector trail 0-6. Two-tenths of a mile later, turn left again at V-2, the Valley Overlook Trail (VOT, colored purple on the park map). Walk another 0.3 mile to trail marker V-3, which is an intersection with the solid-colored RCT. Continue straight (southeast) on the VOT.

About 4 miles from the trailhead, the VOT crosses a small creek drainage. In the spring this is a good place for spotting the wildflowers found at the park, including wood poppies, Solomon's seal, bloodroot, dogtooth violets, Dutchman's britches, and white trillium. The elusive nodding jack-in-the-pulpit can also be found nearby.

On the other side of the creek, bear right (north) to stay on the VOT. A left here would take you on the short yellow connector trail back to the RCT. The VOT stays ridgetop for a while before descending a hillside populated with red cedars. Just after you pass an old concrete filtration plant and before you cross a small wooden bridge, bear left (due east) down the hill to the Blue Hole parking lot below.

Nearby Attractions

At the time of publication, the hiking trails at **Bridges to the Past** and **Tioga Falls** were closed due to bridge construction but were expected to reopen in summer 2013. Most of the 2.3-mile Bridges to the Past Trail is paved and takes you to three scenic stone bridges that were repaired by German POWs in World War II. The 2-mile Tioga Falls Trail can be quite muddy and goes straight up a steep hillside, but is quite beautiful.

To get to both trailheads, take I-265 (KY 841/Gene Snyder Freeway) to Exit 1, turn south on Dixie Highway (US 31W/US 60) toward Fort Knox, and drive about 8 miles. Turn left at the BRIDGES TO THE PAST sign. Follow this road to the parking lot.

Directions

Take I-265 (KY 841/Gene Snyder Freeway) to Exit 1, turn south on Dixie Highway (US 31W/US 60) toward Fort Knox, and drive 13.2 miles. Turn right (west) on KY 1638 and drive 1.8 miles. The entrance to Otter Creek Outdoor Recreation Area will be on your right. From the park entrance gate, follow the signs to the trailhead at Blue Hole, which is about 2.8 miles down dilapidated Lick Skillet Road (don't you just love that name?).

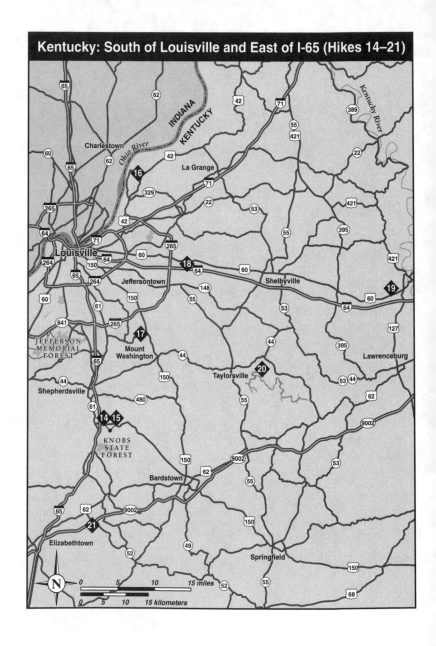

Kentucky: South of Louisville and East of I-65 (Hikes 14–21)

Kentucky:
South of Louisville
and East of I-65

HOW MANY KOI CAN YOU SPOT? *(See Hike 15, Bernheim Arboretum Sampler, page 112.)*

Bernheim Arboretum:
Millennium Trail

SCENERY: ★ ★ ★ ★
TRAIL CONDITION: ★ ★ ★ ★ ★
CHILDREN: ★
DIFFICULTY: ★ ★ ★ ★ ★
SOLITUDE: ★ ★ ★ ★

SUMMER HIKERS MAY WANT TO KEEP IN MIND THE OLD ADAGE "BLACKBERRIES RIPE BY THE FOURTH OF JULY."

GPS TRAILHEAD COORDINATES: N37° 54.623' W85° 39.754'

DISTANCE & CONFIGURATION: 12.5-mile loop

HIKING TIME: 6 hours

HIGHLIGHTS: Ridgetop views, multiple creek crossings, wildflower displays

ELEVATION: 515' at trailhead, ascending to 864' at high point

ACCESS: Millennium Trail hikers must sign in at the visitor center by 10:30 a.m. April–October and by 9:30 a.m. November–March. During the summer, the Millennium Trail closes when the temperatures reach the 90s. Trail closes a half-hour before sunset. Bernheim is closed December 25 and January 1 (see website for specific seasonal hours). Entrance fee is $5/vehicle on weekends and holidays, free at other times.

MAPS: Available at the park and at the website below. A large-scale topographic map with waterproof coating is available for $5 at the sign-in desk. Bernheim also sells a totally cool-looking water bottle with a raised-relief topo map of the park printed on the sides ($20).

FACILITIES: Visitor center, gift shop, café, restrooms, picnic tables, playgrounds

WHEELCHAIR ACCESS: None on the trail

COMMENTS: Leashed pets are welcome; be sure to bring water for them, too. Hiking during peak winter or summer months is not recommended.

CONTACTS: Bernheim Arboretum and Research Forest, 502-955-8512; **bernheim.org**

Overview

The Millennium Trail is the Big Kahuna of all hiking trails at Bernheim Arboretum and Research Forest. Only fit, experienced hikers should attempt this trail—if you're looking for an excellent workout, this one will make you sweat. Use the Millennium to train for a multiday backpacking trip or simply to keep in shape. The best time to hike is in the fall, when colors are at their peak and temps are cooler, or in the spring, when the wildflowers are out. While no single stretch of the Millennium is exceptionally difficult, the sheer length of the trail and the constant ups and downs make for a long, strenuous day.

Route Details

The full Millennium Trail is officially a 13.75-mile loop, starting and finishing at the western edge of the Guerilla Hollow Picnic Area. However, the first mile basically takes you along a field to the edge of the Cypress-Tupelo Swamp and then back along a paved road, Ten Toms Circle. Beginning at the alternative trailhead described next shaves the mileage a bit while keeping all the scenic parts.

After signing in at the visitor center, drive to the Guerilla Hollow Picnic Area and park along the north side of Guerilla Hollow Circle. This will leave your vehicle halfway between the alternative trailhead and the take-out. From here, walk east a very short distance on the road to the point where the yellow-blazed Millennium Trail crosses Guerilla Hollow Road. Pick up the trail east of the road, as it heads clockwise toward Cull Hollow.

As you enter the forest, the trail runs southeast past a small cemetery before heading sharply northeast to the top of Poplar Ridge. The trail then passes through a tall chain-link fence that goes off in either direction. The fence is for keeping deer out of the heart of Bernheim and in the backwoods where they belong. The trail then descends to a small seasonal creek crossing, climbs back to Poplar Ridge, and eventually reaches another creek crossing.

Bernheim Arboretum: Millennium Trail

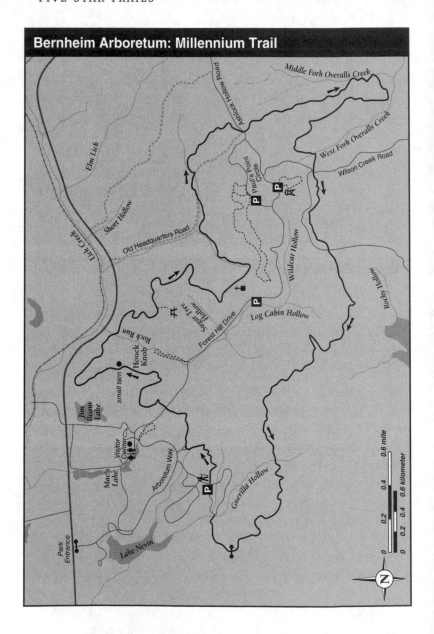

After the second creek crossing (about 0.8 mile from the trail-head), the trail emerges from the woods at Forest Hill Drive, which runs the length of the park. Carefully cross the paved road and continue hiking north to the other side. The next 1.5 miles of trail takes you up a steep creek drainage and around the edge of Houck Knob, before bearing right (southeast) and descending slowly to Rock Run. A portion of this section of the trail parallels KY 245, so you do get some road noise. But the northern slopes of Houck Knob provide one of the many wildflower displays along the trail. Solomon's seal, phlox, larkspur, wood poppies, and bluets are prolific.

About 2.3 miles into the hike, the trail passes under a set of power lines and through a blackberry thicket, followed by a forest of shagbark and shellbark hickories and tulip poplars. Another 0.2 mile brings you to Rock Run, which is a fairly dry crossing except in early spring after a heavy rain. The ascent out of the creek drainage offers hikers a good opportunity to spot jack-in-the-pulpits, as the nodding flower frequently hides under the set of three leaves that form an umbrella, or hood, over the pulpit (technically known as the spadix). In the fall, the flower turns into a cluster of bright-red berries and is equally attractive.

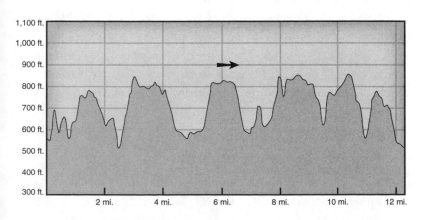

Three miles from the trailhead, a short spur leads to Robert Paul's picnic table and overlook. While the trees block the views most of the year, it's a scenic little spot overlooking Sugar Tree Hollow; a small sign provides an interesting read on Mr. Paul.

A mile from the picnic table is the Jackson Cemetery. Lift the horseshoe hinge and walk on in. After spending a few minutes daydreaming among the tombstones, exit the gate and be on the lookout as the trail bears left (north), where an old access road to the cemetery departs to the right (southeast). From here the trail makes a slow descent into Bingham Valley, along a tributary of Long Lick Creek. Crested iris, pussy toes, false Solomon's seal, and star chickweed feel right at home here.

The alert hiker might notice that on the other side of the creek the trail begins to parallel a gravel road. At 4.75 miles, the trail crosses the creek and turns right (east) on Old Headquarters Road. After a quick 0.2 mile, the trail ducks back into the woods again—turn left (north) to stay on track. Follow the trail up a steep drainage and hike another 0.5 mile to the halfway point of the Millennium, at Ashlock Hollow Road.

Whew. Halfway. And hopefully you're still going strong. Full disclosure: some hikers stop here and drive a shuttle vehicle back to the parking lot. But unless you've planned ahead, look for the yellow blazes and keep on truckin'.

The next 1.7 miles of trail makes a few loops along both the Middle and West Forks of Overalls Creek. When it comes to wildflowers, you'll find all the usual suspects, along with yellow trout lilies and Jacob's ladder. About 7.75 miles from the trailhead, the Millennium crosses Wilson Creek Road. Again, look for the blazes and you'll see where the trail immediately ducks back into the woods once more.

After the trail climbs out of Log Cabin Hollow, the next few miles are mostly featureless, save for some nice ridgetop hiking and beautiful autumnal colors in the fall. At about 10 miles, the trail finally descends into Guerilla Hollow and, like a dairy cow at milking time, most hikers begin to feel the fatigue and are anxious to get back to the barn. At 11.3 miles, the Millennium Trail passes through a tall chain-link fence once again, then bears right (north) along an old grassy access road for 0.2 mile, until you finally reach a trail-sign kiosk. Make one final turn to the right (east), and you'll find yourself back on the road at the Guerilla Hollow Picnic Area. Walk clockwise by turning left on the road to find your vehicle.

Pat yourself on the back. You just hiked the Millennium Trail!

Nearby Attractions

You may or may not be up for more hiking today, but there's a pretty nature area just a few miles from Bernheim that's owned by the Kentucky chapter of The Nature Conservancy. **Pine Creek Barrens Preserve** is 110 acres of open woodland and home to many prairielike flowers that bloom in early summer, including state-endangered Great Plains lady's tresses, Indian grass, little bluestem, purple coneflower, and blazing star (liatrus).

Edged with small limestone cliffs, Pine Creek cuts a lovely figure on the southwest boundary of the preserve. In spring, the small white flowers of the globally threatened glade cress can be found on the bedrock.

From Louisville, drive south on I-65 about 36 miles. Take Exit 116 and turn left (east) on KY 480. After 4.5 miles, turn left (north) onto Pine Creek Trail, toward Wight-Meyer Vineyard & Winery. Drive 0.2 mile and take the first right onto Pine Creek Road, which leads to the preserve. There are no established trails on the preserve, so take a good compass and a topo map, such as USGS *Samuels*.

Directions

From Louisville, drive south on I-65 about 24 miles. Take Exit 112 and turn left (east) at the bottom of the ramp on KY 245 South (Clermont Road). The park entrance will be 1 mile ahead, on your right. The main road leads to the visitor center, where you'll sign in to hike.

15

Bernheim Arboretum Sampler

SCENERY: ★ ★ ★ ★
TRAIL CONDITION: ★ ★ ★ ★ ★
CHILDREN: ★ ★ ★ ★
DIFFICULTY: ★ ★
SOLITUDE: ★ ★

THIS "BRIDGE TO NOWHERE" DELIGHTFULLY TRAVERSES TIME AND SPACE.

GPS TRAILHEAD COORDINATES: See individual trail snapshots

DISTANCE & CONFIGURATION: Five short hikes ranging from 0.3 mile to 1.5 miles each

HIKING TIME: From 10 minutes for Fire Tower Loop to 2.8 hours for all five hikes

HIGHLIGHTS: A bridge through the tree canopy, panoramic views, spring wildflowers, and activities to keep kids engaged

ELEVATION: No significant elevation change except for the Iron Ore Hill Loop (195-foot change in elevation)

ACCESS: Trails open daily at 7 a.m. and close a half-hour before sunset. The visitor center and gift shop are open daily, 9 a.m.–5 p.m. Closed December 25 and January 1 (see website below for specific seasonal hours). Entrance fee is $5/vehicle on weekends and holidays, free at other times.

MAPS: Available at the park and at the website below

FACILITIES: Visitor center, gift shop, café, restrooms, picnic tables, playgrounds

WHEELCHAIR ACCESS: Limited to a number of sidewalks around several of the ponds and along the lake; no trail access

COMMENTS: Leashed pets welcome

CONTACTS: Bernheim Arboretum and Research Forest, 502-955-8512; **bernheim.org**

Overview

Pack the kids in the backseat, tuck Grandma in the front, and head out for a fabulous day of family fun—the 14,000-acre Bernheim Arboretum and Research Forest has something for everyone.

The following sampler weaves together five different trails that provide an overview of what the park has to offer. The preserve was originally developed by distilling magnate Isaac Wolfe Bernheim and designed by Frederick Law Olmsted. With a strong focus on education, Bernheim offers plein-air-painting workshops, photography classes, Eco Kids Discovery Days, stargazing, full-moon hikes, O.W.L.S. (Older Wiser Livelier Seniors) outdoor experiences, and lots more.

Route Details

Isaac Wolfe Bernheim, a German immigrant, arrived in America in 1867 with less than $4 in his pocket and even fewer English words in his vocabulary. After a short stint peddling dry goods and various sundries, Bernheim's horse died and he was forced to find a new line of work. Bernheim then moved to Kentucky in 1868, where he became extremely successful in the wholesale liquor and distilling industry. Grateful for the opportunities his adopted home afforded, he bequeathed 14,000 acres of redeveloped farmland for the people of Kentucky to enjoy.

If you've never been to Bernheim, your first stop should be the visitor center. After entering the park, head straight back on the main road and follow the signs. The visitor center was the first certified Platinum LEED Green Building in a multistate region. Inside you'll find lots of nature-themed activities for the kids, including giant floor puzzles, two large aquariums, and a "Please Touch" table. The large glass windows and cozy southern exposure make the kid-size willow furniture inviting for Hobbits and Munchkins alike. The small bookstore, gift shop, and reasonably priced café deserve a second glance. Native plants are for sale on the back deck of the center.

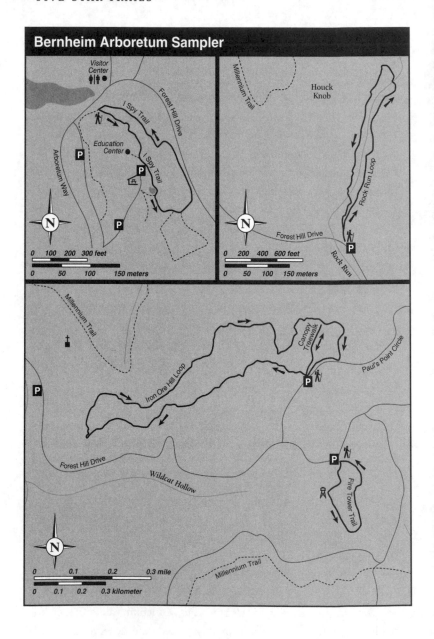

Bernheim Arboretum Sampler

Visitor Center

Forest Hill Drive

I Spy Trail

Education Center

I Spy Trail

Arboretum Way

P

P

P

N

0   100   200   300 feet

0   50   100   150 meters

Millennium Trail

Houck Knob

Rock Run Loop

Forest Hill Drive

Rock Run

P

N

0   200   400   600 feet

0   50   100   150 meters

Millennium Trail

Canopy Treewalk

Paul's Point Circle

P

Iron Ore Hill Loop

P

Forest Hill Drive

Wildcat Hollow

Fire Tower Trail

P

N

Millennium Trail

0   0.1   0.2   0.3 mile

0   0.1   0.2   0.3 kilometer

At the information desk, be sure to pick up at least one map of the park. Although the free photocopied map is more than adequate for this foray, the $5 topographic map is much more interesting and definitely worth the money. If you plan on walking the I Spy Trail, pick up a list of items to look for on the hike.

After leaving the visitor center, drive south on Forest Hill Drive toward Paul's Point Circle. It's less than a 5-minute drive to your first hike.

Canopy Treewalk
(0.3-mile out-and-back; 20 minutes hiking time;
N37° 54.365' W85° 37.714')

This level walk leaves from the small parking area just off Paul's Point Circle. A short hike through the woods leads to a wooden bridge that appears to float in the canopy of oaks and hickories that dominate the surrounding forest. The wooden structure abruptly ends with a north-facing panoramic view of Bingham Valley and the Iron Ore Hill Loop winding below.

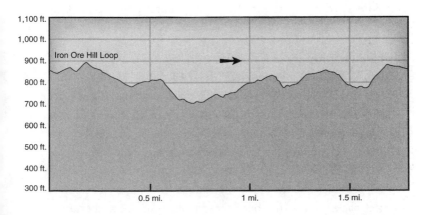

Iron Ore Hill Loop   *(1.5-mile loop; 1 hour hiking time at a kid's pace; N37° 54.364' W85° 37.718')*

If you think your party can hike this one, do it first while everyone is fresh. The 1.5-mile trail travels through a wooded area that is very similar to what you'll experience on many of the longer hiking trails at Bernheim. Oaks and hickories give way to beeches and maples as the trail winds along a north-facing slope that rises above Bingham Valley. Most of the forest has been harvested several times to make charcoal for the pig-iron trade, which flourished here in the mid-1800s.

Fire Tower Loop
(0.5-mile loop; 10–30 minutes; N37° 54.201' W85° 37.621')

This trail can be reached on the other side of Paul's Point Circle. A short, steep ascent from the trailhead brings you to the old fire tower, built in 1929. Sitting atop a 921-foot knob, the 48-foot fire tower was used until 1980. Public access to the tower is restricted to three or four times per month; when it's open (check the website or call the visitor center to confirm), it affords some beautiful views. The trail continues past the fire tower another 0.4 mile through deciduous woods before looping back to the parking lot. After hiking the Fire Tower Loop, return to your car and drive back on Forest Hill Drive toward the visitor center and the Rock Run Loop Trailhead.

Rock Run Loop
(0.5-mile loop; 30 minutes; N37° 54.749' W85° 38.878')

This is one of the most popular hikes at Bernheim. There's a lot packed into this short trail, including two creek crossings, old wagon ruts, and informational signs posted along the slopes of Rock Run. Spring hikers are rewarded with an abundance of wildflowers, many of which were planted in 1932 and cultivated until the 1950s. The spring-fed creek and the limestone and shale outcroppings create the perfect backdrop for the abundance of Dutchman's britches, hepatica, phlox, bloodroot, trillium, and ferns that thrive here.

If your group needs a breather, now would be a good time to take it. Head back to the visitor center, sit a spell, then set out for your final adventure.

I Spy Trail
(0.4-mile balloon; 30 minutes; N37° 55.038' W85° 39.445')

If you've spent any time around kids, then perhaps you've heard of Jean Marzollo's *I Spy* series of books and games, in which the human eye is tested and teased to identify various shapes and items hidden in a visual maze. The I Spy Trailhead is halfway between the visitor center and the education center, just south of Arboretum Way and next to the old stone springhouse. Using the I Spy Trail checklist, have the kids search for 30 items "that do not belong in the forest." Little ones will absolutely love this trail, where they can search for an old toothbrush, a cheese grater, a Slinky, and other items. Be sure to leave everything as you found it for the next group to enjoy.

Nearby Attractions

As a nod to the I. W. Harper brand of bourbon that Isaac Bernheim created, stop at the **Jim Beam American Stillhouse,** just east of the arboretum in Clermont (526 Happy Hollow Road; 502-543-9877; **americanstillhouse.com**). From the Bernheim entrance, travel east on KY 245 South for 0.8 mile. Turn left on Happy Hollow Road and follow the signs for the distillery, which is a stop on the Kentucky Bourbon Trail (see **kybourbontrail.com** for more information).

Once you're safely home, toast to the generosity of Isaac and his wife, Amanda, and to all of their philanthropic endeavors.

Directions

From downtown Louisville, drive south on I-65 about 24 miles. Take Exit 112 and turn left (east) at the bottom of the ramp on Clermont Road (KY 245 South). The park entrance will be 1 mile ahead, on your right.

Creasey Mahan Nature Preserve

SCENERY: ★ ★ ★
TRAIL CONDITION: ★ ★ ★ ★
CHILDREN: ★ ★ ★ ★
DIFFICULTY: ★ ★
SOLITUDE: ★ ★ ★ ★

LET YOUR WORRIES MELT AWAY AS YOU PASS THROUGH THE GATE.

GPS TRAILHEAD COORDINATES: N38° 24.026' W85° 35.392'

DISTANCE & CONFIGURATION: 1.5-mile out-and-back, with more mileage available

HIKING TIME: 45 minutes

HIGHLIGHTS: Nature center, children's programs, frog pond, woodland garden

ELEVATION: 701' at trailhead, descending to 581' at low point

ACCESS: Preserve is open daily, sunrise–sunset. The nature center is open every third Saturday, 10 a.m.–2 p.m. All events are free; donations welcome.

MAPS: Available at the preserve and the website below; USGS *Prospect*

FACILITIES: Picnic tables and shelter, restrooms, swings, recreational fields, nature center, field house

WHEELCHAIR ACCESS: None on trails

COMMENTS: Leashed, well-behaved pets welcome

CONTACTS: Creasey Mahan Nature Preserve, 502-228-4362; **creaseymahannaturepreserve.org**

Overview

While Creasey Mahan Nature Preserve may be quiet during the week, most weekends are filled with activity, laughter, and fun. The staff provides a welcome that's warm enough to melt the fleece on your back and put a smile on your face. Under their energetic leadership, the trail system has been enlarged and a new woodland garden has been developed. Dedicated to recreation, education, conservation, and preservation, Creasey Mahan appeals to everyone from trail runners to curtain crawlers.

Route Details

If this is your first time to the Creasey Mahan Nature Preserve, a quick glance at its calendar of events (find it online at **creaseymahannature preserve.org**) may influence your planning. The preserve offers a variety of programs each month, such as Snakes!, National Squirrel Appreciation Day, and tree identification and care. The small campground and fire pit are rented out most weekends by local Boy Scout troops. Workshops are frequently offered, ranging from wildflower identification to raptor rehabilitation to master gardening.

Inside the nature center, four life-size dioramas are filled with taxidermic delights, showcasing Kentucky's woodlands, wetlands, fish, and early Native American life. Herons, waterfowl, owls, sandhill cranes, bears, and foxes are among the species represented. Neatly displayed Indian artifacts include incense burners, a hair roach, and an eagle pipe. A bird blind with two-way glass overlooks a wildlife-habitat garden, testing visitors' knowledge of spicebush, passionflower vine, sneezeweed, and other native plants. The bird-nest collection is outstanding, particularly the nests of the chimney swift and mud barn swallow. Who needs Netflix with all this fun?

But even with all of these goings-on, Creasey Mahan is a hiking destination as much as it is a community center, with 8.5 miles of trails ranging from open meadows to woodland forests to creekside strolls. A good hike for the younger ones begins at the nature center,

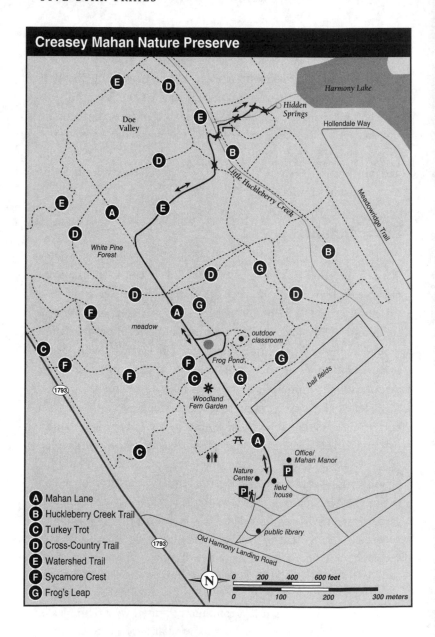

Creasey Mahan Nature Preserve

Harmony Lake

Hollendale Way

Hidden Springs

Doe Valley

Little Huckleberry Creek

Meadowridge Trail

White Pine Forest

meadow

outdoor classroom

Frog Pond

ball fields

Woodland Fern Garden

Office/ Mahan Manor

Nature Center

field house

public library

Old Harmony Landing Road

1793

1793

A Mahan Lane
B Huckleberry Creek Trail
C Turkey Trot
D Cross-Country Trail
E Watershed Trail
F Sycamore Crest
G Frog's Leap

N

| 0 | 200 | 400 | 600 feet |
| 0 | 100 | 200 | 300 meters |

travels past the Woodland Fern Garden and Frog Pond, then follows Little Huckleberry Creek before ending at Hidden Springs. At about 0.75 mile one-way (1.5 miles round-trip), this hike provides lots of interesting diversions to keep the kids engaged.

Beginning at the parking lot, walk northeast between the nature center and the field house, and pass under the wooden trellis, before turning left (northwest) along Mahan Lane (labeled as Trail A on the preserve map). As you pass under a canopy of wild cherry, the picnic area will be to your left (just west of the trail) and the recreational fields to your right (east). Just ahead, another wooden arch leads to the hiking trails.

Shortly after you pass under the second wooden arch, the new Woodland Fern Garden will be on your left (west). In the winter of 2011 and spring of 2012, scores of new native trees and thousands of native wildflowers and ferns were planted here, complemented by a small arched bridge and tumbling creek. Feel free to take a side trip through this woodland wonderland.

Mahan Lane continues past the Woodland Fern Garden to the Frog Pond, on your right. Take time to quietly circle the pond and

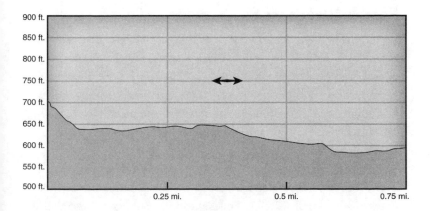

catch a glimpse of the bullfrogs, red-eared sliders, or widow skimmers that reside here. Multiple benches provide a quiet respite for reflection or a staging area for a quick snack.

As you continue down Mahan Lane, the canopy diversifies from cherry into locust and cedar before descending a small hill through a patch of white pines. At the bottom of the hill, about 0.4 mile from the trailhead, turn right (northeast) onto the Watershed Trail (Trail C on the preserve map). This trail doglegs left (north), down a short but steep hillside to a small waterfall, over a small bridge, and across Little Huckleberry Creek. In just a few yards, turn right (northeast) and cross the small wooden bridge that traverses the creek. This short stretch of trail immediately Ts into the Huckleberry Creek Trail. A quick left and then a right will take you to Hidden Springs. You'll pass three more bridges and a small set of benches. The springs are just ahead, bubbling below an earthen berm that supports a small pond.

From this point you can retrace your steps back to the parking lot, completing your 1.5-mile walk; more-adventurous hikers can take a variety of other trails back to your starting point. Either way, your day at Creasey Mahan will have left you a little more relaxed and a little more appreciative of what nature has to offer.

Nearby Attractions

If you're looking to lengthen your hiking day, **Morgan Conservation Park** is just 20 minutes from Creasey Mahan, near La Grange. The park's 4.3 miles of trails wind among a 252-acre tract of primary and secondary successional woods, wetlands, and old agricultural fields. In springtime, the Creekside Trail, a short path connecting to the 2.2-mile Primary Loop Trail, offers an impressive wildflower and waterfall display.

Exit Creasey Mahan on US 42, turn left (east), and drive 13.4 miles. Hang another left (north) on KY 524, which becomes 18 Mile Creek Road; the park will be 1.3 miles ahead, on your right. (*Note:* There are two turnoffs onto KY 524 from US 42. If you took the first one, onto KY 524/Westport Road, you turned too soon.) For more information, contact Oldham County Parks & Recreation, 502-225-0655; **oldhamcounty.net.**

Directions

From the intersection of I-71 and I-265 (KY 841/Gene Snyder Freeway), drive north on I-265 for 2.2 miles. Turn right (north) on US 42 toward Prospect. After 6 miles, turn left (north) at the large water tower onto KY 1793, and drive 1 mile. Turn right (east) on Old Harmony Landing Road. The preserve is 0.3 mile ahead, on your left.

17

Fairmount Falls

SCENERY: ★ ★ ★ ★ ★
TRAIL CONDITION: ★ ★ ★ ★
CHILDREN: ★ ★ ★
DIFFICULTY: ★ ★
SOLITUDE: ★ ★ ★ ★

AN INCREDIBLE ARRAY OF SPRING WILDFLOWERS SURROUNDS FAIRMOUNT FALLS.

GPS TRAILHEAD COORDINATES: 38° 5.506' W85° 34.728'

DISTANCE & CONFIGURATION: 1.1-mile balloon

HIKING TIME: 1 hour

HIGHLIGHTS: Waterfall, spring wildflowers

ELEVATION: 612' at trailhead, ascending to 694' at high point

ACCESS: Park is open daily, 8 a.m.–sunset. Admission is free, but to visit you must secure a permit in advance. Download a PDF permit application from the website on the next page, print it, and submit it by mail or fax.

MAPS: Available at the website on the next page; USGS *Mount Washington*

FACILITIES: Picnic table at trailhead

WHEELCHAIR ACCESS: None

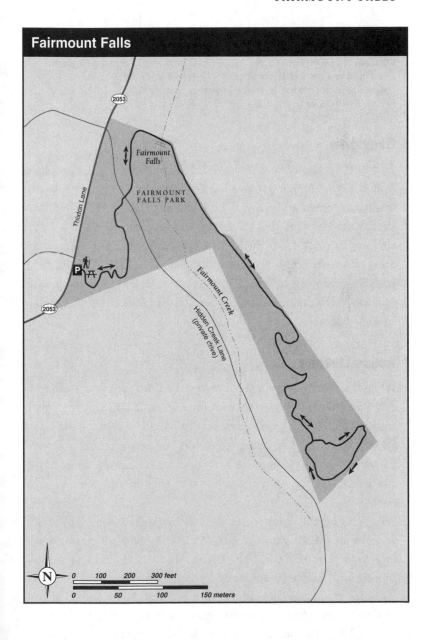

Fairmount Falls

2053

Thixton Lane

Fairmount Falls

FAIRMOUNT FALLS PARK

2053

Fairmount Creek

Hidden Creek Lane (private drive)

P

N

| 0 | 100 | 200 | 300 feet |

| 0 | 50 | 100 | 150 meters |

COMMENTS: Once you've completed the permit process, your information is kept on file, making subsequent visits easy.

CONTACTS: Louisville Metro Parks, 502-368-5404. To download a permit application, go to **tinyurl.com/fairmountfalls** and click the "Fairmount Falls Permit" link; mail your completed application to Natural Areas Management, Louisville Metro Parks, P.O. Box 467, Fairdale, KY 40118, or fax it to 502-368-6517.

Overview

Just outside Louisville, this hidden gem provides a quick respite from the city. Dropping from a height of 40 feet, Fairmount Falls is frequently touted as "Louisville's tallest natural waterfall" (though it should also be noted that the competition is pretty slim). The falls are easy to reach from the trailhead—just 10 minutes away. The short trail is perfect for teaching young children the joy of hiking and providing instant gratification for those with short attention spans. Multiple creek drainages provide an ideal ecosystem for abundant spring-wildflower displays.

Route Details

While this hike requires a bit of pretrip planning, your odds of getting a permit are considerably better than picking a Kentucky Derby trifecta (see "Access" and "Contacts" for details). Louisville Metro Parks keeps visitors capped at three cars and seven people per day. Relatively few people know of this park, but wet springs and glorious wildflower shows can nonetheless result in full capacity on weekends.

Your permit comes with a key code that unlocks the gate at the park entrance. Follow the instructions, lock the gate behind you, and leave your permit on the dash of your vehicle. At the far end of the parking lot, you'll see the trail sign leading to Fairmount Falls.

The trail winds behind the parking lot and past several large boulders before picking up on the other side of Hidden Creek Lane (a private drive). As soon as you cross the road, you can hear the falls, drawing you deeper into the woods. Several short trails take you to the rim of a small gorge, cut by Fairmount Creek as it winds down to Floyds Fork. While the rim provides excellent vistas for photo ops, a short scramble down the rim will allow you a closer look from the base of the falls.

Spring visitors will frequently be treated with tumbling water and cool spray, while winter hikers can watch the falls as if in stop motion. However, from midsummer to late fall, the creek frequently dries up as mosquitoes and gnats take center stage. Timing is everything.

Just above the falls, the trail crosses the creek to the other side of the small gorge. As you read this, you've probably drawn two very important conclusions: One, the more fortunate you are to see a heavy flow of water falling over the lip of the gorge, the wetter your boots will get as you cross the creek. Second, given that the trail crosses about 10 feet from the edge of the 40-foot falls, one wrong step could be disastrous. Keep children and other loved ones close at hand.

After crossing the creek, you'll be walking southeast on the wooded trail, with a small subdivision on your left and Fairmount Creek far below on your right. In 0.2 mile, the trail splits into a small loop, rendering the trail like a small balloon with a very long tail. It's easier to take the loop clockwise, so bear left (east) at the junction.

The loop brings you down to another smaller creek drainage. Fairmount Falls is popular with spring hikers due to the abundance of wildflowers here. Trillium, wild yam, bloodroot, wild ginger, and mayapple abound. Wild columbine and fern tend to prefer the rocky crags of the boulders casually strewn about, while a second creek coming in on your left provides plenty of moisture year-round. The rich environs also provide a perfect habitat for mushrooms and fungi.

After completing the loop, turn left (west) on the trail and retrace your steps back to the falls and the parking lot. Break out that picnic basket you packed and think about making a four-part montage of the falls for your photo album, with one picture taken in each season.

On your way home, stop by your favorite local bookstore and finally spring for that book on wildflowers you've been lusting over. Store it in your daypack, preloaded for your next hike at Fairmount Falls.

Directions

From Louisville, head south on Bardstown Road (US 150 East/US 31 East). Three miles south of I-265 (KY 841/Gene Snyder Freeway), turn right (west) on Thixton Lane (KY 2053) and drive 1 mile. Just before the road makes a sharp right turn, you'll see a small gravel lot to your left, almost hidden behind some trees. Park in front of the cable gate. Using the key code that came with your permit, unlock the cable. Pull inside and park, then relock the gate behind you. Reverse these steps upon departing.

18

The Parklands of
Floyds Fork: Coppiced Woods

SCENERY: ★ ★ ★ ★
TRAIL CONDITION: ★ ★ ★ ★ ★
CHILDREN: ★ ★ ★
DIFFICULTY: ★ ★
SOLITUDE: ★ ★

ACORNS AND DEER SCAT OFFER GOOD EVIDENCE OF WHAT YOU'LL FIND ALONG THE TRAIL.

GPS TRAILHEAD COORDINATES: N38° 13.798' W85° 27.991

DISTANCE & CONFIGURATION: 1.6-mile loop, with more mileage readily available

HIKING TIME: 45 minutes

HIGHLIGHTS: Overlook of Floyds Fork, multiple creek and lake views

ELEVATION: 586' at trailhead, ascending to 720' at high point

ACCESS: Daily, sunrise–sunset; free admission

MAPS: Available at the website below; USGS *Fisherville*

FACILITIES: Picnic tables, restrooms

WHEELCHAIR ACCESS: None on dirt trails. However, the adjacent Louisville Loop offers several miles of paved trail (all of which is graded at less than 10% slope).

COMMENTS: Dogs must be leashed on trails but may roam off-leash in the Bark Park.

CONTACTS: 21st Century Parks, Inc., 502-584-0350; **theparklands.org**

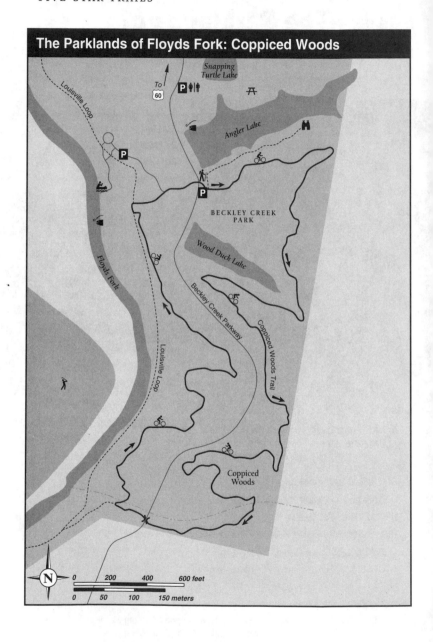

The Parklands of Floyds Fork: Coppiced Woods

Snapping Turtle Lake

To 60

Angler Lake

BECKLEY CREEK PARK

Wood Duck Lake

Louisville Loop

Floyds Fork

Beckley Creek Parkway

Louisville Loop

Coppiced Woods Trail

Coppiced Woods

N

| 0 | 200 | 400 | 600 feet |
| 0 | 50 | 100 | 150 meters |

Overview

The Parklands of Floyds Fork is the newest and largest outdoor recreational venue in Greater Louisville. And as the brochure and website say, "This is not a park. This is a new idea of what a park can be. This is gonna be great." You have to smile at that. The first "soft" (unpaved) trail, Coppiced Woods, opened in November 2012, with more than 100 miles of new trails to be completed by 2016. By then you'll be able to hike, bike, paddle, horseback-ride, or simply relax on nearly 4,000 acres of public green space.

Route Details

The Parklands of Floyds Fork is part of the vision put forward by the nonprofit 21st Century Parks, a major player in bringing private and public resources together to protect, nurture, and improve the park system in Jefferson and surrounding counties. The Parklands is being developed at the same magnitude that Frederick Law Olmsted envisioned for his network of urban-Louisville parks, but it will be sandwiched between the outlying suburbs of the Derby City and the bedroom communities to the east.

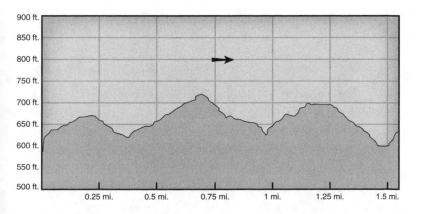

The Parklands will comprise five connected parks—Beckley Creek, Pope Lick, The Strand, Turkey Run, and Broad Run—that will be linked by Floyds Fork and the Louisville Loop (a paved multiuse recreational trail). The master plan also includes 22 miles of canoe trails along Floyds Fork, ball fields, playgrounds, picnic shelters, fishing holes, and more.

The Coppiced Woods Trail is in the northernmost park, Beckley Creek, which surrounds the William F. Miles Lakes. As soon as you enter the park, you'll notice many signs touting the rejuvenation of the adjacent meadows and woodlands. While Olmsted was well known for his expansive green lawns, ornamental trees, and specimen shrubs, The Parklands leans heavily toward the eradication of invasive species and the establishment of indigenous ones. Honeysuckle, pear, and fescue are out; native grasses and wildflowers are in.

As a side note, a coppiced wood is an old forestry-management tool in which every 20–25 years trees are cut stump-high and the wood harvested, typically for poles. The remaining stump then regenerates new branching, and the cycle begins again. There is some evidence that this management can be beneficial for certain kinds of woodland creatures, though it's not a popular or common strategy anymore.

The Coppiced Woods Trailhead lies just east of the road, next to the parking lot described in the Directions. Be forewarned: this parking area is extremely small (holding only six to eight vehicles)—a much larger lot sits just across the road and down the hill. The single-track loop trail begins here and leaves the back right-hand corner of the lot, heading east along a small meadow before entering a stand of hickories and oaks, with a few maples and eastern red cedars mixed in. Most of the oaks here are bur (alternately spelled *burr*) or mossy-cup oaks, easily distinguished in the fall by their furry little caps.

After a scant 0.2 mile, the trail makes a short switchback up to the other side of the small meadow you first saw from below. The summer crop of black-eyed Susans and Queen Anne's lace is supplemented with yellow goldenrods and purple asters later in the year. The trail descends gradually along the drainage that forms a small pond, one of many water sources for the resident deer population. Quiet footsteps and silent voices might reward the vigilant hiker with a brief glance at the six-point buck that lives in these parts.

The trail then slips between several old barbwire fencerows before bearing left (west) and roughly paralleling the eastern side of Miles Parkway, heading southeast. About 0.8 mile from the trailhead, you'll cross three shallow creekbeds before the trail ducks under a stone-clad bridge carrying cars overhead. You're now walking on the opposite (west) side of the parkway, heading toward Floyds Fork.

A few yards past the bridge underpass, the trail turns abruptly right across the creek and travels east once more. After a heavy rain, this creek rumbles along quite noisily, and a 6-foot waterfall flows just downstream from where you crossed.

A few more gentle switchbacks along the trail bring you to a small ridge overlooking Floyds Fork. The views are best from late fall to early spring, when most of the leaves are young or off the trees and the white bark of the sycamores reflects in the water below. In the spring, the blooms of white dogwood and pink redbuds dot the forest. You have several good vantage points to choose from along this ridge, so walk slowly and enjoy the sights.

Periodically along the trail you may see several old deer stands, as evidenced by dilapidated two-by-fours still nailed, yet hanging precipitously, to the crotches of mature trees. The profusion of oaks guarantees the nonstop barking of the gray squirrels that thrive in these woods. Their chatter mimics the woman in line ahead of you at the supermarket, still talking on her cell phone when she reaches the cashier.

Soon the trail leaves the overlook and descends gently to a paved trail that follows Floyds Fork. At 1.45 miles, turn right (north) on the paved trail, and almost immediately bear right (east) again as you walk back up the short road leading to the parking lot.

Nearby Attractions

The **William F. Miles Lakes** are stocked spring and fall with channel cats, largemouth bass, bluegill, and rainbow trout. The occasional crappie might also make an appearance. The lakes here are quite popular among local anglers on weekends and after work.

Paddlers might enjoy a trip down **Floyds Fork.** In addition to the canoe launch at Miles Lake, the Cane Run Canoe Launch at 6500 Echo Trail and the Fisherville Canoe Launch at 14520 Old Taylorsville Road provide easy access.

Directions

From I-265 (KY 841/Gene Snyder Freeway), take Exit 27, heading east on US 60 (Shelbyville Road). Drive 2 miles and, just past the Valhalla Golf Club, turn right (south) on Blue Heron Road (Miles Parkway). Drive another 0.6 mile to the small parking lot on the left (east) side of the road. Start here to walk the loop trail clockwise.

19

Salato Wildlife Education Center

SCENERY: ★ ★ ★
TRAIL CONDITION: ★ ★ ★ ★ ★
CHILDREN: ★ ★ ★ ★ ★
DIFFICULTY: ★
SOLITUDE: ★ ★

CONSTELLATIONS OF SPOTS DAPPLE THESE WHITE-TAILED FAWNS.

GPS TRAILHEAD COORDINATES: Main Trail, N38° 10.670' W84° 55.392';
Pea Ridge Trail, N38° 10.712' W84° 55.585'

DISTANCE & CONFIGURATION: 1.25-mile double loop (includes both a paved figure-eight path around the wildlife exhibits and an unpaved loop trail combining the Habitrek and Prairie Trails). An additional 2.5 miles of hiking utilizing the Pea Ridge Trail are also available.

HIKING TIME: 1.5 hours (generously estimated for short toddler strides)

HIGHLIGHTS: Indoor education center and outdoor exhibit area of native flora and fauna

ELEVATION: 855' at trailhead, descending to 784' at low point

ACCESS: Open March–late November, Tuesday–Friday, 9 a.m.–5 p.m.; Saturday, 10 a.m.–5 p.m. Closed on state holidays and seasonally (see website below for details). Free to hike; see website for fees to enter the education center.

MAPS: Available at the website below and at the education center; USGS *Frankfort West*

FACILITIES: Restrooms, picnic tables and shelters, small fishing lake

WHEELCHAIR ACCESS: Yes, with 0.5 mile of paved trail in the outdoor exhibit area

COMMENTS: Check the website for special events such as wildflower walks, live-owl shows, and native-plant sales. Salato is also popular for school groups and summer camp outings.

CONTACTS: Kentucky Department of Fish and Wildlife Resources, 800-858-1549;
tinyurl.com/salatowec

Salato Wildlife Education Center

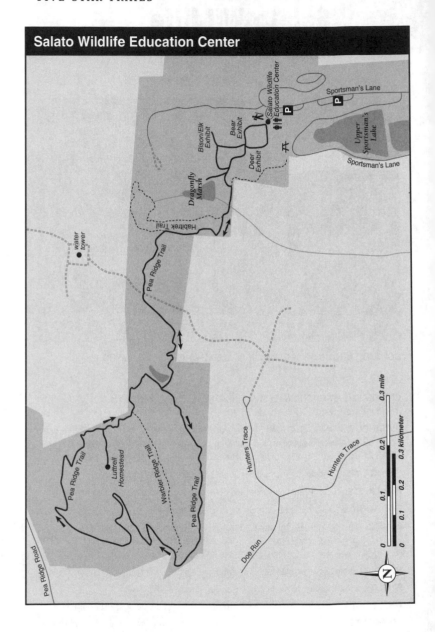

Overview

This one has "kids" written all over it. Pack up the li'l taters and give them a taste of native Kentucky. Both indoor and outdoor exhibits showcase the flora and fauna of the Bluegrass. Owned by the Kentucky Department of Fish and Wildlife, Salato gives the kids a chance to run with wild abandon while teaching many of the lessons only Mother Nature can offer. Big kids will also enjoy hiking the Pea Ridge Trail for its history and scenic beauty.

Route Details

Before hiking, you may want to start your adventure at the main building of the education center. The information desk can provide maps, an Animal Tracks Audio Tour, and all kinds of wildlife pamphlets and paraphernalia.

The education center alone can be a destination on cold or rainy days when you don't want to hike. Just past the information desk, stuffed owls, geese, hawks, and other avian critters dangle from the ceiling as you walk past exhibits showcasing the variety of Kentucky's ecosystems. At the end of the hall, the hanging sculptures change to flying fish such as muskellunge, stripers, rainbow trout, and largemouth bass.

Both cold and warm freshwater tanks let you see native fish up close in their natural habitats. While the serpentarium cases might make some guests squirm, the collection of stuffed raccoons, deer, beavers, foxes, and other mammals are a taxidermist's dream come true. There are also several learning stations where kids can "catch" catfish, count the points on a buck, or observe flying squirrels sleeping soundly.

The large glass doors at the end of the hall lead to the outdoor exhibits. From here a wide paved trail takes you past live exhibits of an American eagle, black bears, wildcats, bison, deer, wild turkeys, and elk. A waterfall and creek exhibit features live fish.

Ramps provide access for strollers and wheelchairs, and benches are scattered generously around the path. It's not unusual to see grandparents pushing strollers while passing along a bit of nature appreciation to the next generation.

While the paved trail is basically a 0.5-mile figure-eight configuration with several spurs shooting in various directions, kids tend to zigzag across the area, going back again and again to see their favorite animals. Patches of wildflowers and grasses native to the Bluegrass, including black-eyed Susan, purple coneflower, and butterfly weed, link the live-animal exhibits.

After you've seen the fauna, young hikers may want to try a short dirt trail. Close to Dragonfly Marsh, a well-marked wooded walkway leads to both the Habitrek and Prairie Trails. Together, these trails form a 0.7-mile loop of relatively flat terrain. Given enough time and encouragement, very young children can complete these trails. Even in the dry of summer, moist areas showcase deer and raccoon prints, and finches can be seen feasting on coneflower seeds.

Hardier hikers can take the 2.5-mile Pea Ridge Trail, a balloon that follows several creek drainages and low rock walls before ambling past the old Luttrell homestead. From the middle of the Habitrek Trail, turn left (west) onto the out-and-back portion of the Pea Ridge balloon. In less than 0.5 mile, you reach the loop part of the trail (which in turn is bisected by the Warbler Ridge Trail).

At the loop intersection, turn left (southwest) to follow the Pea Ridge Trail clockwise. In the spring, this area is populated with wildflowers, including trilliums, wild ginger, Virginia bluebells, trout lilies, fire pinks, and Jacob's ladder. In 0.45 mile, the Warbler Ridge Trail bisects the loop. If you take Warbler Ridge, your hike will be shortened by 0.6 mile. Alternately, you can stay on the Pea Ridge Trail to drop down into another creek drainage before climbing to a high spot along Pea Ridge itself. This is a good place to spot wild turkeys, box turtles, and deer roaming free.

The Luttrell family homesteaded this land before the Civil War, and many of their ancestors still live in the area. You'll observe evidence of their farming operations along several portions of the trail. Stone fences are the remnants of fields having been cleared before plowing. In other places, huge piles of rocks were stacked within creek drainages to reduce erosion and capture running water.

A spur takes hikers a short distance off the Pea Ridge Trail to the site of the old Luttrell log cabin. All that remains are several stone structures, a large notched beam, and several vernal pools formed in depressions where the outhouse and an outbuilding were located.

Returning to the Pea Ridge Trail, you'll pass a small pond in a few hundred yards, alerting you to the intersection of the loop and the out-and-back section. Turn left (southeast) back onto the main stem of the Pea Ridge balloon to get back to the Habitrek Trail and the education center.

Nearby Attractions

If the weather is good, bring a picnic basket and ye olde fishing pole. Salato's small lake is well stocked, and fishing is free for kids under age 16. Free poles and tackle are available first-come, first-served at the education center; otherwise, it's BYOB—bring your own bait.

Hungry? Turn right (west) on US 60 upon leaving Salato and travel 20 miles to feast at **Claudia Sanders Dinner House** in Shelbyville (3202 Shelbyville Road; 502-633-5600). Colonel Harland Sanders's wife didn't miss a trick in learning how to make finger-lickin' chicken. Visit **claudiasanders.com** for menus and hours.

Directions

From Louisville, take I-64 East toward Frankfort about 42 miles. At Exit 48 (Lawrenceburg/Graefenburg), turn left (north) on KY 151. Drive 1.1 miles and turn right (east) on US 60. Drive 4.2 miles and turn left (north) onto Sportsman's Lane, formerly known as Game Farm Road (*note:* many GPS units and online mapping services still use the old name). The education center and parking area are at the rear of the property.

20

Taylorsville Lake
State Park: Lakeview Vista Trail

SCENERY: ★ ★ ★ ★
TRAIL CONDITION: ★ ★ ★ ★
CHILDREN: ★ ★ ★
DIFFICULTY: ★ ★ ★
SOLITUDE: ★ ★ ★

ENJOY TAYLORSVILLE LAKE ANY TIME OF YEAR.

GPS TRAILHEAD COORDINATES: N38° 1.492' W85° 15.819'

DISTANCE & CONFIGURATION: 3.1-mile loop, with longer options

HIKING TIME: 1.25 hours

HIGHLIGHTS: Beautiful lake views, fall colors

ELEVATION: 730' at trailhead, descending to 581' at low point

ACCESS: Daily, sunrise–sunset; free admission

MAPS: Available at the park information center

FACILITIES: Picnic shelters, restrooms, campground, boat ramp

WHEELCHAIR ACCESS: None

COMMENTS: All trails accommodate hikers, equestrian riders, and mountain bikers. Leashed pets welcome.

CONTACTS: Taylorsville Lake State Park, 502-477-8713; **parks.ky.gov/parks /recreationparks/taylorsville-lake**

Overview

The Lakeview Vista Trail is a beautiful loop that skirts open meadows, runs through mature hardwoods, and dances along the edge of Taylorsville Lake. A relatively level hike, this is one that older kids can do while throwing rocks and shooting arrows. With a host of options available, the hike can easily be extended to accommodate those with stronger stamina. But timing is everything. Try to avoid midsummer, when the Jet-Ski traffic is heavy and the humidity is high. Both spring and fall afford the best lake views, offering either delicate wildflowers or autumn colors for visual interest.

Route Details

The closest parking to the trailhead is next to the picnic shelters, 2.1 miles from the main road (KY 248). The trail begins just south of the park road, directly across from Shelter 2. Hit the restrooms and load your daypack before carefully crossing the road. Boaters use this same access road to get to the Possum Ridge Boat Ramp, and none of us want to be flattened on the pavement (like a possum, that is).

Once safely on the other side of the road, you'll see a sign indicating THE OLD HILL CLIMB. To hike the Lakeview Vista Trail counterclockwise, bear right (west) onto the trail. The path winds behind the caretaker's house before passing a small wooden sign: SALT RIVER VISTA LOOP 2 MILES. Relax—you're on the right track. On the official state-park map, this trail is identified as the Lakeview Vista Trail, and generally speaking they're one in the same. Continue along the path through a small dogwood grove and then a mixed cedar–sycamore thicket. The latter is extremely unusual, given that cedars typically prefer sandy, well-drained soils, while sycamores don't mind wet feet in the least.

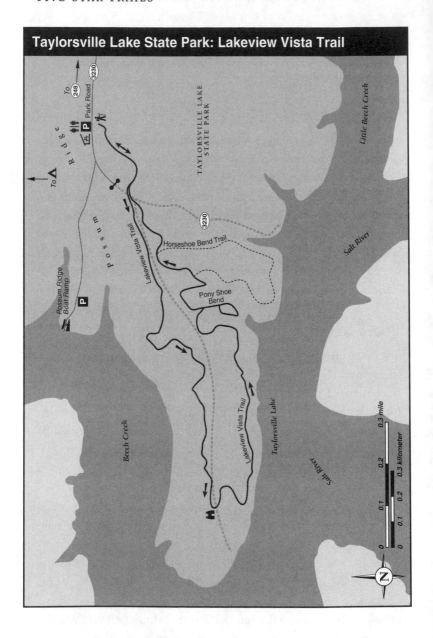

Taylorsville Lake State Park: Lakeview Vista Trail

About 0.25 mile from the trailhead, you'll come to an old cinder roadbed with one end blocked by a red farm gate. Turn left (south) and then take a quick jog right at the sign indicating the Salt River (that is, Lakeview Vista) Trail as the path continues west.

So why all the SALT RIVER signs? Built by the U.S. Army Corps of Engineers, Taylorsville Lake was formed in the early 1980s by damming the Salt River as part of a larger flood-control effort. Early settlers built a number of saltworks along the riverbanks, producing on average 50 pounds of salt for every 400 gallons of processed water. The lake itself is named after Richard Taylor, one of the early land barons who owned a gristmill in the vicinity. He donated 60 acres of nearby land to build the small town of Taylorsville.

Back on the trail, the Lakeview Vista Trail continues ridgetop along a transitional meadow, frequently roamed and bedded by the resident white-tailed-deer population. Walk quietly and you'll have a good chance of spotting a rafter of turkeys that frequent this area. The trail then ducks into the hardwood forest, while glimpses of the lake can be seen through the trees to your right.

If you've managed to hike this trail in the autumn, the fall palette will be filled with orange sassafras, yellow maples, sienna oaks, and

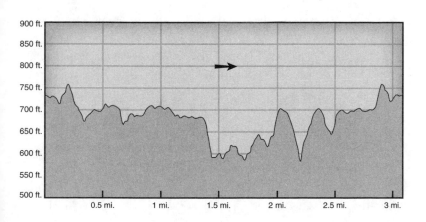

golden-brown poplars. The maniacal cry of a pileated woodpecker or the squawk of a heron may be heard almost any time of the year.

About 1.25 miles from the trailhead, you'll reach a scenic overlook (marked on the park map) with a clear view of the lake to the west. Here you'll find a picnic table, a garbage can, a small hitching post, and a line of young walnut trees, one of which is studded with mistletoe. (When it comes to standing under the mistletoe, we leave that to your discretion and choice of company.)

As you look across the lake to the opposite hillside, you might notice the roofs of a small residential development above the Taylorsville Lake Marina. From this vantage point, the wide, grassy path leading toward a small utility enclosure and the beckoning lakeshore might lure the adventurous hiker. But be forewarned: beyond the grass, the hiking gets rough quickly and the best views are clearly from the top.

Leaving the scenic overlook, the trail loops back to the left (east). In a few yards, the route splits into the Lakeview Vista and Ridge Runner Trails. At this point, the Lakeview Vista Trail dissolves almost completely into the woods—stay on the Ridge Runner Trail, which bears right (south) at this junction and follows closer to the lakeshore.

Covered with a light coating of fine gravel, the Ridge Runner Trail begins a slow series of descending switchbacks, punctuated by short sections of split-rail fence. The park should be applauded for these trail improvements, which have worked to keep horse damage to a minimum. Here, the southern slopes cater to the black-locust and hickory trees that are plentiful along the path. This section of the trail affords wonderful lake views, particularly in the spring and fall. The sound of small motorboats may be heard as fishermen chase that elusive crappie or largemouth bass.

About 2 miles from the trailhead, the path climbs back to the ridgetop, where large hedge apples litter the service road dividing the ridge. Here the Ridge Runner Trail rejoins the Lakeview Vista Trail in a seamless transition. In a short distance, a small OVERLOOK REST

AREA sign just to the right (south) of the trail leads to a short 0.2-mile loop and another small hitching post. This steep trail is known as Pony Shoe Bend. The views here are unimpressive, but the climb back up is good for your calf muscles.

Continuing east, you'll notice another loop trail just south of where you're hiking. On your right you'll pass two signs for Lakeview Vista Trail 2, also known as the Horseshoe Bend Trail. This pleasant 0.7-mile loop descends back down to the lakeshore, then climbs back to the main trail. Adding this loop to the described hike results in a 3.6-mile loop.

If you stay on the Lakeview Vista Trail, another 10 minutes of walking brings you back to the old cinder roadbed. Turn left (north) on the road and you'll see the same red farm gate from before. Turn right (east) at the gate to return to the trailhead. Now that the lake views are gone, the 5-minute walk back to your vehicle seems anticlimactic. The next time everyone in the office skips out early on a Friday afternoon to catch the races, you can be back walking these trails in less than an hour's drive.

Nearby Attractions

With more than 24 miles of multiuse trails, Taylorsville Lake State Park offers a host of other hikes. For shorter trails only open to hikers, the **Wildlife Viewing and Pete Campbell Trails** (at 0.5 and 1.4 miles, respectively) are good options. If you're looking for a longer hike, park at the visitor center and combine the **Wildwood Trace and Legends Run Trails** to create a 6-to-8-mile loop.

Directions

From downtown Louisville, take I-64 East toward Frankfort. About 12.5 miles east of I-265 (KY 841/Gene Snyder Freeway), turn right (south) on Exit 32A (KY 55) toward Taylorsville and drive 4.1 miles. Turn left (east) on Finchville Road (KY 148). In 6.6 miles, turn right (west) on KY 44. Drive 4.2 miles before turning left (south) on Briar

Ridge Road (KY 248). After 1.9 miles, turn right (south) on Park Road (County Road 3230) and drive 2.1 miles to the trailhead.

Alternately, from the intersection of Bardstown Road (US 150 East/US 31 East) and I-265 (KY 841/Gene Snyder Freeway) in south Louisville, take Bardstown Road 6.7 miles south toward Mount Washington. Turn left (east) on KY 44 and drive 17.4 miles. Bear right (south) on Briar Ridge Road and drive 1.9 miles. Turn south (right) on Park Road (County Road 3230) and drive 2.1 miles to the trailhead.

21

Vernon-Douglas State Nature Preserve

SCENERY: ★ ★ ★
TRAIL CONDITION: ★ ★ ★ ★
CHILDREN: ★ ★
DIFFICULTY: ★ ★ ★
SOLITUDE: ★ ★ ★ ★ ★

EVEN "FUN GUYS" ENJOY CONDO LIVING.

GPS TRAILHEAD COORDINATES: N37° 44.003' W85° 42.469'

DISTANCE & CONFIGURATION: 3.5-mile balloon

HIKING TIME: 1.5 hours

HIGHLIGHTS: Second-growth forest, birding, spring wildflowers

ELEVATION: 474' at trailhead to 823' at high point

ACCESS: Daily, sunrise–sunset; free admission

MAPS: Available at the website below

FACILITIES: None

WHEELCHAIR ACCESS: None

COMMENTS: No pets

CONTACTS: Kentucky State Nature Preserves Commission, 502-573-2886;
tinyurl.com/vernondouglas

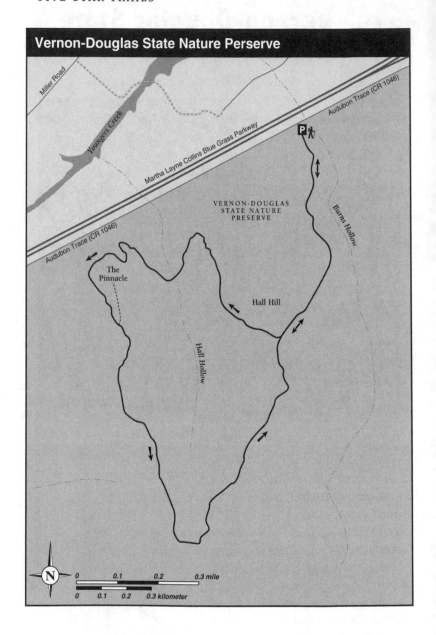

Vernon-Douglas State Nature Perserve

Miller Road

Youngers Creek

Audubon Trace (CR 1046)

Martha Layne Collins Blue Grass Parkway

P

Audubon Trace (CR 1046)

VERNON-DOUGLAS
STATE NATURE
PRESERVE

Burns Hollow

The
Pinnacle

Hall Hill

Hall Hollow

N

0   0.1   0.2   0.3 mile

0   0.1   0.2   0.3 kilometer

Overview

Vernon-Douglas Nature Preserve, just south of the ever-popular Bernheim Arboretum and Research Forest (see Hikes 14 and 15), rarely sees a hiker. Donated to the Audubon Society of Kentucky in 1972 and now managed by the Kentucky State Nature Preserves Commission, this 730-acre tract protects a large second-growth forest in the Knobs region of central Kentucky. The trail traverses low-lying creeks and dry rocky ridges, supporting a wide variety of flora and fauna. Pileated woodpeckers and hooting owls drown out the occasional road noise from the Martha Layne Collins Blue Grass Parkway.

Route Details

The trail kiosk is hidden behind the trees at the rear of the parking lot, in what is known as Burns Hollow. Visitors always seem to find two or three sturdy hiking sticks, left by past hikers, leaning up against one large tree or another. It's a welcoming sign.

    This land once belonged to siblings Eleanor and Ollie Douglas and had been in their family since the early 1900s. Determined

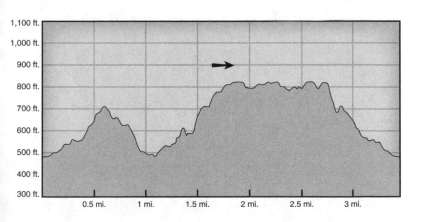

that the land never be logged again, Ollie practiced conservation techniques to protect and preserve the area for future generations to come. Ollie got a little sidetracked when he planted kudzu for erosion control and Virginia pines on the ridgetops, but we don't hold that against him.

The forest comprises magnificent pignut hickory, sweetgum, beech, buckeye, sassafras, and tulip poplar—Kentucky's state tree. About that last one . . .

Not to digress too much, but the tulip poplar was designated Kentucky's state tree in 1956 until Joe Creason, a popular columnist for the *Louisville Courier-Journal* for more than 30 years, launched an all-encompassing campaign to have the Kentucky coffee tree named the state tree. Two years after Creason died, the state legislature acquiesced. But the poplar–coffee tree wars didn't end there: in 1994, the legislature reversed itself again and restored the tulip poplar— also known as the yellow poplar and the tulip tree—as Kentucky's official tree.

Anyway, back to hiking. After taking a minute to read the information posted at the kiosk, follow the trail straight ahead (south) as it climbs the side of a small knob. At this point you may be wondering if you'll hear the sounds of the Martha Layne Collins Blue Grass Parkway the entire hike. Thankfully, on the back side of each knob a large sound eddy forms, sheltering your ears from the sounds of civilization. After about 0.6 mile, the trail splits and forms a loop. Walking the loop counterclockwise is your best bet.

Turning right (west) at this junction takes you down a spiny ridge along an old roadbed through Hall Hollow. The trail flattens a bit as it crosses a shallow creek, which offers the finest opportunity along the trail to see a spectacular spring-wildflower display. Keep an eye out for trillium, bloodroot, columbine, rock cress, and mayapple.

The trail climbs quickly again to the top of a second knob. This is a good time to look for the multitude of 'shrooms and other "fun guys" that populate this preserve. (If you still haven't bought that mushroom-identification book, don't put it off any longer.)

Before you reach the top of the ridge, you'll see a clearly marked trail coming in on your left (you're now about 1.5 miles from the trailhead). This short spur leads you to what locals call The Pinnacle. At 800 feet, the hilltop faces north and overlooks Youngers Valley. In the summer and early fall the views are greatly obstructed by the tree canopy, but at other times of the year you can catch glimpses of distant pastoral landscapes.

The main trail continues along the ridgetop for another 1.5 miles. Here the soils are quite thin and the undergrowth quite sparse. Past ice storms, lightning strikes, and heavy winds have taken their toll, giving the local woodpecker population a perpetual feast. Birds of prey frequent these ridgetops, as do wild turkeys and owls. Halfway along the ridgetop trail, the preserve skirts adjacent farmland, where local agrarians raise corn and cell phone towers to make ends meet.

Once again, the trail quickly descends back to the junction with the out-and-back stem of the balloon. These steep, rocky spines are a good place to spot crinoids, the fossils of ancient marine animals. In some places along the trail, the crinoids are so plentiful they look like pennies tossed across a parking lot. (Leave them where you find them, though.)

Bear right (north) at the junction to walk the final 0.6 mile back to the parking area. If you've borrowed a hiking stick, be sure to return it for the next hiker. And be sure to murmur a word of thanks to Ollie and Eleanor for their vision and passion.

Nearby Attractions

Mountain bikers (as well as hikers) might be interested in the **Youngers Creek Trail,** just a 10-minute drive from Vernon-Douglas. Built for mountain bikers by mountain bikers, the trailhead is 3 miles down Miller Road: after leaving Vernon-Douglas, cross back over the Martha Layne Collins Blue Grass Parkway on Youngers Creek Road, then turn left on Miller Road. With more than 12 miles of single- and doubletrack, Youngers Creek can be tight and technical, with a series of seven leg-burning switchbacks lovingly referred to as the Seven Dwarfs. For more information, see **kymba.org/louisville.**

Directions

From Louisville, head south on I-65. From the intersection of I-65 South and I-265 (KY 841/Gene Snyder Freeway), drive about 20 miles; at Exit 105, turn left (south) on KY 61 and drive 4.1 miles. In the small town of Boston, bear right (west) on KY 61 South/US 62 West and drive 3.8 miles. Turn left (south) on Youngers Creek Road (KY 583). In another 2 miles you'll cross the Martha Layne Collins Blue Grass Parkway. Take an immediate right onto Audubon Trace (County Road 1046). Drive another 0.5 mile and you'll see the small, unmarked gravel parking lot, on your left.

Opposite: **VERNON-DOUGLAS IS A WOODPECKER'S HEAVEN ON EARTH.**

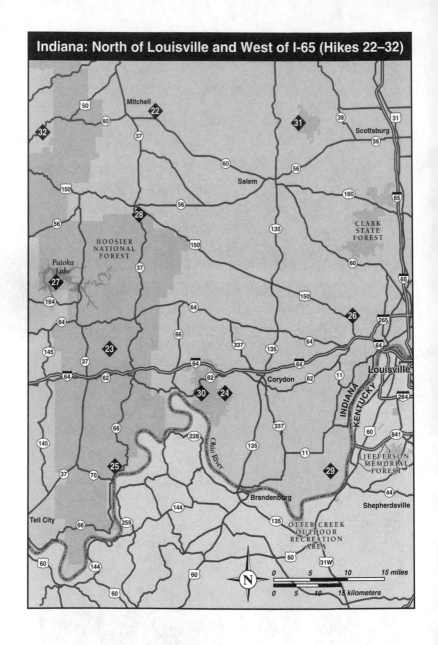

Indiana: North of Louisville and West of I-65 (Hikes 22–32)

Mitchell

Scottsburg

Salem

CLARK STATE FOREST

HOOSIER NATIONAL FOREST

Patoka Lake

Louisville

Corydon

INDIANA

KENTUCKY

JEFFERSON MEMORIAL FOREST

Ohio River

Brandenburg

Shepherdsville

Tell City

OTTER CREEK OUTDOOR RECREATION AREA

N

0   5   10   15 miles

0   5   10   15 kilometers

Indiana:
North of Louisville
and West of I-65

ON YOUR MARK, GET SET, *SLIDE!* *(See Hike 26, Mount St. Francis Lake Trail, page 180.)*

Donaldson's Woods Nature Preserve

At Spring Mill State Park

SCENERY: ★ ★ ★ ★ ★
TRAIL CONDITION: ★ ★ ★ ★ ★
CHILDREN: ★ ★ ★
DIFFICULTY: ★ ★
SOLITUDE: ★ ★ ★

WATCH YOUR STEP HERE—THE STONE CAN BECOME QUITE SLIPPERY WHEN WET OR COVERED WITH SNOW OR ICE.

GPS TRAILHEAD COORDINATES: N38° 44.044' W86° 24.849'

DISTANCE & CONFIGURATION: A 2.5-mile balloon on a very short string (5.5 miles with optional side trip)

HIKING TIME: 1.5 hours

HIGHLIGHTS: Several creeks appear from and disappear into caves as the trail traverses an old-growth forest. Side trip includes nature center and pioneer village.

ELEVATION: 652' at trailhead, ascending to 735' at high point

ACCESS: Trails open daily, sunrise–sunset. Entrance fee: $5/vehicle for Indiana residents, $7/vehicle out-of-state. Annual permits also available (see **in.gov/dnr/parklake/5062.htm**).

MAPS: Available at the website below and the park entrance gate; USGS *Mitchell*

FACILITIES: Campground, historic inn, swimming pool, and picnic shelters

WHEELCHAIR ACCESS: None on the trail

COMMENTS: Timing is everything! This place can be packed on holiday weekends and anytime during the summer. But during the off-season, you may have the trail to yourself.

CONTACTS: Spring Mill State Park, 812-849-4129; **in.gov/dnr/parklake/2968.htm**

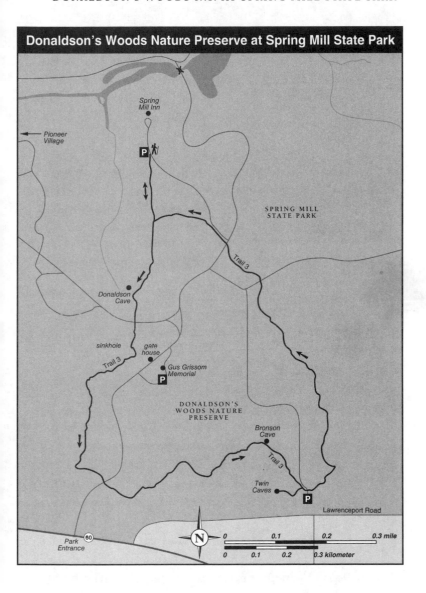

Donaldson's Woods Nature Preserve at Spring Mill State Park

Spring Mill Inn

← Pioneer Village

P

SPRING MILL STATE PARK

Trail 3

Donaldson Cave

sinkhole

gate house

Trail 3

Gus Grissom Memorial

P

DONALDSON'S WOODS NATURE PRESERVE

Bronson Cave

Trail 3

Twin Caves

P

Lawrenceport Road

N

0   0.1   0.2   0.3 mile

0   0.1   0.2   0.3 kilometer

Park Entrance 60

Overview

This park hits on all cylinders. Hiking without getting your boots muddy. Creeks disappearing underground and popping out of caves. Wildflowers. Hot showers. Kids having a blast. With the possible exception of gastronomic delights, if Spring Mill State Park doesn't have it, you may not need it.

But best of all, Spring Mill State Park has a beautiful 2.5-mile loop trail that traverses Donaldson's Woods Nature Preserve and passes through a stand of old-growth forest. The heavily wooded path winds its way past both Bronson and Twin Caves before returning you to the beautiful Spring Mill Inn.

Route Details

If you've never been to Spring Mill State Park, it's worth spending a little time getting to know your surroundings. The park sits upon the Mitchell Plateau, and parts of Spring Mill have more than 100 sinkholes per square mile as a result of the karst geology of the region. The constant flow of groundwater was essential in creating an early-1800s industrial village that at one time housed more than 300 people. These pioneer-age titans of local industry used the power of the water to operate several gristmills, a wool mill, a sawmill, and even a distillery.

By the early 1920s, however, the pioneer village was in a state of considerable disrepair. In the early 1930s, the Civilian Conservation Corps jumped in and began renovating the historical log structures, building exquisite stone walls, and erecting quaint picnic shelters throughout the park. The restored Pioneer Village consists of 20 log buildings, most of which are original to the park. The village (admission is free with your park-admittance fee) is open daily, March–mid-October, 9 a.m.–5 p.m. The three-story limestone gristmill still grinds corn on occasion; park employees, dressed in period clothing, work at the apothecary, loom house, and other shops in the village.

Spring Mill State Park is home to three nature preserves: Donaldson's Woods, Donaldson Cave, and Mitchell Sinkhole Plain.

Although the forest is listed on park brochures as virgin timber, the Indiana Department of Natural Resources notes that the 145-acre Donaldson's Woods is one of only a few "undisturbed" old-growth forests remaining in Indiana, including centuries-old white oaks and massive tulip poplars. Virgin versus undisturbed . . . either way, it's older than you and me put together, and undeniably more stunning to look at.

The main route through Donaldson's Woods Nature Preserve is listed as Trail 3 on state park maps. The trail both begins and ends at the eastern edge of the parking garage adjacent to the Spring Mill Inn. Hikers can access Trail 3 at other points, but parking is easy here and the old inn is fun to explore.

The trail itself is a path of finely crushed gravel 4–5 feet wide. With the exception of a few short sets of stairs and a couple of brief climbs, the trail is relatively flat, following a gently rolling terrain. With all the points of interest along the trail, it's perfect for young kids or anyone with a short attention span.

From the trailhead, the trail splits almost immediately. Bear right (south) to walk the loop counterclockwise and to follow the signage in the most logical order.

The trail quickly rewards spring hikers with a nice display of shooting stars, bloodroot, wild ginger, and trillium before reaching the Donaldson Cave overlook. Although you can't see the cave from here, you can't miss the sound of falling water. Unfortunately, the cave is closed indefinitely because of white-nose syndrome, a fungal disease that has endangered the local bat population.

About 0.3 mile into the hike, the trail crosses the park road close to the entrance gate. A large sinkhole will be on your right. If any little ones are joining you on this trip, it's an excellent time to start that conversation on karst geology, explaining that persistent (typically acidic) waterflows begin to eat away at the carbonate (typically limestone) rock below, leaving a depression or sinkhole in the ground. Once you see one sinkhole, it's easy to recognize the hundreds of other sinkholes that pockmark the face of Spring Mill.

In another 0.5 mile, the trail crosses the main park road. Traffic is usually sparse here, but proceed with caution. You don't want to look like the squirrels that were unsuccessful in crossing busy streets.

Bronson Cave is the next point of interest, about 1.2 miles from the trailhead. Here, one of the many creeks in the park mysteriously appears from nowhere, only to disappear into the adjacent cave. Have a seat on one of the benches or read more about the Mitchell Plateau. You really needn't be in a hurry.

From early spring until midsummer, the woods here are generously studded with mayapple, also known as Adam's apple, mandrake, raccoon berry, wild lemon, Indian apple, duck's foot, and umbrella plant. (Who thinks up all these names?) While the fruit of the mayapple is edible in small amounts, the leaves and roots are poisonous. American Indian lore sadly tells of Cherokees consuming the plant as they marched along the Trail of Tears—unable to face a forced relocation, they chose another fate.

Just past Donaldson Cave, the trail makes a sharp but brief ascent to the small parking lot where the Twin Caves boat tours operate. Immediately to your right is a beautiful circa-1920s stone arch and a set of stairs leading to the caves. During the off-season or off-hours, feel free to descend the steps to explore the area. In the summer, the park service offers tours from this location. Customers are loaded into small flat-bottom boats at the mouth of Twin Caves. Park employees then guide the boat upstream into the cave using their gloved hands to press on the roof of the rock. It's about a 20-minute ride into the cave and out again.

The trail picks up again on the opposite side of the parking lot. The next 0.5 mile showcases some of the oldest trees in the park. In the fall this section of the trail is magnificent, with the pale golden poplars towering over the smaller red- and orange-leafed sugar maples and yellow pawpaw trees. Two more road crossings and you're back to the start of the loop. Turn right (north) at the Y, and you're back to the parking garage and the Spring Mill Inn.

Nearby Attractions

A longer 5.5-mile hike combines **Trails 3, 4, and 5** on the Spring Mill State Park map. Each of these trails is a loop that begins and ends very close to the Spring Mill Inn. Start at the parking garage, just south of the inn, as described at the beginning of the hike profile. Walk south on Trail 3, bearing right (west) at the first Y in the trail. Just past the Donaldson Cave Overlook, bear right (west) on a short spur of Trail 3 that will connect you with Trail 4.

The Trail 4 loop can be hiked in either direction to take you past several points of interest. The trail circles past the Hamer Pioneer Cemetery and Hamer Cave and skirts the southern edge of the Pioneer Village before bringing you back to Trail 3 once again.

Bear right (south) on Trail 3 and complete the loop as described above, taking you past Bronson Cave and Twin Caves, and through Donaldson's Woods. Once you've completed the Trail 3 loop, walk to the north side of the inn and pick up Trail 1, a short spur that will link you with Trail 5, which loops around the lake and nature center before bringing you back to the inn and parking structure.

Directions

From Louisville, take I-64 West across the Ohio River into southern Indiana. At Exit 119 (Greenville/Paoli), turn right (north) on US 150 and drive 15 miles west to Palmyra. Turn right (north) on IN 135 and drive 15 miles to Salem, then turn left (west) on IN 60 and drive 18 more miles. Spring Mill State Park will be on your right, just north of IN 60.

23

Hemlock Cliffs

SCENERY: ★ ★ ★ ★ ★
TRAIL CONDITION: ★ ★ ★ ★
CHILDREN: ★ ★ ★
DIFFICULTY: ★ ★
SOLITUDE: ★ ★

NOT EVEN CINDERELLA COULD SQUEEZE INTO THIS DELICATE LADYSLIPPER.

GPS TRAILHEAD COORDINATES: N38° 16.642' W86° 32.346'

DISTANCE & CONFIGURATION: 1.5-mile loop

HIKING TIME: I hour

HIGHLIGHTS: Large rock houses, imposing cliffs, lush wildflower habitat

ELEVATION: 838' at trailhead, descending to 671' at low point

ACCESS: Anytime year-round; free admission

MAPS: Available for download (free) and for purchase at the website below; USGS *Taswell*

FACILITIES: None

WHEELCHAIR ACCESS: None

COMMENTS: Although kids love this trail, please hike with care, particularly along the cliff overhangs and rock houses.

CONTACTS: Hoosier National Forest, 866-302-4173 or 812-275-5987; **fs.usda.gov/hoosier**

Overview

Hemlock Cliffs is one of the most spectacular natural areas in southern Indiana. The trail quickly takes you into a magical world of rock houses (natural rock shelters), filtered sunlight, verdant ferns, and running water. The most popular time to visit is springtime, when the wildflowers generously litter the trail and cling to the cliffs. Tread lightly—the ecosystem is as fragile as it is beautiful.

Route Details

The only complaint you're likely to hear about Hemlock Cliffs is that there just isn't enough of it to go around. The short 1.5-mile loop trail is about one-third woodland wonder, one-third creekside ooh-ing and ah-ing, and one-third jaw-dropping scenery as the path travels under cliffs and rock houses. Visitors frequently go off-trail to explore all the nooks and crannies the place has to offer. You could spend 2 hours here and still want to hike the loop a second time.

Unfortunately, the natural beauty of Hemlock Cliffs draws hikers from all over, and sometimes solitude is hard to find, particularly during spring weekends. But the area is equally beautiful during other seasons. The high cliffs shelter visitors from the hot summer sun, and multiple caves and springs push cool air into the small gorge. The fall offers an array of color from the beeches, maples, and hickories found here, while winter brings dripping ice formations that hang from the cliffs above.

The loop trail can be walked either clockwise or counterclockwise, and both directions have their advantages. Walking the trail clockwise provides a gradual immersion into the small gorge, while going the other direction gives you immediate access to the main waterfall.

To walk the trail clockwise, begin on the west side of the parking lot, opposite the kiosk. A number of small signs identify trees along the way: red, black, and white oak; pignut hickory; sassafras; red and sugar maple; blackgum; and more. The path travels northwest until

Hemlock Cliffs

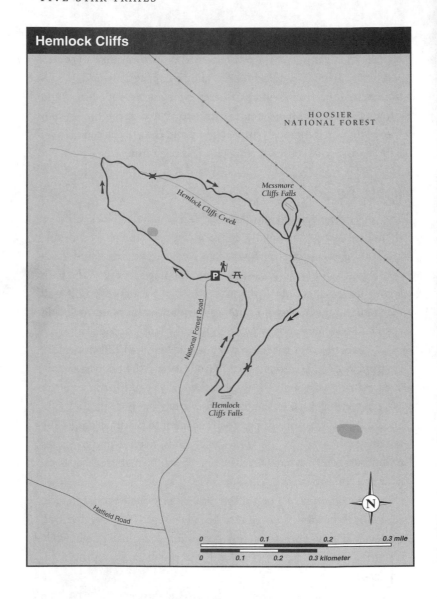

HOOSIER
NATIONAL FOREST

Messmore
Cliffs Falls

Hemlock Cliffs Creek

National Forest Road

Hemlock
Cliffs Falls

Hatfield Road

N

| 0 | 0.1 | 0.2 | 0.3 mile |

| 0 | 0.1 | 0.2 | 0.3 kilometer |

it takes a gentle hairpin curve back to the right (southeast). The trail then runs roughly parallel to a broad but shallow seasonal creek and crosses a small footbridge. Be on the lookout for yellow ladyslippers amid the wide variety of ferns that thrive here.

Past the bridge, about 0.6 mile from the trailhead, the trail forks. Heading left (north) on the loop will lead you up a set of wooden stairs, past white-plumed false Solomon's seal, jack-in-the-pulpit, and wild stonecrop. The trail then takes you along a wide shelf that runs under a large rock house. If heights or drop-offs make you nervous, stop here, enjoy the view, and retrace your steps to the start of the loop. But if you're the adventurous type, continue on the trail—the views up here are wonderful.

The rock house is basically a work of art in action. The trickling water falling from the small creek gently carves various layers of sandstone and limestone, each eroding at different rates. Eventually, long after this book has turned to dust, the rock house will erode until a natural arch is formed, similar to the many natural arches found in eastern Kentucky. Enjoy your time up in the cool rock shelter, watching how the trees filter the light in different

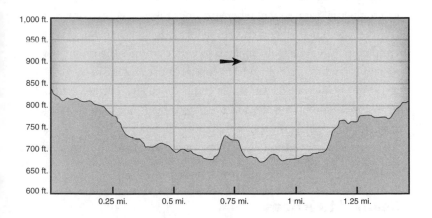

patterns and noticing how the weathering of the iron ore has honeycombed the rock. Carefully continue around the inner perimeter of the rock house and work your way down the rocks to finish the loop back to the main path.

Now back where the trail forked, bear left (south) to continue working your way creekside to the bottom of a small gorge formed by iron-stained cliffs on either side. Both false and true Solomon's seal grow here, along with star chickweed, crested iris, phacelia, white trillium, and alumroot. Wild ginger, the rare wintergreen, sweet woodruff, and a variety of ferns grow almost year-round. A few namesake hemlocks accent the forest canopy, and a sweet breeze always seems to be blowing through here as the cooler air falls, pushing the warmer air higher. An abandoned campsite lies on the other side of the creek, testimony to when rock climbers were permitted to scale and rappel from these cliffs. Hemlock Cliffs is part of the Hoosier National Forest, and camping is permitted as long as sites are 300 feet from the nearest trail, water source, or rock house.

After crossing a second footbridge 1.2 miles from the trailhead, the trail climbs another set of wooden steps. From this vantage point a large seasonal waterfall appears, falling from the cliffs above. Several rogue trails are evident where previous hikers have explored this and the adjacent creekbed and stone formations. While you may be tempted to leave the main trail, do so with caution—the fragile ecosystem balances on a tight fulcrum between use and misuse.

The main trail continues to climb the steep hillside, guiding hikers up a set of stone steps as the path threads between two large stone formations. At the top of this short climb, a small spur on your left takes you above the falls, while a right-hand (north) turn takes you to the parking lot.

Nearby Attractions

If you're interested in visiting the adjacent 100-acre **Saalman Hollow Nature Preserve,** contact The Nature Conservancy. Access is very limited, and you must obtain permission in advance. For more information, call (317) 951-8818 or visit **tinyurl.com/saalman.**

Directions

From Louisville, take I-64 West across the Ohio River into southern Indiana. At Exit 86, turn right (north) on IN 237 toward English. Go 2.6 miles and turn left (west) on Union Chapel Road (County Road 8). Drive another 2.6 miles and bear right (west) on Hatfield Road (CR 8/CR 13). Drive about 1.6 miles until you see the US Forest Service sign for Hemlock Cliffs. Stay straight on National Forest Road, which dead-ends into the parking lot.

24

Indian Creek Overlook

SCENERY: ★ ★ ★ ★ ★
TRAIL CONDITION: ★ ★ ★ ★ ★
CHILDREN: ★ ★
DIFFICULTY: ★ ★ ★
SOLITUDE: ★ ★ ★ ★

WHILE RAVENS LOVE TO SOAR, BLACKBIRDS CAN DO SO FOR ONLY A FEW SECONDS AT A TIME.

GPS TRAILHEAD COORDINATES: N38° 11.683' W86° 14.140'

DISTANCE & CONFIGURATION: 5.8-mile out-and-back

HIKING TIME: 2.5 hours

HIGHLIGHTS: Overlook views of Indian Creek, a log trail shelter

ELEVATION: 865' at trailhead, ascending to 953' at high point

ACCESS: No official hours, but day hikers should be off the trail by sunset. No fees.

MAPS: Harrison-Crawford State Forest, O'Bannon Woods State Park, and USGS *Leavenworth*. If you're obtaining a trail map from either the state forest or the state park, be sure to get one that has the full Adventure Hiking Trail (AHT) outlined, including the far eastern portion of the AHT.

FACILITIES: Shelter with picnic tables and fire pit

WHEELCHAIR ACCESS: None

COMMENTS: Carry plenty of water—creeks are seasonal, and water quality at the on-trail spring may be unreliable.

CONTACTS: Harrison-Crawford State Forest, 812-738-7694; **in.gov/dnr/forestry/4826.htm.** O'Bannon Woods State Park, 812-738-8232; **in.gov/dnr/parklake/2976.htm.**

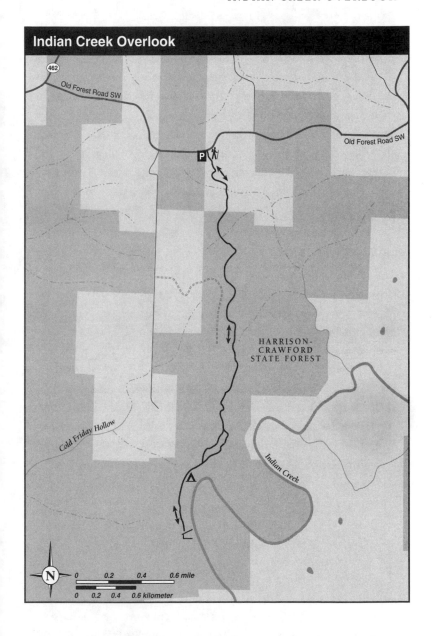

Indian Creek Overlook

462
Old Forest Road SW
Old Forest Road SW
P
HARRISON-
CRAWFORD
STATE FOREST
Cold Friday Hollow
Indian Creek

N
0   0.2   0.4   0.6 mile
0   0.2   0.4   0.6 kilometer

Overview

The Indian Creek Overlook Trail is a section of the 24-mile Adventure Hiking Trail (AHT), which traverses the far southeastern portion of Harrison-Crawford State Forest. The trail passes through scenic hardwood forest, crosses several creek drainages, and climbs to a rocky bluff overlooking Indian Creek and the surrounding valley. This moderate hike leads to a small log trail shelter used by day hikers and backpackers. The old picnic table and stone grill are just begging for a hot fire on a cold winter afternoon; they're also a place to rest your boots and replenish those fluids during the dog days of summer.

Route Details

The Adventure Hiking Trail lies within southern Indiana's Harrison-Crawford State Forest, just 45 minutes from downtown Louisville. Basically one large loop, the AHT can be accessed at numerous points, including several within O'Bannon Woods State Park. Various portions of the trail overlook the Ohio River, the Blue River, and Indian Creek. Overnight backpackers must register with either the Harrison-Crawford or O'Bannon Woods park office. Five overnight shelters sit along the trail, and primitive camping is permitted.

Because of easy trail access, day hikers also use the AHT. However, the trail's configuration makes it impossible to set up a day-hike loop—unless you set up a shuttle in advance, you must follow an out-and-back route. Another complicating factor for day and overnight hikers alike is the fact that Harrison-Crawford is actively managed. The state-forest office periodically shuts down one or more segments of the AHT for timber management, so call 812-738-7694 before you hike to confirm any closures.

The Indian Creek Overlook Trail, easily one of the most beautiful segments of the AHT, runs south from Old Forest Road, through the eastern portion of Harrison-Crawford. Begin by parking in the small lot described in the Directions. The trail leaves from the southern end of the parking area and immediately begins to descend to one of several creek drainages you'll encounter. Here, the hardwood canopy is tall and graceful, with very little undergrowth. This part of the AHT is exceedingly serene. Seasonal-creek crossings will come at 0.3 and 0.6 mile from the trailhead and offer nice wildflower displays in the spring. *Cornus mas* (cornelian cherry dogwood) also blooms here.

About 0.7 mile into the trail, a small spring trickles out from moss-covered rocks and crosses the path. This spring tends to run year-round and is frequently the only water available on this segment of the AHT. As always, purify or filter any water you intend to drink.

After passing the spring, the trail gently ascends the spine of a ridge before crossing an old logging road. Continue to look for the green-and-white trail blazes that mark the AHT. Apparently the AHT has been marked and remarked several times with blazes found on Carsonite posts, trees, large wooden signs, and small metal rounds (about the size of a Dinty Moore beef-stew can). Although the color of the paint can change from Girl Scout green to the fluorescence of a rough green snake, rest assured that the AHT is very well marked.

About 1.3 miles from the trailhead, the path crosses yet another small creek before merging briefly with a horse trail. As long as you keep looking for those green-and-white markers, you'll have no trouble staying on the trail.

At 2.3 miles into the hike, the trail begins to follow a rocky escarpment overlooking Indian Creek. Take a few minutes and sit on one of the many large stones at the edge of the bluff overlooking the valley. On almost any day, ravens will ride the thermals rising up the escarpment from the valley floor. Add a turkey vulture or two and the occasional hawk, and you've got better entertainment than television.

Following the bluff another 0.5 mile brings you to the log shelter used by overnight hikers. Chances are the place will be vacant, allowing you to slip off that pack and enjoy more views of Indian Creek and the valley below. This is the end of the road for the Indian Creek Overlook Trail, and the shelter signals the turnaround point.

A small fire pit and grill are available for those wanting to roast a few hot dogs or nestle foil-wrapped sweet potatoes in newly created coals. If the day is too warm for a fire, just sit. Linger as long as you can before tracing your steps back to the parking lot.

Nearby Attractions

If all that hiking has left you famished, head for the **Overlook Restaurant** in Leavenworth, just 11 miles from the Indian Creek Overlook Trailhead (1153 W. State Road 62; 812-739-4264; **theoverlook .com**). Perched on a spectacular bluff overlooking the Ohio River, the restaurant serves up fine Southern fare. Both the scenery and the deep fryer go nonstop. There's no need to ask for a window seat—the artful arrangement of the three indoor dining rooms, along with an outdoor deck, guarantees that every diner has a gorgeous 180-degree view of the mighty Ohio.

The menu offers a generous selection of fried chicken and fish, ribs, salads, sandwiches, and regional favorites such as the Hot Brown. Save room for dessert—the homemade treats range from coconut cream pie to Death by Chocolate and hummingbird cake. (Supposedly it takes 150 male hummingbirds to equal a pound, but that might not be enough to make this cake stand three layers tall.) The local brews and signature cocktails, such as the Perfect Storm and the Overlooker, might make those two bed-and-breakfasts you passed look even more inviting.

To find the restaurant from the Indian Creek Overlook Trailhead, backtrack 1.3 miles to IN 462. Turn right (north), drive 2.3 miles, then turn left (west) on IN 62. The Overlook is 7.6 miles ahead, on your left. The fastest way back to I-64 from the restaurant is to continue west on IN 62, then east on IN 66—3.3 miles in all.

Directions

From Louisville, take I-64 West across the Ohio River into southern Indiana. At Exit 105 (Corydon), turn left (south) on IN 135 and drive

1.8 miles. Turn right (west) on IN 62 and drive 7 miles. Turn left (south) on IN 462 and drive 2.3 miles. Bear left (east) on Old Forest Road SW and drive another 1.3 miles. A small parking area will be on your right, just before you descend a hill; it's large enough to hold two Subaru Outbacks or three Smart cars. More parking is available where you can find it.

25

Mogan Ridge East

SCENERY: ★ ★ ★ ★
TRAIL CONDITION: ★ ★ ★ ★ ★
CHILDREN: ★ ★
DIFFICULTY: ★ ★ ★ ★
SOLITUDE: ★ ★ ★ ★ ★

FOLKLORE HOLDS THAT THE MAIDENHAIR FERN CAN CURE BALDNESS.

GPS TRAILHEAD COORDINATES: N38° 3.029' W86° 31.230'

DISTANCE & CONFIGURATION: 7.2-mile figure-eight

HIKING TIME: 3 hours

HIGHLIGHTS: Open meadows intermingled with deciduous hardwood forest

ELEVATION: 504' at trailhead, ascending to 777' at high point

ACCESS: Anytime year-round; free admission

MAPS: Available for download (free) and for purchase at the website below; USGS *Derby*

FACILITIES: None

WHEELCHAIR ACCESS: None

COMMENTS: Check **in.gov/dnr/forestry/2711.htm** for current hunting-season dates. Either skip this hike during those times or dress appropriately.

CONTACTS: Hoosier National Forest, 866-302-4173 or 812-275-5987; **fs.usda.gov/hoosier**

Overview

The Mogan Ridge East Trail lies at the southern end of Hoosier National Forest, just north of the Ohio River and west of Louisville. The hike can easily be shortened if you want a little less mileage. While most trails in Hoosier are open to equestrian riders and mountain bikers, Mogan Ridge East is for hikers only. The combined wooded and open meadow trail is excellent for year-round hiking, and the wide path easily accommodates large groups or twosomes who wish to walk side-by-side.

Route Details

Lucky enough to have a Porsche Boxster in your garage? Well, today's the day to get it out. The two-lane back roads to Mogan Ridge are curvy enough to remind you that those tires just might leave the pavement. Driving along the Ohio River Scenic Byway is a great way to experience southern Indiana.

Parking for the trailhead is a small gravel lot big enough for a half-dozen cars. The wildflowers found here are worth the drive, as the prairie trillium, waterleaf, and spiderwort blooming at the pavement's edge prove. The trailhead kiosk offers valuable information, including a posted map, but the map box is frequently empty. It's always a good idea to bring your own.

The trail begins with a gentle descent, leading to a basic figure-eight configuration. Our route twice makes use of the midway connector to turn the loop trail into a slightly longer hike, giving you double the enjoyment of the open meadows and ponds along the connector trail.

The trail becomes a bit rocky in places as the slope falls away, leading you to a small valley formed by Clover Lick Creek. In the spring, the trailsides are filled with a variety of ferns, rue anemones, Jacob's ladder, wild geraniums, and Solomon's seal. At 0.3 mile, bear left (west) to begin a counterclockwise rotation through a transitional meadow. White-tailed deer, a variety of songbirds,

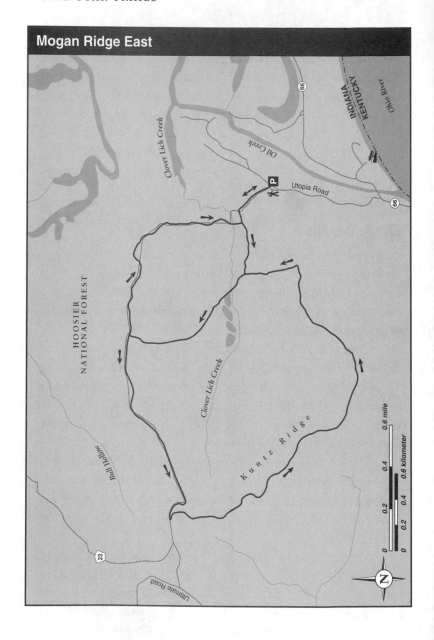

Mogan Ridge East

and signs of an old farming operation will keep your eyes darting left and right.

In another 0.3 mile, the white-blazed main loop intersects the orange-blazed connector trail. Turn right (north) on the connector trail.

Shortly, the trail crosses a small creek, then makes an abrupt but short climb to the first of two small ponds, about 0.7 mile from the trailhead.

Stop and soak in the quiet. No road noise, no jet traffic—only bluebirds and yellow finches to keep the frogs company. The second pond soon appears, positioned just over the next terrace. The hillside affords a great place to stop for a bite to eat or to fish that camera out of your backpack.

The US Forest Service conducts prescribed burns periodically, as evidenced by the stubble. These burns are performed primarily to support wildlife, to maintain the oak and hickory stands by clearing out some of the understory, and to provide open space for all the critters that call this home.

The trail briefly ducks back into the woods, then reappears before another transitional meadow. In late spring, be on the lookout

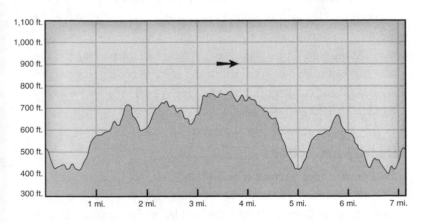

for a fabulous patch of white and pale-pink shooting stars off to your far left (west of the trail). This wildflower is aptly named, as its petals flare backwards, projecting its slender stamens forward. On the other side of the meadow, the trail comes to a T. Turning right (east) will take you back to your vehicle, while turning left (west) takes you counterclockwise along the outer loop.

As you continue on this outer loop, the trail follows a pleasant gravel road. Here the hardwoods are peppered with the occasional pine tree, and the poison ivy is as verdant as the ferns. Stay on this road about 1.1 miles, then bear left (south) to stay on Mogan Ridge East. (Going straight at this junction takes you onto Mogan Ridge West, which is open to horseback use.)

The trail leaves the gravel road and trades it for a dirt trail, which eventually widens to an old country lane. Some interesting rock formations will be on your left as the trail begins to gently climb along Kuntz Ridge. The maples are plentiful here, guaranteeing prime fall color for autumn hikers. The wide, well-marked trails make this hike a good choice in winter, too. Follow the country lane 2.4 miles.

The trail then begins a long, slow descent before it rejoins the connector trail. Again, turn left (north) and follow the connector past the two ponds and through the transitional meadows. Following the connector trail twice lets you not only complete the loop but see the meadows in all their glory.

At the next T, turn right (east) to return to the parking lot. The trail passes through a wonderful stand of pine before reverting to hardwoods and crossing Clover Lick Creek. A final turn left (east) will take you back to your vehicle.

Nearby Attractions

The **German Ridge Recreation Area (GRRA),** with 24 miles of trails, is only 15 minutes away from the Mogan Ridge East Trailhead. The scenic 1.9-mile German Ridge Lake Trail leaves from the picnic area next to the German Ridge Campground, which is heavily used by the horseback-riding crowd. The lake trail, however, is off-limits for equestrian use and loops past a small collection of interesting cliffs and rock formations before circling a small lake and returning to the picnic area. Although the GRRA receives a lot of use, the lake trail itself is lightly traveled.

To reach the German Ridge Lake Trailhead from the Mogan Ridge East Trailhead, take Utopia Road south to return to IN 66. Turn right (south) on IN 66 West and drive 10.8 miles. Turn right (north) on German Ridge Road. The campground turnoff will be 0.8 mile ahead, on your left. Follow the signs to the picnic area.

Directions

From Louisville, take I-64 West across the Ohio River into southern Indiana. At Exit 86, turn left (south) on IN 237 toward Leavenworth and drive 1 mile. Immediately past the Ole Country Store in Sulphur, turn right (west) on IN 66 and drive 11.9 miles. Bear right to continue south on IN 66. Drive 5.8 miles, past the Mano Point boat ramp, cross the bridge, and take an immediate right on Utopia Road. The trailhead parking area is 0.6 mile up this gravel road, past the Ohio River Cabins, on your right.

26

Mount St. Francis Lake Trail

SCENERY: ★ ★ ★ ★ ★
TRAIL CONDITION: ★ ★ ★ ★ ★
CHILDREN: ★ ★ ★
DIFFICULTY: ★ ★
SOLITUDE: ★ ★

JUST HOW INVITING CAN ONE BENCH BE?

GPS TRAILHEAD COORDINATES: N38° 20.122' W85° 54.102'

DISTANCE & CONFIGURATION: 1.8-mile balloon, with more mileage readily available

HIKING TIME: 1 hour

HIGHLIGHTS: Lakeside trail, wildflowers

ELEVATION: 890' at trailhead, descending to 820' at low point

ACCESS: No hours posted, but visiting during daylight is best; free admission

MAPS: Available at trailhead; USGS *Georgetown*

FACILITIES: Picnic shelter, restrooms

WHEELCHAIR ACCESS: None on trails. However, a short gravel road provides direct access to the lake.

COMMENTS: Well-behaved dogs on leash are welcome.

CONTACTS: Mount St. Francis Sanctuary is adjacent to but totally independent of the Mount St. Francis Retreat Center. For more information, contact the Southern Indiana Botanical Society, 812-923-8224; **southernindianabotanicalsociety.org.**

Overview

Mount St. Francis Sanctuary, just 20 minutes northwest of down-town Louisville, is the perfect place for an after-work stroll or a weekend hike with the family. Next to the Mount St. Francis Retreat Center, the sanctuary and its several miles of wooded paths are open to the public. Teeming with wildflowers in spring and rich with fall colors in autumn, the lake trail is an easy 1.8 miles. Longer trails are available for those wanting a deeper spiritual experience and a more rigorous retreat from the trials and tribulations of everyday life.

Route Details

In the late 19th century, 400 acres of woods, fields, and lakes were kindly donated by Joseph and Mary Anderson to the Conventual Franciscan Friars. The Franciscans established a residence here and later a high school seminary for those with the passion to join the order. The seminary was named for St. Francis of Assisi, patron saint of animals and the environment and founder of the Franciscan Order of Catholic friars.

The Mount St. Francis Sanctuary, a religious nonprofit entity, was established more than 100 years after the Andersons' bequest, with the goal of preserving 375 acres of the property and, accord-ing to the sanctuary's literature, "to provide a welcoming space for a variety of people to walk, pray, play and enjoy creation." The rest of the property remains under the auspices of the Franciscan brothers, including a chapel, a retreat center, a friary, a youth center, and the Mary Anderson Center for the Arts. The Southern Indiana Botanic Society (SIBS) works with both the sanctuary and the monastery to sustain the Garden of Remembrance Memorial Program, the Native Woodland Wildflower Gardens, and the Botanical Garden at Mount St. Francis. Brochures describing the sanctuary and SIBS, as well as hiking maps, are available at several trailhead locations. In general, the trails are very well marked. With such good signage, hikers don't need divine providence to find their way around.

Mount St. Francis Lake Trail

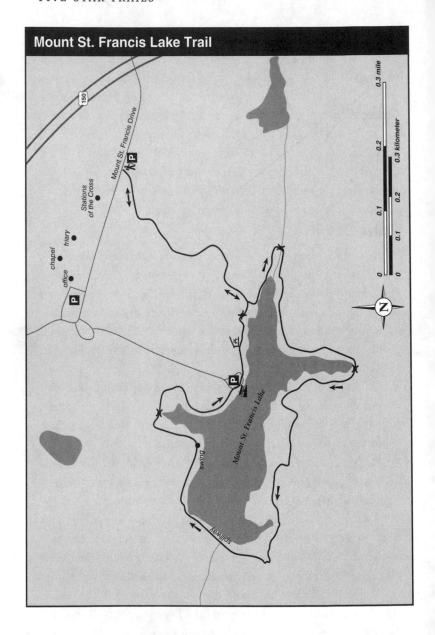

To hike the Mount St. Francis Lake Trail, begin at the small parking lot on your left shortly after you enter the sanctuary. If this is your first time here, pick up a trail map and the Native Woodland Wildflower Garden brochure. The trail to the lake leaves just west of the small lot and initially follows a paved path (Trail 1 on the sanctuary map) down through the woods. In a little more than 0.1 mile, the path arrives at a small woodland garden. An inviting wooden bench offers hikers a spot of peace and tranquility.

The lake trail is perfect for spring hikers with a healthy obsession for wildflowers. Maintained by SIBS, the small woodland garden is chock-full of native species found throughout Mount St. Francis, identified with signs that correspond with the brochure available at the trailhead. It's wonderful to be able to freshen up on the difference between Virginia bluebells and wild blue phloxes, cinnamon and maidenhair ferns, and celandine poppies and large merrybells. The brochure includes the common and botanical names, heights, bloom times, and color characteristics of 19 wildflowers and 3 native shrubs found in the sanctuary. However, the watchful eye might discover several other kinds of wildflowers not on this list.

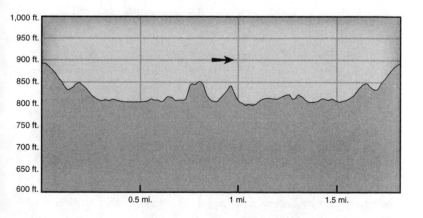

Continue hiking another 0.2 mile to reach the lakeshore and a small wooden bridge. To walk the trail clockwise, turn left (east) here and follow the edge of the lake (you're now following Trail 3 on your sanctuary map). Bluets love the sun exposure here, their dainty pale-blue flowers clustered along the path. Be on the lookout for recent beaver activity, as evidenced by gnawed stumps and branches on either side of the trail. Bluegills and striped bass are easily seen in the shallows, among the cattails and other grasses bordering the lake. Throughout the summer, jewelweed, or touch-me-not, grows thickly in the marshy headwaters.

After a few minutes (about 0.1 mile) of walking you'll cross a second bridge. Don't be too intrigued by the path (marked Trail 2) that leads uphill to your left, as it dead-ends in a few hundred yards. Stay on the trail to your right (west) as it hugs the shoreline. Here, spring hikers will be greeted with yellow trout lilies, cheerful white star chickweed, crested irises, Solomon's seal, and more bluets. There's something about hiking Mount St. Francis in the spring, particularly around Easter, that ensnares even the most diehard agnostic.

A third wooden bridge lies just around the corner, about 0.65 mile from the trailhead. Red-eared sliders, the ubiquitous tortoise found in local ponds and streams, frequently sun themselves here, while bullfrogs scramble for the murky bottom. *Plop-plop.* Take a seat on the bench and contemplate.

Continue right (north, then west) on the trail, hugging the lake's southern shoreline. Keep an eye out for the yellowish-brown stubs of squawroot, a parasite that attaches to the roots of oak trees. Across the opposite shore you'll see a colorful variety of small fishing boats and canoes, reserved for members of the Mount St. Francis Fishing Club and resident friars. The roof of the small picnic shelter is also visible.

At the far western edge of the lake, the trail crosses a grass-covered spillway before heading north and east to complete the lake loop. The field to your left (north) is often dotted with bright-yellow wild mustard, a beautiful, albeit invasive weed found across

Indiana and Kentucky. And how can you pass up that swinging bench?

The trail encircles one last finger of the lake. Please tread softly as you pass the prayer hermitage at the water's edge. The path follows the periphery of one more mustard-studded field, home to a multitude of redwing blackbirds. Two small docks extend into the lake. Be mindful of the sign proclaiming NO SWIMMING EXCEPT WITH A FRANCISCAN FRIAR. No kidding. That's what it says.

Walk beyond the picnic shelter and the sculpture climbing the tree at the water's edge. Cross one last bridge before turning left (north) and walking back up the paved trail to the parking lot. Stop by the woodland garden and see how many native wildflowers you can recognize. And try to remember how many others you saw on the trail that aren't growing here.

At the top of the hill, you should see your vehicle. If you have time, look for the small sign across the road from the parking lot, leading walkers to two short loops that encircle the Stations of the Cross and a small sculpture garden. Nod to St. Francis, enshrined in his stone grotto; pause at the sight of the reclining figure at the edge of the gurgling spring; and thank an industrious Eagle Scout for his contribution to the world of the sacred.

Nearby Attractions

If you're up for a longer hike, Mount St. Francis has seven other trails to choose from. Most of them can be accessed from the lake area, but a more efficient way is to park on the opposite side of the retreat center. To reach this alternate trailhead, continue on the entrance road you came in on, driving past the chapel and the youth center to the far northwestern edge of the sanctuary, by the team-building course. Park in the large lot that overlooks the open field. A small gravel road leads to Trails 8 and 9, marked with a sign and a box that holds more brochures and maps. Weaving together portions of Trails 6, 8, 9, and 10 creates a scenic 2.4-mile woodland loop.

Hiking west on Trail 8 will take you through open woods and across two small creek drainages. A hard left at the next intersection will take you onto Trail 10, as you travel southeast along a larger creek drainage, a tributary of Little Indian Creek. This portion of the trail will reward spring hikers with prairie trillium, crested iris, bicolored dwarf larkspur, and wild blue phlox. The ever-watchful eye might even spot the elusive jack-in-the-pulpit camouflaged among last year's maple and oak leaves. The woods are equally beautiful in the autumn, with the golden poplar leaves mingling with the reds and oranges of the maples and the yellow beech trees.

At the next intersection, stay east on Trail 6 until it dances along the edge of yet another mustard-punctuated open field. Finally, bear east again on Trail 9 and hike the last few hundred yards before returning to your vehicle.

Directions

From Louisville, take I-64 West across the Ohio River into southern Indiana. After 4 miles, take Exit 119 (Greenville/Paoli) and turn right (north) on US 150 West. At the third stoplight (about 2 miles from the interstate), turn left into Mount St. Francis.

27

Patoka Lake Trail

SCENERY: ★ ★ ★ ★ ★
TRAIL CONDITION: ★ ★ ★ ★ ★
CHILDREN: ★ ★
DIFFICULTY: ★ ★ ★ ★
SOLITUDE: ★ ★ ★

TOTEM ROCK, ONCE USED FOR CHURCH SERVICES, IS MORE OF A ROCK HOUSE.

GPS TRAILHEAD COORDINATES: N38° 24.406' W86° 40.587'

DISTANCE & CONFIGURATION: 6.1-mile loop

HIKING TIME: 3 hours

HIGHLIGHTS: Large rock house, unusual rock formations, intermittent lake views

ELEVATION: 720' at trailhead, descending to 540' at low point

ACCESS: Trails open daily, sunrise–sunset. Entrance fee: $5/vehicle for Indiana residents, $7/vehicle out-of-state. Annual permits also available (see **in.gov/dnr/parklake/5062.htm**).

MAPS: Available at park entrance, visitor center, and the website below; USGS *Cuzco*

FACILITIES: Restrooms and nature center at trailhead

WHEELCHAIR ACCESS: None on trail

COMMENTS: Check **in.gov/dnr/forestry/2711.htm** for current hunting-season dates. Either skip this hike during those times or dress appropriately.

CONTACTS: Hoosier National Forest, 866-302-4173 or 812-275-5987; **fs.usda.gov/hoosier**

Patoka Lake Trail

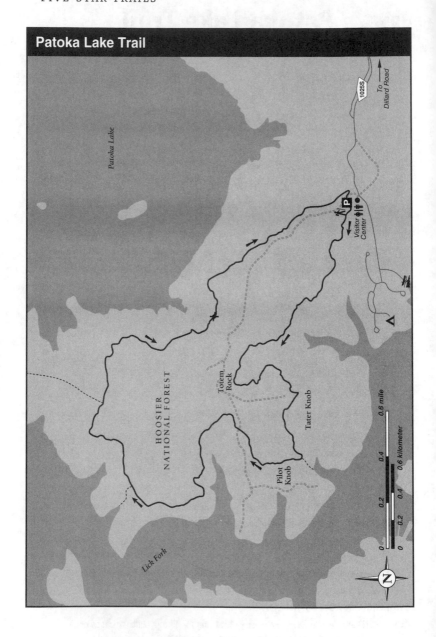

Overview

The Patoka Lake Trail consists of a large loop that leaves from the visitor center and encircles a prominent peninsula offering intermittent lake views. The forested trail passes under Totem Rock, a large rock shelter previously used by American Indians, and other interesting rock outcroppings. The trail crosses many seasonal creeks, creating a roller coaster of a hike. Multiple shortcut trails accommodate those wanting less mileage. The visitor center provides an interesting geological history of Totem Rock.

Route Details

The Patoka Lake hiking area encompasses nearly 1,000 acres of southern Indiana uplands, surrounded by water on three sides. The mature beech–maple and oak–hickory forest includes several rock shelters, fascinating rock formations, an old pine plantation, and numerous meadows in various stages of succession.

The lake was formed in the late 1970s, when the Patoka River was dammed for flood control and to provide a local water supply;

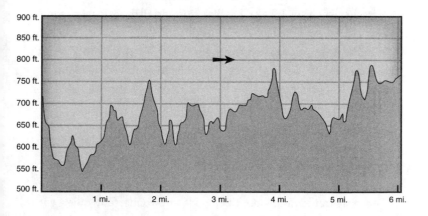

today it affords general recreational opportunities and a wildlife habitat. The main trail at Patoka Lake traverses what is known as the Wickliffe Formation, layers of rock laid down 325 million years ago, and the younger Mansfield Formation, which created Totem Rock and other rock houses.

The trail begins on the west side of the parking lot, behind the visitor center. Before starting out, you may want to wander inside the center to learn more about the history and geology of the area. Be sure to refill those water bottles and take advantage of the miracles of indoor plumbing before heading out for a few hours of hiking.

The Patoka Lake Trail, or the Main Trail as it's labeled on park maps, is officially 6.5 miles long and is marked every 0.5 mile with trail signs. The trail is actually closer to 6.1 miles, however, not counting both spurs to the lake. An old farm road runs the length of the peninsula, and hikers have several opportunities to cut their walk short and return to the visitor center. In addition, the sign at the trailhead kiosk indicates that the trail is marked with orange and white blazes, where in reality the main trail is red-blazed and the shortcuts are orange-blazed. Despite these caveats, the trail is otherwise very well marked and easy to navigate.

Most people take the main trail clockwise, since the red blazes are fresher when you hike in that direction and all the signage assumes hikers will be walking that way. The trail immediately immerses you in a deciduous forest of mixed hardwoods, with a string of rock formations on the left (south). In late spring the beautiful white blooms of shooting stars cluster on the ridgetops, along with the deep-lavender wood sorrel and the cottony tufts of pussy toes.

The trail begins with a multitude of ups and downs as it crosses over several seasonal creeks. About 0.6 mile from the trailhead, your first lake view appears. Of course, the best views are from late fall to early spring, when the trees are bare. With the exception of summer, when boat traffic ramps up, the woods are wonderfully quiet, with only the squawking of blue jays, the drumming of woodpeckers, or the chattering of squirrels to keep you company.

At this point, the trail has moved off the Wickliffe Formation and onto the Mansfield Formation, which, geologically speaking, was laid down in an era when dragonflies with 3-foot wingspans and 15-foot-long salamanders haunted these woods. Totem Rock, a popular hiking destination, appears less than 1.5 miles from the trailhead. This large rock house, or shallow cave opening, provided shelter for many American Indians who lived in this area, and later for livestock who roamed the surrounding fields. The sandstone is distinctive, with its honeycomb weathering and broad cross-bedding, which looks like intricate wood-grain patterns. The stone is stained brown and red in places, due to manganese and iron having leached from the rock.

Just beyond the rock house, wild turkeys like to seek shelter. Their gobbles are constant in late spring and early summer, reminding hikers of Ben Franklin's choice for the national bird and of that venerable Kentucky bourbon. Deer and small game also take refuge here and in other pockets across the peninsula. A short distance from Totem Rock, the trail crosses a small field. Turn right here and look for the small sign that reads MAIN TRAIL, with an arrow pointing to the spot where the path ducks back into the woods.

About 2 miles from the trailhead, the first of two spurs leaves the main trail for a short junket to the lake. Hiking Patoka Lake Trail in the summer can be a bear, with noisy boats, high humidity, and flying insects. But if you do find yourself here at that time of the year, be sure to throw a bathing suit in your pack for some cool relief from the heat.

Just past the spur you'll discover a picturesque set of rocks that forms a bit of a narrows, where at an earlier time the rocks were perhaps one before being cleaved in two. Take a few minutes to explore the interesting formations that have been sculpted over the millennia. Ferns, jack-in-the-pulpits, and star chickweed abound on this section of trail.

A second spur to the lake comes just after the halfway spot in the loop. In early spring and late fall, this section of shoreline provides a good vantage point for waterfowl viewing as various ducks and geese migrate through the region. It's an easy place to while away some time, soaking sore feet in the cool water or grabbing a bite to eat.

After another 1.5 miles of woodland hiking, the trail passes through the edge of another successional field, left over from the farming heyday of Patoka. Most of the peninsula is now considered a climax forest, with distinct stands of beech–maple (harboring more-shade-tolerant and moisture-loving plants) and oak–hickory (thriving on more-upland soils, which tend to be drier and thinner).

About 4.5 miles from the trailhead, you'll find evidence of a small pine plantation. White, red, and scotch pines were planted 20–40 years ago as a conservation practice to control erosion and provide windbreaks. Although a little controversial now (given that these woods were primarily deciduous hardwoods), the pines serve as important cover and food for wildlife in the area. Hikers will also pass a small sign prohibiting admittance to a bald-eagle nesting area adjacent to the lakeshore.

The last mile of the trail follows an old logging road that runs next to and atop numerous rocky outcroppings. Here, the walking is easy and shooting stars appear once again. The trail brings you back to the opposite side of the parking lot.

Nearby Attractions

If you have any energy left, the lake trail ends where the 0.75-mile **Garden Rock Loop Trail** begins. This yellow-blazed wooded path takes you along the rocky outcroppings you saw from above during the last half-mile of the Patoka Lake Trail. The rock formations here are extremely interesting and unusual to southern Indiana. Late-spring hikers will enjoy the jack-in-the-pulpits, phacelias, and mayapples.

A short spur takes hikers to a very small rock shelter, framed by wild ginger, false Solomon's seal, and a variety of ferns. Drooping grapevines give the trail a prehistoric feel, rendering those images of dragonflies and salamanders even more real.

The trail wanders through a western mesophytic forest of oak, hickory, and ash before transitioning to a beech–maple climax forest. Fall hikers will enjoy the variation in fall color as the reds and browns of one forest are traded for the yellows and oranges of another.

Directions

From Louisville, take I-64 West across the Ohio River into southern Indiana. At Exit 79 (Tell City/French Lick), turn right (north) on IN 37 and drive 7 miles. Turn left (west) on IN 64 and drive 1.1 miles. Turn right (north) on IN 145 and drive 1.3 miles. Turn right on Dillard Road (County Road 221) and continue to the park entrance.

28

Pioneer Mothers Memorial Forest

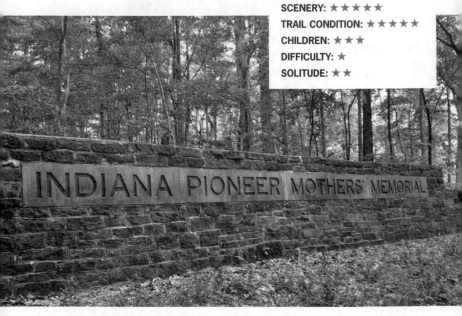

SCENERY: ★ ★ ★ ★ ★
TRAIL CONDITION: ★ ★ ★ ★ ★
CHILDREN: ★ ★ ★
DIFFICULTY: ★
SOLITUDE: ★ ★

THIS STONE SIGN IS BUT A MERE TODDLER COMPARED WITH MANY OF THE TREES FOUND HERE.

GPS TRAILHEAD COORDINATES: N38° 32.064' W86° 27.484'

DISTANCE & CONFIGURATION: 1.5-mile out-and-back

HIKING TIME: 45 minutes

HIGHLIGHTS: Old-growth forest

ELEVATION: 821' at trailhead, descending to 623' at low point

ACCESS: Anytime year-round; free admission

MAPS: Available for download (free) and for purchase at the website below; USGS *Paoli*

FACILITIES: None

WHEELCHAIR ACCESS: None

COMMENTS: The trail can be reached from US 150 as well as IN 37; the latter entrance, however, is more accessible.

CONTACTS: Hoosier National Forest, 866-302-4173 or 812-275-5987; fs.usda.gov/hoosier

Overview

What a great place to make you feel young again! Pioneer Mothers Memorial Forest is 88 acres of old-growth woods just outside Paoli, Indiana. The ancient trees stand in silent testimony to the centuries they have survived on this earth. Their stubby arms and towering canopies prove that old lives have a grace all their own.

Route Details

What gift of nature should we leave our children? Many would argue that we must leave nature just as we found it. But others maintain that a growing population and its attendant demand for goods and services call for the consumption of at least some natural resources.

One compromise is to set aside parcels of land to protect an entire ecosystem. And that's exactly what the Cox family did. The land here is pretty much the way Joseph Cox found it when he first purchased it in 1816. He set aside 88 acres (of a larger 258-acre tract) to preserve as old-growth forest. What an amazing vision he had!

The land eventually passed to his grandson, also named Joseph Cox, and upon his death in 1940 the property was sold for $23,000 to the Wood-Mosaic Company of Louisville. After the sale was advertised in the local paper, the community launched a massive fundraising effort and, together with the US Forest Service, bought the land back from the lumber company at the same purchase price. Donations from the community mandated that no trees ever be cut from the parcel and, in acknowledgement of a $5,900 donation from the Indiana Pioneer Mothers Club, that a rock-wall memorial be built.

So what's the difference between old-growth and virgin forest? Theoretically, a virgin forest has never been exploited by mankind: no mining, no timbering, no agrarian use. Obviously, the number of forests on Earth today that would qualify as virgin are few and far between.

Alternatively, an old-growth forest is just that—old. The trees and accompanying ecosystem have been left undisturbed for

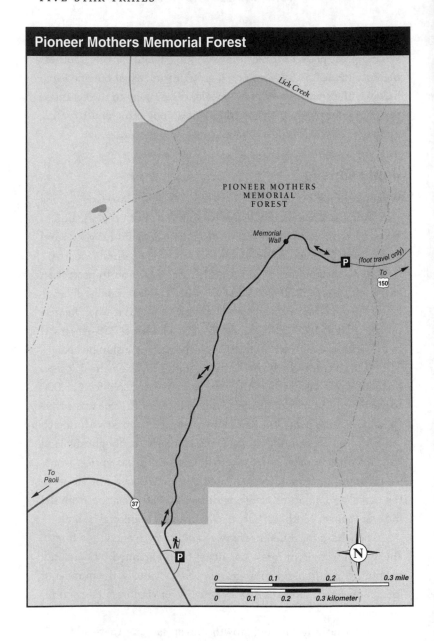

Pioneer Mothers Memorial Forest

Lick Creek

PIONEER MOTHERS
MEMORIAL
FOREST

Memorial
Wall

P (foot travel only)

To
150

To
Paoli

37

P

| 0 | 0.1 | 0.2 | 0.3 mile |

| 0 | 0.1 | 0.2 | 0.3 kilometer |

N

sufficient time that the forest has returned to its native, or virginal state, leading to a high level of biodiversity and a full range of growth and decline. That's exactly what you'll find at Pioneer Mothers. Young trees. Old trees. New growth. Decay.

So how do you tell the age of a tree? Of course, cutting it down and counting its rings is one approach, albeit deadly for the patient at hand. We could also drill into the base of the trunk, remove a core sample, and use sophisticated DNA sampling to provide a best estimate. But that also creates a pathway for insects and disease.

Then again, we could sit quietly and observe the differences between big trees and little trees. An old tree that has stood the test of time truly does stand as evidence of endurance. These trees have withstood heavy winds, scathing fires, ice storms, and other natural maladies. Their trunks reach for the light as their arms have been lost to survival. Branches become stubs, and knots form where wounds were suffered. Root flare, where the trunk emerges from the earth, is another indicator of age in the woodland.

When entering Pioneer Mothers Memorial Forest, don't expect to see the aged giants of the redwood forest or the twisted trunks of

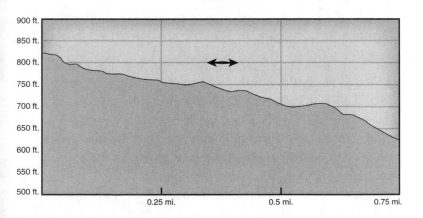

400-year-old bonsai. The differences between the young and old trees are much more subtle here, as girth is not the only litmus test for determining age.

The trail begins at the north end of the parking lot, not far from a busy state highway. Of course, when some of these trees first sprouted, the road was but a set of wagon-wheel tracks or an animal trail at most. The path descends a small hill, blocking out much of the vehicle noise as it follows a narrow ridge. Black walnut, yellow poplar, white oak, hickory, and ash thrive amid the blooms of dwarf larkspur, bloodroot, and wood poppy.

Though spring is beautiful here, winter hiking is perhaps more impressive, as the trees' stark silhouettes transform these behemoths into modern-art sculptures.

Hiking a little more than a half-mile from the trailhead brings you to an old rock wall engraved with INDIANA PIONEER MOTHERS' MEMORIAL. Does that refer to the women who first settled these lands? Or to the early trees whose seeds and young sprouts have populated these forests?

The trail ends in a small, abandoned parking lot accessed by a closed road that joins US 150. You'll probably want to turn around here and stroll the 0.75 mile back to your vehicle.

Nearby Attractions

If you're looking for a longer hike in the region, try a section of the 12.7-mile **Youngs Creek Trail.** Also part of Hoosier National Forest, it's just a few miles south of Pioneer Mothers. Although the trail is open to horseback riders and mountain bikers, it's in very good condition owing to ongoing maintenance. The area is beautiful and only occasionally used. Much of the surface is graveled, adding a delicate crunch to your hiking step.

Several parking areas and trailheads are available, and maps can be downloaded from the website in "Contacts" (page 194). Perhaps the prettiest section of Youngs Creek lies off IN 37 and County

Road 550 South. From Pioneer Mothers, turn left (south) on IN 37 and drive 5 miles. Turn right (west) on CR 550 South and drive 1.3 miles to the intersection with Burma Road (CR 450/CR 525 South). Limited parking is available on the left (south) side of CR 550.

The 3.6-mile balloon trail starts at the end of the parking lane and travels along a seasonal-creek bed flush with color in the fall and wildflowers in the spring. Hike 0.5 mile until you come to a T, where the balloon starts. Turn right (south) to walk the loop counterclockwise. In 0.3 mile, the trail Ts again. Bear left (southeast) and hike 2.4 miles. This section of the trail will take you up a small drainage and back down again.

At the next trail intersection, bear left (south) again; another 0.4 mile of hiking brings you back to the start of the loop. Turn right (north) here to backtrack the final 0.5 mile to your vehicle.

Directions

From Louisville, take I-64 West across the Ohio River into southern Indiana. At Exit 119 (Greenville/Paoli), turn right (north) on US 150 West and drive 38 miles. In Paoli, turn left (south) on SW First Street (IN 37). Just outside of town, the parking area for Pioneer Mothers Memorial Forest will be on your left. (*Note:* The eastern entrance for Pioneer Mothers is off US 150, just before you reach Paoli. However, the access road is closed and has limited parking, forcing you to walk an old abandoned road.)

SCENERY: ★ ★ ★
TRAIL CONDITION: ★ ★ ★
CHILDREN: ★ ★ ★
DIFFICULTY: ★ ★ ★
SOLITUDE: ★ ★ ★ ★ ★

A RELATIVE NEWCOMER TO THE HIKING CIRCUIT, RABBIT HASH CONTINUES TO APPRECIATE STRUCTURAL IMPROVEMENTS.

GPS TRAILHEAD COORDINATES: N38° 2.878' W85° 57.543'

DISTANCE & CONFIGURATION: 2.6-mile out-and-back, with a 3.7-mile alternate route

HIKING TIME: 1.5 hours

HIGHLIGHTS: Ridgetop trail to creekside hiking

ELEVATION: 792' at trailhead, descending to 578' at low point

ACCESS: Daily, sunrise–sunset; free admission

MAPS: A topographic trail map is available at **tinyurl.com/rhtmap**; USGS *Kosmosdale*

FACILITIES: None

WHEELCHAIR ACCESS: None

COMMENTS: No pets

CONTACTS: The Nature Conservancy Blue River Project Office, 812-737-2087; **tinyurl.com/rabbithashtrail**

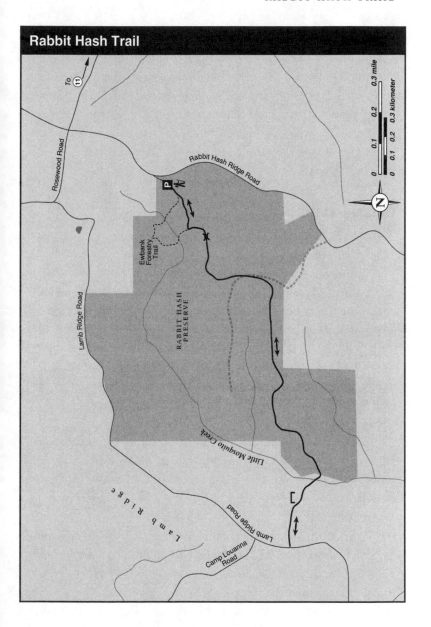

Rabbit Hash Trail

Overview

Rabbit Hash is part of a cluster of nature preserves known as the Harrison County Glades, owned and managed by The Nature Conservancy. This out-and-back trail traverses part of Rabbit Hash Ridge before descending to Little Mosquito Creek. Just 40 minutes from downtown Louisville, Harrison County, Indiana, is home to 91 rare plant species and 138 rare animal species. Deer, turkeys, and, yes, rabbits are plentiful.

Route Details

Rabbit Hash. A colorful little river town? A cool motorcycle destination? A wild-game stew?

However Rabbit Hash Preserve got its name, it represents The Nature Conservancy's effort to protect the rare plants and animals that thrive here. The 400-acre preserve is further sheltered by the 58-acre Thomas Ewbank conservation easement on one side and by 205 acres managed by the Southern Indiana Forest Bank, a Nature Conservancy–run financial entity that helps private-land owners preserve woodland property, on another. Park next to the sign in the open field, and you stand an excellent chance of not seeing another person.

This hike earns five stars for solitude, and they're well deserved. With the exception of a hooting owl, a chattering squirrel, or an amped-up pileated woodpecker, the woods offer serenity. The trailhead is next to the conservancy sign, on the far southwestern edge of the field.

The first things you may notice are the dozen or so large anthills that border the field and the first section of trail. And by *large* I mean these colonies could consume a small calf. OK, that may be a slight exaggeration, but you might want to avoid walking on them unless you want to be a character in the next Stephen King novel. Ignore the signs to the Ewbank Trail for now, and head down the main path instead.

In about 0.3 mile, the Rabbit Hash Trail crosses a wooden bridge at a seasonal creek before climbing to the northern reaches of Rabbit Hash Ridge. The path is mostly singletrack except for the intermittent merger with an old roadbed. The trail then runs along the ridge of something akin to a two-humped camel, with the first hump being much larger than the second. But in general, the hiking in this section is relatively flat to rolling.

After the second hump, the trail descends sharply along a series of quick, short switchbacks to Little Mosquito Creek. The creek is pretty and interesting to explore. Many wildflowers thrive along the steep embankments of this miniature gorge, including a variety of ferns, crested irises, and mayapples.

The creekbed forms the far western boundary of the preserve and is 1.3 miles from the trailhead. So if you stop here and turn around, your hike will be 2.6 miles round-trip.

But if you like to bushwhack, Commission Ministries (which owns the land on the other side of the creek) has generously permitted hikers to continue hiking west by climbing out of the drainage to Lamb Ridge. While there is no designated trail, hikers can follow the smaller drainage just upstream of where the preserve trail reaches the creek. The climb is straight up from the creek, encircles a few sinkholes, and reaches a small wood bench. Follow the old grassy road to Lamb Ridge Road, about 0.3 mile above the creek. During the summer, oxeye daisies, fleabane, monardia, and ground cedar grow. Unless you've left a shuttle here, turn around and retrace your steps back to the parking lot.

If you're interested in forestry-management practices, the 0.3-mile Ewbank Trail may be of interest. This short loop is just off the main Rabbit Hash Trail, near the trailhead. Narrative signs describe different wood species, undesirable-tree control, and best management practices. If you hike the entire Rabbit Hash Trail, climb to Lamb Ridge Road, and walk the Ewbank Trail, you'll have hiked 3.7 miles.

Nearby Attractions

The **Harrison County Glades,** including Buena Vista Glade, Teeple Glade, Mosquito Creek Preserve, and Klinstiver Glade, can be explored as a suite of hikes, several in the same day. The website below provides limited driving directions and maps for the other preserves in this area. The Blue River Project Office of The Nature Conservancy (812-737-2087) can also be extremely helpful.

The **Sally Reardon Woods,** part of the Mosquito Creek Nature Preserve, is particularly beautiful, and while it has no designated trails, you're free to explore. Walking downhill from the large brown sign, you can hike down to Mosquito Creek. Or you can park at the bridge on Mosquito Creek Road and walk downstream for several miles. There you'll find the remains of two old stone mills.

Teeple Glade does have a designated trail, but it's difficult for The Nature Conservancy to maintain. The small glade—an opening in the forest with prairielike plants—lies about a mile from Keen Hill Road. During May and June, coneflower, shooting star, blazing star (liatris), and little bluestem bloom here. But be ready for the ticks and mosquitoes that thrive in these woods, too.

For more information, see **tinyurl.com/harrisoncountyglades.**

Directions

From downtown Louisville, take I-64 West just across the Ohio River to New Albany, Indiana. At Exit 123, turn immediately right (south) on Scribner Drive, then right again (southwest) on West Main Street, which becomes IN 111 (River Road) and follows the Ohio River. Drive southwest on IN 111 for 11.2 miles. Turn right (west) on IN 211 and drive 2 miles. Turn left (south) on IN 11, drive 1.7 miles, then turn left (south) again to stay on IN 11. Drive 2.6 miles. Where IN 11 doglegs right (west), go straight on Rosewood Road SE, still heading south. After 2.7 miles, turn left (east) on Rabbit Hash Road SE (also signed as Rabbit Hash Ridge Road SE). The preserve is 0.4 mile ahead, on your right.

Rocky Ridge Trail at O'Bannon Woods

SCENERY: ★ ★ ★ ★
TRAIL CONDITION: ★ ★ ★ ★ ★
CHILDREN: ★ ★ ★
DIFFICULTY: ★ ★
SOLITUDE: ★ ★

HOW FORLORN CAN ONE ASS LOOK?

GPS TRAILHEAD COORDINATES: N38° 11.689' W86° 17.542'

DISTANCE & CONFIGURATION: 2.5-mile balloon

HIKING TIME: 1 hour

HIGHLIGHTS: Beautiful creek drainages, wildflowers, interesting stone formations

ELEVATION: 680' at trailhead, descending to 571' at low point

ACCESS: Daily, 7 a.m.–sunset. Entrance fee: $5/vehicle for Indiana residents, $7/vehicle out-of-state. Annual permits also available (see **in.gov/dnr/parklake/5062.htm**).

MAPS: O'Bannon Woods State Park, USGS *Leavenworth*

FACILITIES: Campgrounds, nature center, picnic tables, grills, shelters, equestrian trails, and swimming pool

WHEELCHAIR ACCESS: Not on this trail, but there is a universal access trail on the park property.

COMMENTS: O'Bannon is popular on weekends during late spring and early fall, and all week long during the summer. Timing is everything if you're looking for a secluded outdoor experience. The O'Bannon Woods State Park map lists the Rocky Ridge Trail at an even 2 miles, but it's actually a tad longer, at 2.5 miles.

CONTACTS: O'Bannon Woods State Park, 812-738-8232; **in.gov/dnr/parklake/2976.htm**

Rocky Ridge Trail at O'Bannon Woods

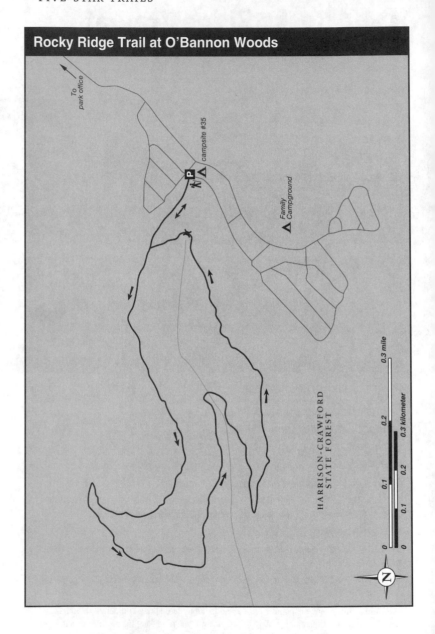

Overview

O'Bannon Woods State Park is a rustic version of an all-inclusive resort, without the tiki huts dotting the shoreline or the umbrellas in your drinks. Hiking, camping, swimming, fishing, historical sites, nature center—all securely nestled in the crook of the Blue River where it empties into the Ohio. What more could you want? Bring the kids. Bring the tent. Bring some adventure to your life. One of several park trails, Rocky Ridge is only 45 minutes away from downtown Louisville.

Route Details

Formerly known as the Wyandotte Woods State Recreation Area, the 2,000-acre O'Bannon Woods State Park is surrounded by the 26,000-acre Harrison-Crawford State Forest. The park was developed in the early 1930s by the Civilian Conservation Corps (CCC), which built many of its roads, stone shelters, and picnic areas. Bordered by the Blue River on the west, Potato Run on the east, and the Ohio River on the south, O'Bannon is characterized by a rugged terrain crisscrossed with hiking and equestrian trails.

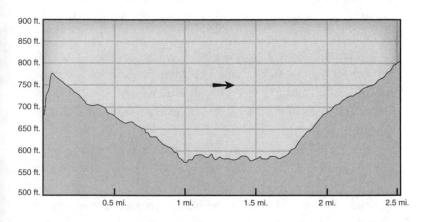

In addition to hiking, O'Bannon Woods State Park offers four different campgrounds (two catering specifically to the horse crowd), a swimming pool (with a set of crazy spiral slides), a nature center, a 1830s homestead, and terrific views of the lazy, rolling Ohio. A fire tower stands guard at the park entrance, and those willing to brave the stairs will be rewarded with commanding views of the countryside.

Rocky Ridge is one of nine hiking trails in the park. At a little more than 2 miles, it's also the longest trail in O'Bannon Woods, leaving several other hiking opportunities for the younger ones and for those with less stamina. The Rocky Ridge Trail leaves from Campsite 35 in the Family Campground, at the northern end of the park. Hikers may enter the campground and park near one of the bathhouses to gain access to the trail. Alternately, you can park at one of the many empty campsites in the off-season.

The trail is relatively easy to follow as it winds through hardwood forest and across several creek drainages. From the trailhead, Rocky Ridge travels west atop a small ridge as it heads toward the Blue River. After about 0.1 mile of walking, the loop portion of the trail begins. To get the best views of the creeks and stone formations, walk the loop counterclockwise by staying straight at the intersection and continuing west. Follow the trail past several small rocky outcroppings and bear west (left) again to avoid the spur trail heading east toward the fire tower.

The trail begins a gradual decline to the first creek crossing. The rock formations only become more interesting. Spring hikers are rewarded with cutleaf toothwort, yellow trout lilies, rue anemones, and several kinds of violets. As the trail emerges from the drainage, note the beautiful moss-covered rocks to the left (south).

Rocky Ridge continues to follow the contours of the land as the trail rises and falls over smaller creeks and crosses several wooden bridges. While the creeks are dry most of the year, spring and early summer offer views of tumbling brooks and the sound of water gurgling over rocks. The fall colors are equally beautiful as the forest is populated with oaks, maples, beech, and hickory.

About 2.2 miles from the trailhead, the trail completes its loop portion. At the intersection, turn right (east) and walk the last 0.1 mile back to the campground.

Nearby Attractions

O'Bannon Woods offers plenty of hiking opportunities besides Rocky Ridge. Family-friendly trails include the **White-Tailed Deer Trail** (1 mile), the **Sharp Spring Trail** (1 mile), and the **Tulip Valley Trail** (2 miles).

A more rugged option is the **Ohio River Bluff Trail,** a 1.5-mile hike along the river at the far southern end of the park. This loop can be accessed at several points, including Shelter House 2, which sits atop a rocky bluff overlooking the Ohio. Hike east down to the horse trail and continue walking to the lower parking lot and picnic area. From there, hike west under the edge of the bluff, climb the rocky escarpment, and go up the rock staircase built by the CCC. At the top of the bluff, you'll be back at Shelter House 2.

Another rugged yet scenic hike is the 1.75-mile **Cliff Dweller Trail,** which follows Potato Run (a seasonal-creek bed) and then a spring-fed creek before descending under a rocky bluff. Here, Indians collected bluish-gray chert, or flint, which they used to make tools and weapons such as spear points, arrowheads, and knives. The Cliff Dweller Trail begins and ends at the Pioneer Shelter House.

The **Charles C. Deam Nature Preserve** (divided into two separate tracts) lies just outside the southern park boundary, along the Ohio River, and is accessed via the Adventure Hiking Trail (AHT), which connects O'Bannon Woods State Park with the rest of Harrison-Crawford State Forest (see Hike 23, page 162). The Deam Preserve was created to protect the Allegheny woodrat, which inhabits the rocky ledges found here. When the leaves are off the trees, this section of the AHT offers scenic views of the Ohio River, but the rest of the year the trail is less inviting.

The **Hickory Hollow Interpretive Center** at O'Bannon Woods is filled with the totally cool exhibits that kids love. Several large display boxes hold beautiful feather, moth, and butterfly collections. Numerous small mammals and large animal heads are mounted and hung on the walls. Live displays include a large snapping turtle, looking menacing in his aquarium, and a rough green snake whose fluorescent hue beats Kermit the Frog's hands-down. On rainy days, the one-way bird window and the table with activities and crafts will easily entertain your crew.

Just out the back door of the nature center is a re-created mid-19th-century farmstead, complete with a restored 1850s hay press and barn. On holiday weekends during the summer, the park offers living-history events, with participants in era-appropriate clothing, wooden toys for the rug rats to play with, weaving demonstrations, and the like. A 1-mile gravel section of a universal-access trail runs past the homestead.

Directions

From Louisville, take I-64 West across the Ohio River into southern Indiana. At Exit 105 (Corydon), turn left (south) on IN 135 and drive 1.8 miles. Turn right (west) on IN 62 and drive 7 miles. Turn left (east) on IN 462, which becomes Old Forest Road. The park office is another 2.9 miles ahead, at the park boundary.

31 # Spurgeon Hollow Loop

SCENERY: ★ ★ ★
TRAIL CONDITION: ★ ★ ★ ★ ★
CHILDREN: ★
DIFFICULTY: ★ ★ ★
SOLITUDE: ★ ★ ★ ★

EVEN THE DEAD STAND SENTRY FOR THE LIVING.

GPS TRAILHEAD COORDINATES: N38° 42.785' W86° 2.631'
DISTANCE & CONFIGURATION: 8.4-mile loop
HIKING TIME: 4 hours
HIGHLIGHTS: Deep woodland and ridgetop trail, scenic creek crossings, lake views
ELEVATION: 543' at trailhead, ascending to 973' at high point
ACCESS: No official hours, but day hikers should be off the trail by sunset; free admission

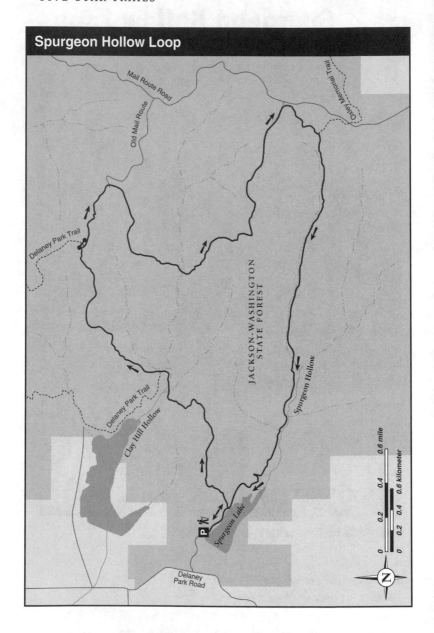

Spurgeon Hollow Loop

MAPS: A full-color waterproof map of the entire Knobstone Trail can be purchased from the Indiana Department of Natural Resources by calling 317-232-4200 ($4 plus 7% tax, including shipping). A PDF version of the same map can be downloaded free at **in.gov/dnr /outdoor/4224.htm.** USGS *Kossuth.*

FACILITIES: None

WHEELCHAIR ACCESS: None

COMMENTS: Check **in.gov/dnr/forestry/2711.htm** for current hunting-season dates. Either skip this hike during those times or dress appropriately.

CONTACTS: Jackson-Washington State Forest, 812-358-2160; in.gov/dnr/forestry/4820.htm

Overview

If you've ever wanted to hike part of the 58-mile backcountry Knob-stone Trail, Spurgeon Hollow is an excellent choice. Two loops form the northern terminus of the Knobstone—the Delaney Park and Spurgeon Hollow Trails. While portions of the southern section of the Knobstone Trail suffered damage from the 2012 tornado that swept through south-central Indiana, the northern section remains relatively unscathed. The Spurgeon Hollow Trail combines relatively flat ridgetop and creekside hiking with intermittent steep climbs and

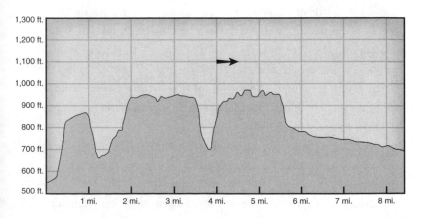

descents. While the trail is well marked and easy to follow, it may not be a good choice for the faint-of-heart hiker.

Route Details

The Knobstone Trail follows much of the Knobstone Escarpment northwest from Deam Lake, just east of I-65 and south of Henryville, to Delaney Park, just north of Salem. Considered a thru-hiking or linear trail, the Knobstone is frequently used for multiday backpacking trips and as a training ground for those wanting to do longer jaunts, such as the Appalachian Trail. For day hikers, most of the Knobstone Trail consists of out-and-backs leaving from one of eight different trailheads. But at the northern terminus, two adjacent loops—the Delaney Park and Spurgeon Hollow Trails—provide more interesting options.

The loop beginning at the Delaney Park Trailhead can be quite busy, particularly from late spring to early fall, as the park is popular with campers, fishermen, and picnickers. A small admission fee is charged as well. On the other hand, the Spurgeon Hollow Trailhead receives considerably less use, the trail covers much of the same hiking area, and parking is free.

The Spurgeon Hollow Trail leaves from the far southeastern corner of the parking lot, near the lake and the trailhead sign. Before heading out, be sure to carry plenty of water—the creeks tend to run dry as the year progresses. Follow the trail 0.2 mile as it hugs the northeastern shoreline of Spurgeon Lake. You'll pass a small camping spot on your left, which typically has extra jugs of water stashed for the thru-hikers.

To begin the loop, turn left (north) at the trail sign to Delaney Park to hike the trail clockwise. The soil is very acidic, as evidenced by the ground cedar, ferns, and pines that thrive here. The trail immediately begins a very sharp ascent to a narrow ridgetop. Viburnum, wood sorrel, alumroot, and wild roses become increasingly prolific as the soil underfoot becomes dry and rocky. A 0.25-mile slog will bring you to the top of the ridge and, during the warmer months, a much-needed breeze.

The trail runs ridgetop for a few hundred yards, past a small pond balanced among the hardwoods. As part of the Knobstone Trail, Spurgeon Hollow is blazed with blue and white paint and has mile markers placed at appropriate intervals. Just past mile marker 44, be on the lookout for these blazes, as the trail bears left (northeast) and descends the other side of the ridge to Clay Hill Hollow and the upper drainage of the lake at Delaney Park. At the bottom, a seasonal creek crossing is blanketed with jack-in-the-pulpits, puttyroot, and wood poppies in late spring. The blue and white blazes make the path easy to follow as the trail crosses the creek several more times.

About 1.3 miles from the trailhead, the Spurgeon Hollow and Delaney Park Trails converge and share a section of trail. Turning left (west) at this intersection will take you to the Delaney Park Trailhead, while going right (north) lets you continue on what is both the northern side of the Spurgeon Hollow Trail and the southern side of the Delaney Park Trail. So choose the latter option to continue climbing out of the creek drainage and reach the ridgetop once more. The trail briefly drops along a small but gentle saddle before climbing to the next ridge.

This section of the trail is relatively flat as it follows the ridgetop for nearly a mile. Here the trees belie their age. The thin soils and exposure to the elements have kept the trunks of the oaks and hickories relatively small in circumference. But the lack of lower limbs and the gnarled stubs along their trunks indicate that the trees here are older than they might appear.

Soon the trail merges with an old logging road, lined with blackberry thickets. The ridge changes in character as pines and large poplars become more prevalent. At 2.4 miles from the trailhead, the route Ts just before a green iron gate. Turning left (north) would take you back around the Delaney Park Trail. Bear right (southeast) to follow the Spurgeon Hollow Trail.

Almost immediately, the trail begins to narrow as you take the path less traveled. A long, slow descent takes you through wild-turkey haunts and pileated-woodpecker territory. The trail then returns to the creek that runs through Clay Hill Hollow, even farther upstream from where you crossed it the first time. But almost immediately the trail climbs once again, reminding you why people find the Knobstone a good proving ground for the Appalachian Trail.

Another 1.6 miles of hiking brings you to the last big trail intersection, with more choices to be made. Bearing left (south) here will take you to the Oxley Memorial Trailhead. Instead, bear right (west) to complete the final portion of the Spurgeon Hollow Trail. From this junction it's 3 miles back to the parking lot, but the hiking is easy as the trail follows the Spurgeon Lake creek drainage. The path is mostly flat and rewards spring hikers with a wonderful wildflower display of more wood poppy, jack-in-the-pulpit, wild ginger, dwarf larkspur, trillium, and phlox. The ferns along the trail grow easily thigh-high by the Fourth of July. Be forewarned that this section of the trail can also get quite buggy in the summer, when gnats, mosquitoes, and chiggers come out in full force.

The trail finishes lakeside once more as the tail waters of Spurgeon Lake come into view. It's easy walking here, albeit a bit boggy after a heavy rain. Once back at the parking lot, remove those hot boots and soak your feet in the cool waters of the lake. Check for ticks. Watch the frogs jump. And think about what other sections of the Knobstone you might want to hike next.

Nearby Attractions

Twin Creek Valley, a pretty little preserve owned by The Nature Conservancy, is just west of Salem. The 188-acre property is filled with limestone outcroppings, scenic creeks, beautiful waterfalls, and several caves. A combination of karst geology and woodland forest, Twin Creek Valley is particularly fetching in the spring, when a riot of wildflowers peeks from every nook and cranny. Columbine, trillium, jack-in-the-pulpit, crested iris, mayapple, and squawroot are everywhere.

Unfortunately for some, Twin Creek Valley has no established trails. A few lightly trodden paths, created by humans and wildlife, crisscross the preserve, but a sense of adventure and a good compass are essential. And a topo map (USGS *Smedley*) is worth its weight in gold.

At the intersection of IN 60 and IN 56 west of Salem, bear right (west) on IN 60 and drive 3.5 miles. Turn right (north) on Dog Trot Road and drive 3 miles; then turn left (west) on Wonder Valley Road. Drive another 1.5 miles to Wonder Valley Christian Camp. Shortly after entering the camp, park on the left (south) side of the road, just after the basketball courts. (This small parking area, owned by The Nature Conservancy, holds only a couple of cars—if it's occupied, ask the Wonder Valley caretaker if you can use their parking area, also near the ball courts. It shouldn't be a problem as long as camp isn't in session.) You should see an old wooden sign announcing the preserve, tucked back in the trees. The preserve boundary lies south and west of the sign.

Directions

From Louisville, take I-65/US 31 North across the Ohio River into southern Indiana. At Exit 7, turn left (west) on IN 60 and drive 22 miles to Salem. Once in Salem, turn right (north) on IN 135, bear right around the lively town square, and continue north on IN 135. After 4 miles, turn right (east) on North Delaney Park Road. Drive another 4.5 miles and, immediately after you cross an old iron bridge, turn left (north) to stay on Delaney Park Road. Drive another 5.8 miles and turn right (east) at the sign to Spurgeon Hollow. The gravel road dead-ends in 0.3 mile, at the lake and at the trailhead.

32

Tank Spring

SCENERY: ★ ★ ★ ★ ★
TRAIL CONDITION: ★ ★ ★ ★
CHILDREN: ★ ★
DIFFICULTY: ★ ★ ★
SOLITUDE: ★ ★ ★ ★

TANK SPRING IS A DELIGHTFUL JUMBLE OF ROCKS, FERNS, AND FALLEN TIMBERS.

GPS TRAILHEAD COORDINATES: N38° 41.416' W86° 42.456'

DISTANCE & CONFIGURATION: 3.6-mile balloon

HIKING TIME: 2 hours

HIGHLIGHTS: Spring-fed creeks tumbling from sandstone cliffs

ELEVATION: 510' at trailhead, ascending to 841' at high point

ACCESS: Daily, sunrise–sunset; free admission

MAPS: USGS *Huron*

FACILITIES: None

WHEELCHAIR ACCESS: None

COMMENTS: Pets allowed off-leash

CONTACTS: Martin State Forest, 812-247-3491; **in.gov/dnr/forestry/4822.htm**

Overview

This scenic hike is well worth the 1.5-hour drive from Louisville, particularly considering the other hiking opportunities in the area. Tank Spring is in southern Martin State Forest, just east of Shoals, Indiana. The hike climbs ridgetop before descending to Tank Spring, just south of Beaver Creek. The wildflowers, sandstone cliffs, and ice-cold water serve as natural complements to the human history of the springs.

Route Details

Water flowing from Tank Spring (originally known as Green Spring) was used to fill a large vessel along the tracks serving the old Baltimore and Ohio Railroad (yes, *that* B&O Railroad—Monopoly, anyone?). The trains stopped at the now-extinct town of Willow Valley to draw the clear, cold water into their steam engines, enabling them to pull their commerce just a bit farther across the countryside. As the steam era faded, the town of Willow Valley dried up long before Tank Spring did.

The trailhead is reached from a small parking lot where only a modest state-forest sign announces its location. The hike begins with a very steep 0.4-mile ascent, making it difficult to both walk and talk. Save your breath until you've reached the ridgetop, where the trail levels and briefly joins an old logging road. Look out for the yellow blaze and the sign indicating that the trail leaves the road and ducks back into the woods, heading due north.

The ferns are prolific here and provide a lush, green groundcover nearly year-round. Poplar, oak, and hickory dominate the tree canopy. The trail descends 0.4 mile (losing all the elevation you worked so hard to obtain) and crosses four small tributaries. Keep looking for the yellow blazes—you'll be on the right track and should end up on the other side of a large creek drainage.

About 1.2 miles from the trailhead, sandstone cliffs will appear on your right (east), with a spring-fed creek tumbling from the

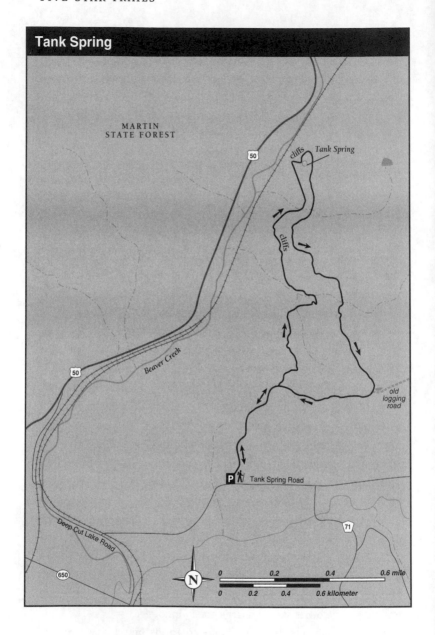

Tank Spring

MARTIN
STATE FOREST

50

cliffs

Tank Spring

cliffs

50

Beaver Creek

old
logging
road

P Tank Spring Road

71

Deep Cut Lake Road

650

N

0   0.2   0.4   0.6 mile

0   0.2   0.4   0.6 kilometer

heights above. The cool water glitters as it flows down through the rocks and creates a beautiful microecosystem of wild ginger, phacelia, jack-in-the-pulpit, and maidenhair fern. In the spring the wildflowers are spectacular, but when the trees are bare, the enhanced views of the towering cliffs are equally incredible.

About 1.5 miles from the trailhead, a second cliff bowl is formed by Tank Spring. Gigantic white trillium, more wild ginger, bloodroot, and Solomon's seal grace the area. Spend all the time you need exploring the mossy logs, fern-studded boulders, and sparkling water as it rushes down the hillside. Does hiking get any better than this?

The trail climbs the ridge that runs above the springs, then takes a roller-coaster ride down various creek drainages and back up again. Almost 2.3 miles into your hike, the trail leaves the creeks and begins its last ascent to the final ridge. At the top (at 2.7 miles), bear right (due west) to rejoin the same logging road you walked in on. Hike down the last 0.4 mile back to your vehicle. We only wish the trail had been longer.

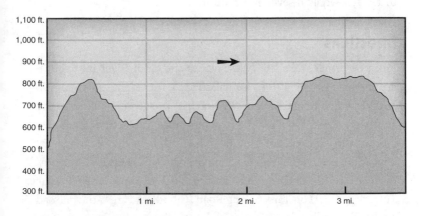

Nearby Attractions

Martin State Forest has several other trails, most of which receive very little use. The 1.25-mile **Woodland Education Trail** includes several short spurs that lead to the Willow Valley Fire Tower and the Tower Hill Shelterhouse, both of which were built by the Civilian Conservation Corps in the 1930s. The 0.25-mile **Arboretum Trail** identifies almost 60 different tree species. Finally, 7 miles of mountain-biking trails along fire lanes are also available for hiking.

Visit **in.gov/dnr/forestry/4822.htm** for a more detailed listing of trails and a trail map. All trailheads can be reached from the main entrance of the park, at the intersection of US 50 and IN 650. A primitive campground and three small fishing lakes are also on the grounds. Be aware that Martin State Forest conducts prescribed burns for management of wood and support of wildlife; call 812-247-3491 to confirm any trail closings.

The nearby town of **Shoals** is renowned, according to local boosters, for its "Gypsum, Catfish, and World-Famous Jug Rock." That last point of civic pride—an interesting stone formation—is just 0.9 mile north of the US 50–IN 650 junction. (Of course, if someone named Mandy hadn't spray-painted a peace sign and her name on the rock in 1991, it would be even more stunning.)

Directions

From Louisville, take I-64 West across the Ohio River into southern Indiana. At Exit 119 (Greenville/Paoli), turn right (north) on US 150 West and drive 60.2 miles. Turn right (east) on US 50 and drive another 4 miles. You'll see the main entrance to Martin State Forest on the left (west) side of the road—instead, turn right (east) on IN 650. After 1 mile, the road dead-ends at the U.S. Gypsum Company. Turn left (north) on Deep Cut Lake Road (CR 67) and drive 0.2 mile. Turn right (east) on Tank Spring Road (CR 54) and cross the railroad tracks. The trailhead parking lot is about 0.5 mile ahead, on your left (north of the road).

SOFT YELLOWS AND GLOWING ORANGES WORK IN TANDEM TO ILLUMINATE THE CHICKEN MUSHROOM.

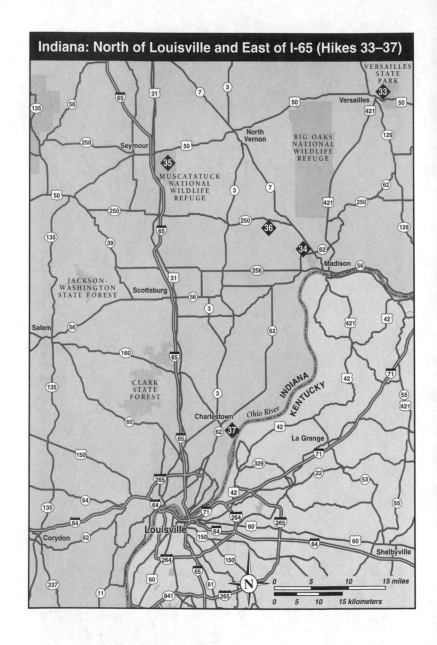

Indiana: North of Louisville and East of I-65 (Hikes 33–37)

Indiana:
North of Louisville
and East of I-65

LAKE LINDA EXUDES TRANQUILITY.
(See Hike 35, Muscatatuck National Wildlife Refuge, page 238.)

33

Bridges of Versailles

SCENERY: ★ ★ ★ ★ ★
TRAIL CONDITION: ★ ★ ★ ★ ★
CHILDREN: ★ ★
DIFFICULTY: ★ ★ ★
SOLITUDE: ★ ★ ★

IF YOU LISTEN QUIETLY, THE CLOP OF HORSE HOOVES AND THE CREAK OF WAGON WHEELS STILL RESONATE WITHIN THE COVERED BRIDGE.

GPS TRAILHEAD COORDINATES: N39° 4.881' W85° 14.179'

DISTANCE & CONFIGURATION: 5-mile loop

HIKING TIME: 2.5 hours

HIGHLIGHTS: Tranquil lake views, multiple creeks, and footbridges

ELEVATION: 791' at trailhead to 965' at the high point

ACCESS: Daily, sunrise–sunset. Entrance fee: $5/vehicle for Indiana residents, $7/vehicle out-of-state.

MAPS: Available on-site and at the website below

FACILITIES: Restrooms, picnic shelters and tables, playgrounds, campground, nature center, swimming pool, boat launch

WHEELCHAIR ACCESS: None

COMMENTS: Leashed dogs welcome

CONTACTS: Versailles State Park, 812-689-6424; **in.gov/dnr/parklake/2963.htm**

Overview

This wooded trail crosses 14 footbridges to traverse 5 miles of creek-side and ridgetop trail in Indiana's second-oldest state park, which covers nearly 6,000 acres, including a 230-acre lake. In addition to hiking trails, Versailles State Park has almost 17 miles of mountain-biking trails and 25 miles of horseback-riding trails. The park can be quite busy during the summer, but the hiking trails are fairly deserted during the shoulder seasons. Just remember to pronounce it "Ver-*sayles*," or you'll end up 12 miles southwest of Paris.

Route Details

The following 5-mile loop weaves together the park's three hiking paths: Trails 3, 2, and 1, in that order. If you or any member of your group begins to tire, the loop can be easily shortened—for example, by eliminating Trail 1.

The trail begins near the nature center and camp store, adjacent to the boat launch at Versailles Lake. After parking, take a few minutes to soak up the beauty of the lake, the open space, and the surrounding woods. In addition to the usual gaggle of geese and balding of ducks, great blue herons enjoy standing on the lakeshore picnic tables, quietly observing their domain.

Just east of the parking lot, on the other side of the main park road, you'll see the trailhead for Trail 3. It's an easy hike, 5 feet wide and quite level, running east–west along Fallen Timber Creek. Both herons and pileated woodpeckers seem to haunt this area, squawking and kuk-kuk-kukking their displeasure with having their day interrupted. At the far eastern end of the route, Trail 3 crosses Fallen Timber Creek three times. When the water is high, be prepared to take off your boots and wade shin-deep across, or test out those new Gore-Tex linings. When water levels are low, you can jump from rock to rock thanks to those who've crossed before you. If need be, throw in a few more rocks and you're good to go. Surprisingly, although the trail has 14 bridges, none are located here. At less than 1 mile each way,

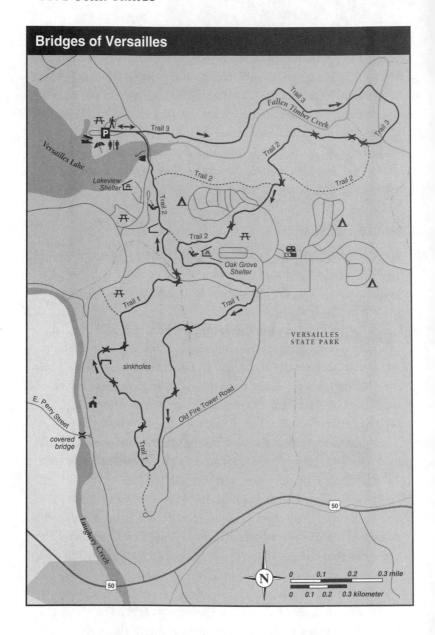

Bridges of Versailles

Trail 3 is a good out-and-back for youngsters without the stamina to do the entire loop.

As you continue on the 5-mile loop, Trail 3 climbs slightly before intersecting Trail 2, which is basically a figure-eight lying on its side. At the intersection, about 1.5 miles from the trailhead, turn right (west) on Trail 2 and cross the small footbridge before continuing your gentle climb. You will now be hiking west, following Fallen Timber Creek, but at a higher elevation.

The trail then rejoins the other half of the first loop of Trail 2. Bear west again by turning right. Walk a short distance and then head southwest by bearing left at the next fork. Although this may sound confusing, when you match the directions with the map, it's very easy to navigate. The trail then crosses the road to Campground A before ducking back into the woods once again. From here the trail meanders south of the campground before it connects with Trail 1, about 4.2 miles from the trailhead.

A short connector trail promenades between a small corridor of large, flat stones, taking you south toward the Oak Grove Shelter. Many shortcuts exist between Trail 1 and the Oak Grove Shelter,

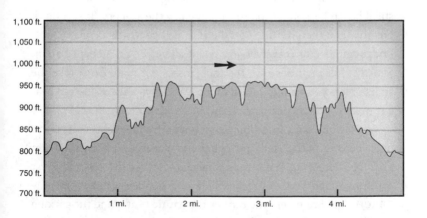

playground, and picnic area. Again, pull out your map, reorient yourself, and pick up Trail 1 just south of the shelter. You can hike the Trail 1 loop in either direction, but clockwise is easiest and affords the best views.

Trail 1 is the longest of the three trails, at just over 2 miles, and the least hiked. It's interesting how the trees get larger and the understory changes within such a small geographic area as you move from one trail to another. Here you can measure the age of the woods by the girth of the grapevines and the size and number of woodpecker holes. The prolific oak trees provide an ample food supply for the deer, turkey, and small mammals that inhabit this section of the park.

You may have seen several small sinkholes in the first loop of Trail 2; they grow significantly larger in the Trail 1 loop. You could tell your kids that the sinkholes are the footprints of the trolls who live under all the footbridges. Or you could impress your friends with your knowledge: sinkholes, you could say, are commonly formed when acidic water (for example, from decaying oak leaves) dissolves the underlying carbonate rock (such as limestone), creating voids and cavities. These conditions prevail across many parts of Kentucky and southern Indiana.

By now, about 4.8 miles from the trailhead, you should see a small bench beckoning you to sit and enjoy the scenery. Take a quick breather and then continue on the trail as it gently descends to footbridge number 11 (have you lost count already?), an L-shaped affair. Shortly after footbridge 12, the trail crosses the road. Don't take the stairs unless you want to return to the Oak Grove Shelter. Instead bear left (northwest) and left again until you see a marker for Trail 2.

Stay on Trail 2 for as long as you can—frequent shortcuts try to take you over to the Trailside Shelter and playground along the main park road. However, Trail 2 runs parallel to the road before ending just south of Fallen Timber Creek. Follow the wooden walkway and the BEACH sign. From here you can see the nature center and the parking lot. Slip on that Speedo or leopard-print bikini and enjoy standing on the lakeside picnic tables, quietly observing your domain.

Nearby Attractions

Versailles State Park offers a natural taste of America's heartland and the essence of wholesome fun. Next time you come, bring a canoe (or rent one) and explore Versailles Lake. Slap a slice of country ham on a croissant for an easy picnic lunch and enjoy the best of the rustic and the citified.

As you leave the park, be sure to stop at the **Busching Bridge**, built in 1885. Restored in 2005, the covered bridge crosses Laughery Creek, and the road passes a bison farm on the other side.

Directions

From downtown Louisville, take I-65 North across the Ohio River into southern Indiana. After 6.7 miles, take Exit 6A to merge onto I-265 East, toward Clark Maritime Center. Shortly before I-265 ends (after about 3 miles), exit on IN 62 East, heading left (northeast). Stay on IN 62 East almost 42 miles, then turn left (north) on US 421 and drive 22 miles until you reach the town of Versailles. Turn right (east) on US 50. The entrance to Versailles State Park will be 2.4 miles ahead, on your left.

34

Clifty Falls

SCENERY: ★ ★ ★ ★ ★
TRAIL CONDITION: ★ ★ ★ ★ ★
CHILDREN: ★ ★ ★
DIFFICULTY: ★ ★ ★
SOLITUDE: ★ ★

THE STONEWORK AT THE PARK IS POETRY IN MOTION BY WAY OF ITS FORM AND FUNCTION.

GPS TRAILHEAD COORDINATES: N38° 46.209' W85° 26.232'

DISTANCE & CONFIGURATION: 3.8-mile loop

HIKING TIME: 2.5 hours

HIGHLIGHTS: Multiple waterfalls, intimate canyon setting, spring wildflowers

ELEVATION: 834' at trailhead, descending to 538' at low point

ACCESS: Park is open daily, 7 a.m.–11 p.m.; trails close at sunset. Entrance fee: $5/vehicle for Indiana residents, $7/vehicle out-of-state.

MAPS: Available at park entrance and the website below

FACILITIES: Restrooms, picnic tables and shelters, nature center, playground, campground, swimming pool

WHEELCHAIR ACCESS: Clifty Falls Overlook is ADA-compliant; however, the stone wall precludes views for those in wheelchairs.

COMMENTS: Leashed dogs are allowed in Clifty Falls State Park but not in Clifty Canyon Nature Preserve, in which this hike takes place.

CONTACTS: Clifty Falls State Park, 812-273-8885; **in.gov/dnr/parklake/2985.htm**

Overview

Within Clifty Falls State Park, the 178-acre Clifty Canyon Nature Preserve presents southern Indiana at its finest. This loop trail, which takes in views of all three of the preserve's waterfalls, follows the western edge of a small, intimate canyon formed by Little Clifty Creek before crossing the stream and climbing to the eastern rim. Autumn hikers are rewarded with the gorgeous colors of mature hardwoods, while spring hikers are treated to a profusion of wildflowers such as hepatica, blue-eyed Mary, Dutchman's britches, and trillium (including the large, showy white variety). Multiple options exist for those wanting either shorter or longer hikes.

Route Details

The Clifty Creek Loop combines five trails—8, 2, 5, 6, and 7, in that order—for a traverse of the northern half of Clifty Canyon Nature Preserve. The park is dissected by Clifty Creek as it flows toward the Ohio River, forming a long, narrow gorge. Only one trail in the park, Trail 2, crosses the creek, allowing you to travel from one side of the gorge to the other. Because most of Trail 2 lies in the actual creekbed, spring hikers will want to come prepared with waterproof boots.

The loop begins at the small picnic area immediately to the west of the North Gate park entrance, off IN 62. You can also reach the trailhead via the South Gate entrance, off IN 56. Leave your vehicle in the picnic area near the Trail 8 trailhead parking lot, and start at the kiosk.

After leaving the picnic area, Trail 8 descends a short set of wooden stairs before crossing a small tributary of Little Clifty Creek. The ruckus of barking dogs and vehicular traffic soon subsides as the sound of falling water rises from the small canyon below. The trail follows the western edge of the creek along an old roadbed and past Big Clifty Falls, although no views are apparent from this side of the gorge.

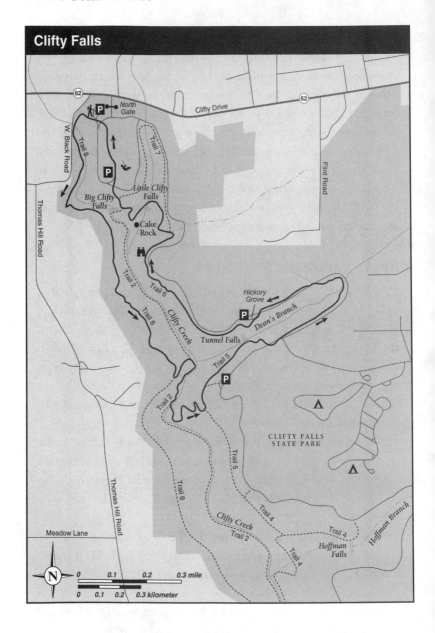

Clifty Falls

62
North Gate
Clifty Drive
62
W. Black Road
Trail 8
P
P
Trail 7
Flint Road
Little Clifty Falls
Big Clifty Falls
Cake Rock
Thomas Hill Road
Trail 2
Trail 6
Trail 8
Hickory Grove
Dean's Branch
P
Clifty Creek
Tunnel Falls
P
Trail 5
Trail 2
CLIFTY FALLS STATE PARK
Trail 5
Meadow Lane
Thomas Hill Road
Trail 8
Trail 4
Clifty Creek
Trail 2
Trail 4
Hoffman Falls
Trail 4
Hoffman Branch

N

0   0.1   0.2   0.3 mile
0   0.1   0.2   0.3 kilometer

About 1 mile from the trailhead, the trail descends once again. At the bottom of the hill, bear left (east) and continue down toward the creek. At the creek crossing, looking upstream, you'll see a NO EXIT sign as Trail 2 eventually dead-ends at the base of Big Clifty Falls. If you want to take a side trip on Trail 2, you can hike north up the creekbed to the falls, adding a little more than a mile (round-trip) to your day. Although the view of Big Clifty Falls is quite beautiful, walking in the creekbed can be difficult, especially when water levels are high.

To continue on our loop trail, turn right (south) on Trail 2 and follow the creek downstream for a scant 0.15 mile. Again, you'll be hiking in the creek itself. It's very rare for a trail to actually run in a creek due to the possibility of damaging such a fragile ecosystem, but enjoy the glimpses of fossils and fish as you jump from one interesting rock to another. Soon you'll see a cable running across the creek with a sign pointing left (east) toward Trail 5. Take the trail up a challenging set of switchbacks as you climb out of the gorge on the opposite side of the creek.

After ascending a small set of wooden stairs, the trail Ts with a wooden walkway running north and south. Turn left (north) on Trail

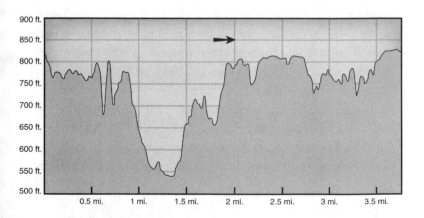

5 toward Tunnel Falls. You're very close to an old railroad tunnel that is currently closed due to white-nose syndrome, a fungal disease that has infected the resident bat population. The Madison and Indianapolis Railroad Company built the 600-foot-long tunnel in 1852. The project was abandoned in bankruptcy, but its legacy includes parts of the trail system you're now walking on. About 0.2 mile of hiking brings you to the Tunnel Falls Overlook.

At 83 feet high, Tunnel Falls is the highest waterfall in the park. Summer foliage may obstruct views from the overlook, so this may be a good time to remind yourself that the journey is the reward. In general, the waterfalls in the park are best viewed in late winter and early spring, when water flows are at their highest and the trees haven't yet leafed out.

To continue the loop, follow the stairs to the road and the Tunnel Falls Trail 5 parking lot. Turn left (northeast) and walk the left shoulder of the park road (facing traffic). Be sure to walk on the broad shoulder itself and not in the road. Although walking along the road is not ideal, the well-worn path along the shoulder provides ample evidence of other hikers doing the same.

In 0.5 mile you'll be at the Hickory Grove Trail 6 parking area. Follow Trail 6 past Lookout Point until you reach Trail 7, which splits several times but always rejoins itself shortly thereafter. The bridge across Little Clifty Falls is scenic, but you must take the lower trail, marked RUGGED, for the best waterfall views. Despite their names, both Big and Little Clifty Falls stand 60 feet high.

Trail 7 follows the ridgetop past Cake Rock before climbing a final set of stairs for an overlook view of Big Clifty Falls. Again, winter and spring hikers may enjoy the best views of the falls. Just north of Big Clifty Falls are a picnic pavilion, bathrooms, and play field. Cut north across the parking lot until you see the Trail 8 picnic area and your vehicle.

Nearby Attractions

A fourth waterfall, **Hoffman Falls,** lies in the south-central part of Clifty Falls State Park. From the North Gate, continue driving south on the park road until you reach the Hoffman Falls parking area. A short hike leads to an overlook and a bridge over Hoffman Branch, just above the falls.

Upon leaving the South Gate of the park, turn left (east) on IN 56 East and drive a short distance to historic downtown **Madison,** on the Ohio River. This scenic riverfront town is filled with small shops, cafés, and beautiful old homes. The fall Madison Chautauqua Festival of Art is well worth the drive.

Directions

From downtown Louisville, take I-65 North across the Ohio River into southern Indiana. After 6.7 miles, take Exit 6A to merge onto I-265 East, toward Clark Maritime Center. Shortly before I-265 ends (after about 3 miles), exit on IN 62 East, heading left (northeast), and drive 37.2 miles. Clifty Falls State Park will be on your right.

35

Muscatatuck National Wildlife Refuge

SCENERY: ★★★★
TRAIL CONDITION: ★★★★★
CHILDREN: ★★★★
DIFFICULTY: ★★
SOLITUDE: ★★★

COULD YOU IMAGINE A FAMILY OF SEVEN LIVING HERE TODAY?

GPS TRAILHEAD COORDINATES: See individual hike snapshots

DISTANCE & CONFIGURATION: Five short loops, 3.9 miles total

HIKING TIME: 3 hours

HIGHLIGHTS: Migrating waterfowl, including sandhill cranes and trumpeter swans

ELEVATION: No significant elevation change on any of the featured trails

ACCESS: Daily, 1 hour before sunrise–1 hour after sunset; free admission

MAPS: Available at the nature center

FACILITIES: Nature center, restrooms

WHEELCHAIR ACCESS: Yes, at the nature center and on the paved 0.4-mile Chestnut Trail. An interpretive auto tour is also available.

COMMENTS: Time your visit carefully. In the quiet of winter, the refuge can provide solace for some and boredom for others. Similarly, the heat and humidity of summer, coupled with swarming mosquitoes and gnats, can discourage hikers. Muscatatuck is open for a limited hunting season; call the refuge for current hunting schedules. A good pair of binoculars might be a wise addition to your daypack.

CONTACTS: Muscatatuck National Wildlife Refuge, 812-522-4352;
fws.gov/refuge/muscatatuck

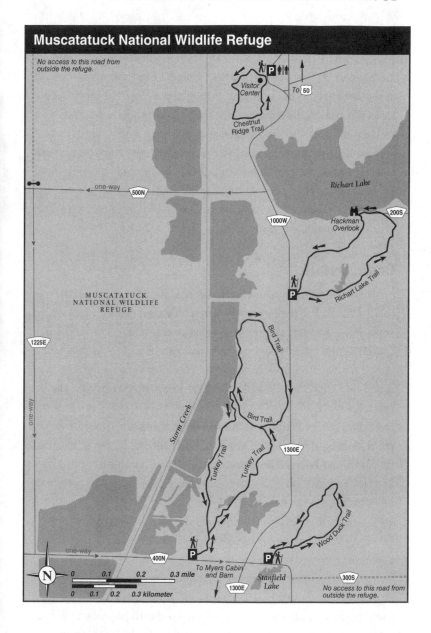

Muscatatuck National Wildlife Refuge

No access to this road from outside the refuge.

Visitor Center

To 50

Chestnut Ridge Trail

one-way

500N

1000W

Richart Lake

Hackman Overlook

200S

MUSCATATUCK NATIONAL WILDLIFE REFUGE

1225E

one-way

Richart Lake Trail

Bird Trail

Storm Creek

Bird Trail

Turkey Trail

Turkey Trail

1300E

Wood Duck Trail

one-way

400N

To Myers Cabin and Barn

Stanfield Lake

1300E

300S

No access to this road from outside the refuge.

N

| 0 | 0.1 | 0.2 | 0.3 mile |
| 0 | 0.1 | 0.2 | 0.3 kilometer |

Overview

Established in 1966, Muscatatuck National Wildlife Refuge provides 7,800 acres of restored wetlands as a landing ground for waterfowl and other birds as they migrate through south-central Indiana. The U.S. Fish and Wildlife Service has worked diligently at Muscatatuck to convert farmland to a mixed ecosystem of forest, aquatic, and grassland habitat. The proposed 3.9-mile hike encompasses five of the trails at Muscatatuck, an American Indian word meaning "land of winding water." Spring and fall may be the best times to see the migratory waterfowl as they travel between South America and northern Canada.

Route Details

After entering Muscatatuck National Wildlife Refuge, drive 0.4 mile to the Charles E. Scheffe Visitor Center. Start your visit by picking up some maps and learning more about the refuge. Big kids and small will enjoy the birding room, which has lots of hands-on displays, a bird window with one-way glass overlooking several feeders, a video describing Muscatatuck, and a small gift shop with an excellent selection of books.

Before the 19th century, this region was primarily swamp forest that frequently flooded. By the 20th century, however, most of this land had been clear-cut and drained for agricultural purposes. The U.S. Fish and Wildlife Service now uses a sophisticated system of pipes and pumps to keep water flowing in and out of the refuge, creating a natural wetlands for the roughly 15,000 migrants who pass this way. Muscatatuck can be a civil engineer's dream or nightmare, depending on the weather.

The migratory waterfowl residing at the refuge include wood ducks, mallards, northern shovelers, and hooded mergansers. Along the fencerows and open meadows, indigo buntings, American redstarts, and Baltimore orioles are frequently seen. In 1998, trumpeter swans were introduced to the refuge; more-recent visitors include sandhill cranes. These cranes, with their flamboyant courtship rituals, are among the largest birds on earth and usually arrive at the refuge in late October and again in March. Call 812-522-4352 to find out if the cranes are present.

A careful examination of the hiking brochure indicates eight trails in the refuge. However, the two longest, the East River Trail and the West River Trail, were recently closed due to persistent flooding and, for safety's sake, are not expected to reopen. The following description covers five of the remaining open trails, presented in the order in which visitors would normally drive through the refuge.

Chestnut Ridge Trail *(0.4-mile loop; 15 minutes hiking time; N38° 57.578' W85° 47.922')*

This paved trail starts directly behind the visitor center and has a small interpretive pamphlet available. Benches provide a nice respite if the insects aren't too aggressive.

After your walk, drive south on the main road (County Road 1000W) and turn right (west) on the one-way gravel road (CR 500N) just across from Richart Lake. Park signs then direct you left (south) on CR 1225E and left again (east) on CR 400N. Multiple turnouts are available for parking and viewing the waterfowl. (*Note:* The county roads listed here and following aren't marked on the refuge map, nor are they marked on the roads themselves, but I've marked them on our trail map for navigational purposes.) The parking lot for your next hike is on your left, just north of CR 400N.

Turkey Trail and Bird Trail *(1.9-mile figure-eight; 40 minutes hiking time; N38° 56.438' W85° 48.123')*

These two trails, just east of Storm Creek, are accessed from the southern parking area, as indicated on our trail map. The eastern parking lot is no longer open (and thus isn't shown on the map), so if you want to hike Bird Trail, you have to hike Turkey Trail first.

Start at the Turkey Trailhead and walk counterclockwise (heading right, or northeast). You'll immediately notice huge sassafras trees on both sides of the trail. With the noisy gravel underfoot, you'll likely scare off the deer that abound here before you can see them. Shortly you'll come to a small pond, edged with large bald cypress, their skinned knees protruding from the ground and water. Just past the pond, Turkey Trail joins Bird Trail. Continue straight (west) until Bird Trail departs north. Follow the Bird Trail loop clockwise until it rejoins Turkey Trail. You can then follow the western half of Turkey Trail through sycamores, sweetgums, poplars, and oaks.

After your hike, continue driving on the gravel road a few yards until it intersects the main road. Turn right (south) on CR 1300E, toward the Myers homestead.

Side Trip: Myers Cabin and Barn
(Just a short stroll and a few minutes back in time)

The Myers cabin was built between 1880 and 1885 by Louis Myers and his family of seven, using beech logs harvested off the land. The first floor includes a living area and the parents' bedroom. A summer kitchen was set up on the back porch. The five kids slept upstairs unless it was too hot, in which case they slept outside. Louis's wife, Nancy, lived here until she died in 1948.

The barn is built of poplar logs held together with wooden pegs. One of the Myers sons became a nurseryman and planted the seedless hybrid persimmon trees growing across the road from the cabin. Fall visitors will enjoy the juicy fruit and a taste of yesteryear.

After exploring, drive the main road (CR 1300E, which becomes CR 1000W) back north to the Wood Duck Trail, just north of Stanfield Lake. The parking lot will be just east of the road, on your right.

Wood Duck Trail
(0.5-mile balloon; 15 minutes hiking time;
N38° 56.416' W85° 47.874')

Perhaps the prettiest wooded path in the refuge, this small loop can be walked clockwise or counterclockwise. Interpretive signs identify pawpaw, swamp chestnut oak, a truly magnificent white oak, and many other native species. Some of the larger beech trees are used as nesting spots by wood ducks.

To reach the final hike, drive north on the main refuge road until you see the trailhead, just south of Richart Lake.

Richart Lake Trail   *(0.9-mile loop; 20 minutes hiking time; N38° 57.054' W85° 47.794')*

Yet another loop, this trail can be hiked two ways, but many hikers like to save the best for last. So head out counterclockwise and circumvent the large meadow. Once lakeside, turn left (west) to get to the Hackman Overlook. The views of Richart Lake are lovely, and many shorebirds can be seen wading in the shallows.

Nearby Attractions

On your way home, stop by the **Freeman Army Airfield Museum** in Seymour. Focusing on World War II aircraft, the airfield once served as a training ground for the Tuskegee Airmen. See **freemanfield.org /images/data/museum.htm** for hours and other details.

Directions

From downtown Louisville, take I-65 North across the Ohio River into southern Indiana and drive 50 miles. At Exit 50A, turn right (east) on US 50 toward North Vernon. The main entrance to Muscatatuck Wildlife Refuge will be 2.6 miles ahead on your right, just south of US 50.

36

Pennywort Cliffs

SCENERY: ★ ★ ★ ★
TRAIL CONDITION: ★ ★
CHILDREN: ★ ★ ★
DIFFICULTY: ★ ★ ★
SOLITUDE: ★ ★ ★ ★ ★

PAWPAW TREES, ALSO KNOWN AS "POOR MAN'S BANANA," GROW AT PENNYWORT CLIFFS.

GPS TRAILHEAD COORDINATES: N38° 49.054' W85° 32.224'

DISTANCE & CONFIGURATION: 3.5-mile "starfish loop"

HIKING TIME: 1.5 hours

HIGHLIGHTS: Solitude, the elusive pennywort, spring wildflowers, and a small waterfall

ELEVATION: 702' at trailhead, ascending to 755' at high point

ACCESS: Daily, sunrise–sunset; free admission

MAPS: None

FACILITIES: None

WHEELCHAIR ACCESS: None

COMMENTS: Dogs welcome if leashed and kept on-trail. Wetlands serve as primo mosquito breeding grounds late spring and summer—you may prefer to avoid those times of year.

CONTACTS: The Nature Conservancy, Indiana Field Office, 317-951-8818; **tinyurl.com/pennywortcliffs**

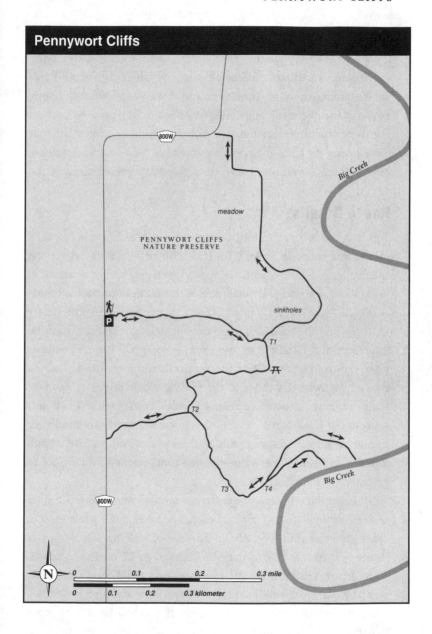

Pennywort Cliffs

800W

Big Creek

meadow

PENNYWORT CLIFFS
NATURE PRESERVE

sinkholes

T1

T2

T3   T4

Big Creek

800W

N

| 0 | | 0.1 | | 0.2 | | 0.3 mile |

| 0 | 0.1 | 0.2 | 0.3 kilometer |

Overview

If solitude is what you want, Pennywort Cliffs Nature Preserve delivers. Its unmarked trails follow old roadbeds through mature hardwoods, linking the hardy hiker to meadows, small sinkholes, bubbling streams, and eventually Big Creek. At 216 acres, the preserve is small but designed to protect the rare pennywort, an aquatic plant that grows along the cliffs and springs in the area. A 30-foot waterfall lies off-trail; access is recommended through official guided hikes.

Route Details

This is a hike where you might want to bring breadcrumbs or a GPS unit to find your way around. The trail configuration is best described as a five-legged starfish, with one appendage trying to regenerate itself. Bring along a friend and you'll double the number of people hiking here on any given day. It's nice to know that places like this still exist.

To find the trailhead(s), check your mileage carefully from the intersection of IN 250 East and County Road 800 West. From this intersection, it's 0.9 mile to the first trail-access point, basically a mowed pathway; 1.4 miles to the middle access point, or primary trailhead; and a little more than 1.5 miles to the last access point, near an old black barn. The trail described begins at the middle, or primary trailhead. You can park on the shoulder of the road or pull into the small entrance, where there's room for one full-size SUV or perhaps two Mini Coopers.

From the trailhead, the path runs straight ahead (directly east) under a canopy of tulip poplar, beech, and sweetgum, while ground cedar grows at your feet. About 0.3 mile of walking will bring you to the first of many Ts in the trail (marked as T1 on the accompanying map). Bear slightly left (northeast) at the T, and work your way past two small sinkholes (also on your left) and up a gentle hill. Wild turkeys love this place, and quiet hikers will be able to identify the distinctive yelping and clucking of the hens. The trail then passes through a small pine grove populated with young oaks and poplars before following the eastern edge of a meadow. In the fall, this meadow is beautifully anointed with yellow goldenrod, purple ageratum, and white snakeroot.

To digress a bit: White snakeroot is quite toxic. If eaten by cattle, the poison (tremetol) is passed to humans through the consumption of meat and milk, causing a condition known as milk sickness. Nancy Hanks Lincoln (mother of Abraham) is believed to have died of the illness. Impress your friends with this piece of toxicological trivia the next time you pass this way.

The meadow portion of the trail ends at CR 800 West (the first trail-access point identified previously). Take a look around and head back the way you came, just past the two small sinkholes, to T1. Back at the intersection, bear left (south) on the trail.

After a few minutes of walking, you'll see an old picnic table on your left (east of the trail). Have a seat and just soak up the stillness. In time you might notice the small monument to Mary G. Clashman, who gave this property to The Nature Conservancy in 2002. Close by you'll spot another small marker with dog tags on a chain collar— Mary was also the founder of the nonprofit Jefferson County Animal Welfare Fund in Madison. What curiosities the forest holds.

Continuing down the same path, bear right (west) at the next intersection (T2 on the map). This section of the trail holds some of the largest beech trees known to humankind. The trail also leads you to CR 800 West (the last trail-access point noted above). Once you've reached the road, backtrack to T2. Turn right (south) at T2 to walk toward T3. Although the trail appears to go straight, instead head left (east) at T3 to reach T4. Look carefully and you'll notice hanging from a branch a small strip of yellow plastic tape that confirms which trail to take.

At T4, you'll find yourself atop a small ridge. The right branch follows a narrow ridgetop. Here the path gets lost among other animal trails, but keep heading down the spiny ridge and it will take you to Big Creek. In late summer, look for the small, round, shiny leaves and delicate white blooms of pennywort along the limestone cliffs bordering the creek.

Alternately, at T4 you can bear left on an old roadbed. Walk as far as you can, until deadfall blocks your path and another strip of yellow plastic tape flags a small trail leading to a creek and a 12-foot waterfall. From here you can continue down the roadbed and cross the tributary for additional scenic views of Big Creek. In the spring this entire area is flush with wildflowers, including jack-in-the-pulpit, Virginia bluebell, wild ginger, and wood anemone.

You've now seen most of what Pennywort Cliffs has to offer when it comes to trails. Occasionally authorized guides lead trips to Pennywort, promising more views of the secrets the preserve quietly protects. Contact the Indiana Field Office of The Nature Conservancy (see "Contacts," page 244) for more information on guided walks.

Nearby Attractions

As you leave the preserve, drive north again on CR 800 West and turn east on IN 250. In 0.7 mile you'll pass back through the village of Lancaster and the site of **Eleutherian College.** The abolitionist Baptists who founded this school in 1848 envisioned a utopian society in which education and the arts would be available to all, regardless of gender or race. The magnificent stone school building was completed in 1856. Nearby is the **Lyman Hoyt House,** whose owner was a well-known conductor for the Underground Railroad. To set up a tour of either site, call 812-866-7291 or e-mail **eleutheriancollege2012@hotmail.com;** for additional information, visit **eleutheriancollege.org.**

Directions

From downtown Louisville, take I-65 North across the Ohio River into southern Indiana. Drive 30 miles. At Scottsburg, take Exit 29 right (east) on IN 56 and drive 7 miles until IN 56 merges with IN 3, bearing left (north). Drive another 9 miles on IN 3; just before you reach the small town of Paris Crossing, turn right (east) on IN 250 and drive 6 miles. Turn right (south) on County Road 800 West. Drive 1.4 miles to the primary trailhead, which will be on the left (east) side of the road.

Rose Island Loops

SCENERY: ★ ★ ★
TRAIL CONDITION: ★ ★ ★ ★ ★
CHILDREN: ★ ★ ★
DIFFICULTY: ★ ★ ★
SOLITUDE: ★ ★ ★

A COMMANDING VIEW OF FOURTEENMILE CREEK FROM ATOP THE PORTERSVILLE BRIDGE

GPS TRAILHEAD COORDINATES: N38° 25.638' W85° 37.777'

DISTANCE & CONFIGURATION: 5-mile double loop

HIKING TIME: 2 hours

HIGHLIGHTS: Multiple creek views, historic bridge, spring wildflowers

ELEVATION: 661' at trailhead, descending to 427' at low point

ACCESS: Daily (including holidays), 7 a.m.–sunset. Entrance fee: $5/vehicle for Indiana residents, $7/vehicle out-of-state. Annual permits also available (see **in.gov/dnr/parklake /5062.htm**).

MAPS: Charlestown State Park, USGS *Charlestown*

FACILITIES: Restrooms, picnic tables, water, and campsites in the park; no facilities at the trailhead

WHEELCHAIR ACCESS: Short paved section at the trailhead

COMMENTS: Pets must be leashed. Guided wildflower walks are advertised locally.

CONTACTS: Charlestown State Park, 812-256-5600; **in.gov/dnr/parklake/2986.htm**

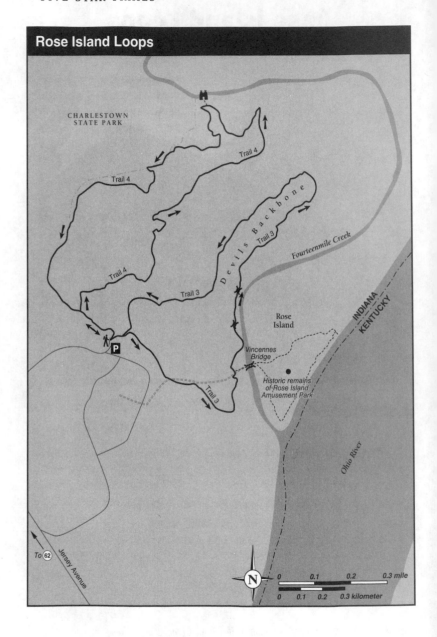

Rose Island Loops

CHARLESTOWN STATE PARK

Trail 4

Trail 4

Trail 4

Trail 4

D e v i l s   B a c k b o n e

Trail 3

Trail 3

Fourteenmile Creek

Trail 3

Rose Island

Vincennes Bridge

Historic remains of Rose Island Amusement Park

Trail 3

INDIANA
KENTUCKY

Ohio River

To 62

Jersey Avenue

P

N

0   0.1   0.2   0.3 mile

0   0.1   0.2   0.3 kilometer

Overview

The Rose Island Loops nestle along Fourteenmile Creek in Charlestown State Park, an easy 20 miles north of downtown Louisville. Sharing the same trailhead, each loop passes through a small meadow before descending to the creek and back up again. In the spring, Fourteenmile Creek and adjacent tributaries yield spectacular waterside wildflower displays that include wild geranium, trillium, bluebells, bloodroot, and many rare species found only here.

The hike also provides close-up views of Devonian fossil outcroppings and several examples of karst-sinkhole geology. A short hike across a restored bridge leads to the remains of the historic Rose Island Amusement Park, where Fourteenmile Creek flows into the Ohio River.

Route Details

Established in 1996, Charlestown State Park originally was part of the Indiana Armory Ammunition Plant (INAAP). Subsequent land donations from the INAAP have allowed the park to grow to more

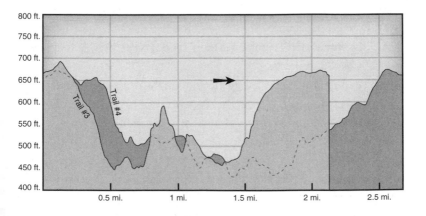

than 5,100 acres, making it the third-largest state park in Indiana. Improvements include the building of trails, picnic areas, a campground, and a boat launch on the Ohio River.

The Rose Island Loops comprise Trails 3 and 4, which share a trailhead and parking area just east of the main park road. At the far end of the lot, a small kiosk displays a trail map (none for the taking) and several old photos of Rose Island Amusement Park. Beyond the gate, the paved road signals the start of both loops.

To hike Trail 3 counterclockwise, follow the paved road, which begins northeast of the lot, about 0.3 mile toward Fourteenmile Creek. The road quickly descends among towering yellow poplars, sycamores, and maples. Soon the beautifully restored 1912 Vincennes Bridge spanning the creek comes into view. At this point, the trail leaves the road and heads north into a forest of deciduous hardwoods. Turn left (north) just before the bridge to follow the trail along Fourteenmile Creek.

After crossing two small footbridges, the trail continues along the bottomland as the main creek disappears from view. Up along the small ridge to your left (west), a string of low rocky outcroppings will appear. Known as Devils Backbone, this ridge was most likely formed by the combined effects of glaciation and erosion as Fourteenmile Creek flowed into the Ohio River. With perhaps less scientific rigor yet more colorful appeal, local legend has it that the ridge was once part of a stone fortress built by Prince Madoc and early Welsh explorers in the 12th century.

As the trail makes a U-turn from northeast to southwest, the moss-covered rocks of Devils Backbone will stay on your left as you steadily ascend out of the creek drainage. The trail tops out with a distant view of the southern banks of the Ohio River. A short (0.2-mile) walk through a transition meadow of grasses and red cedars brings you back to the blacktop road. Turn right (southwest) to find the start of Trail 4.

This second Rose Island Loop begins a few yards north of the trailhead parking lot. To hike the loop counterclockwise, turn right (northeast) at the beginning of the Trail 4 loop for the best creek views. The trail traverses a flat half-mile of transitional meadow (again, primarily grasses and cedar thickets) before descending into a deciduous hardwood forest of hickories, maples, and beeches draped with ancient grapevines. If you've brought kids along, try to keep a straight face and tell them this is where the *Tarzan* movies were filmed.

A little more than a mile from the trailhead, a small spur appears on your right (just north of the trail), providing an overlook of Fourteenmile Creek. The trail then meanders along several smaller tributaries. Spring hikers will love the sound of rushing water and the spectacle of blooming wildflowers. (All the intertwining tree trunks might have you humming "Love Shack," especially if you're familiar with the accompanying video, which starts out with the B-52's driving through the forest in a Chrysler "that's as big as a whale.") From here the trail ascends once again, back through the same transitional meadow. Turn right (south) on the blacktop road to get back to the parking lot.

If you still have some energy after hiking the Rose Island Loops, take a short jaunt to the remains of the historic Rose Island Amusement Park. Technically not an island but a spit of land formed by the junction of Fourteenmile Creek and the Ohio River, the trail begins just across the restored Vincennes Bridge. Charlestown State Park finished renovating the bridge and opened a rough 0.75-mile loop trail around the property in 2011. Interestingly, the 1912 bridge was not original to the site, but rather replaced a swinging bridge once used by visitors to the amusement park.

In 1923, local businessman David B. G. Rose purchased the park, originally called Fern Grove and built around 1880. He immediately launched a series of improvements, including a swimming pool, a roller coaster, a merry-go-round, an ice plant, and an alligator pit. Pony rides cost a nickel. Visitors could arrive aboard the steamboat *Idlewild* (now the *Belle of Louisville*) from the Kentucky side of the river, while Hoosiers arrived via the suspension toll bridge. The hiking trail takes you along the river to the original steamboat landing, where three stone pillars remain, and the old swimming pool, which would now be eerily at home in a horror movie.

After Mr. Rose sank his heart and $250,000 of his cash into Rose Island, he managed to keep it afloat throughout the Great Depression. But it was the Great Flood of 1937 that did in the amusement park, inundating it with 10 feet of water. The damage was so devastating that Rose Island never reopened.

Nearby Attractions

Next to the new boat launch, **Trail 6** takes hikers on a 2.3-mile loop atop a bluff overlooking the Ohio River and Twelvemile Island. The trailhead is across the road from the Riverside Overlook, at the far southern edge of the park. The trail crosses a small footbridge over a waterfall before descending to the bluff bottom. The wildflowers here rival those along the Rose Island Loops.

If you happen to be hiking on a Sunday from April through October and you want to grab some brunch first, drive an additional 11 miles north on IN 62 East to New Washington. Turn right on Main Street to find **A Step Back** (409 E. Main St.; 812-293-BACK (2225) or 293-4395; **astepback.net**). Operating out of a historic two-story brick schoolhouse, the restaurant serves a huge spread of comfort food from 11 a.m. until 3 p.m. A free museum upstairs showcases, among other things, an authentic Conestoga covered wagon from the early 1800s, a rope bed, and an antique washing machine. The walls of the school are four bricks thick, and the windows hold their original fish-eye glass.

Directions

From downtown Louisville, take I-65 North across the Ohio River into southern Indiana. After 6.7 miles, take Exit 6A to merge onto I-265 East, toward Clark Maritime Center. Shortly before I-265 ends (after about 3 miles), exit on IN 62 East, heading right (northeast). Charlestown State Park will be 8.5 miles ahead, on your right.

Appendixes & Index

CANADA GEESE AND OTHER WATERFOWL ARE PLENTIFUL AT VERSAILLES LAKE.
(See Hike 33, Bridges of Versailles, page 226.)

Appendix A:
Outdoor Retailers

Bass Pro Shops
basspro.com

RIVER FALLS MALL
951 E. Lewis and Clark Parkway
Clarksville, IN 47129
812-218-5500

Cabela's
cabelas.com

OLD BROWNSBORO CROSSING
(opens spring 2013)
9607 Old Brownsboro Road
Louisville, KY 40207

Dick's Sporting Goods
dickssportinggoods.com

OXMOOR CENTER
7900 Shelbyville Road
Louisville, KY 40222
502-420-6400

RIVER FALLS MALL
951 E. Lewis and Clark Parkway
Clarksville, IN 47129
812-288-2194

SPRINGHURST TOWN CENTER
3555 Springhurst Blvd.
Louisville, KY 40241
502-429-0776

STONEYBROOK SHOPPING CENTER
3500 S. Hurstbourne Parkway
Louisville, KY 40299
502-499-9029

Quest Outdoors
questoutdoors.com

CLIFTON
2330 Frankfort Ave.
Louisville, KY 40206
502-893-5746

ST. MATTHEWS
4600 Shelbyville Road
Louisville, KY 40207
502-290-4589

THE SUMMIT
4340 Summit Plaza Drive
Louisville, KY 40241
502-326-0424

River City Canoe & Kayak
814 Cherokee Road
Louisville, KY 40204
502-384-3737
rcckonline.com

Appendix B:
Hiking Clubs

Kentucky & Indiana Single Hikers and Walkers
tinyurl.com/kishaw

Louisville Hiking Meetup
www.louisvillehikingmeetup.com

Orienteering and Adventure Racing Louisville
meetup.com/orienteering-louisville

Outdoor Women of Louisville
meetup.com/outdoorwomenoflouisville

Sierra Club, Greater Louisville Group
P.O. Box 415
Floyds Knobs, IN 47119
louisville.sierraclub.org

Appendix C:
Public and Private Agencies

Frederick Law Olmsted Parks
502-456-8125
olmstedparks.org

Indiana Division of Nature Preserves
317-232-4200
in.gov/dnr/naturepreserve

Indiana Division of State Parks and Reservoirs
317-232-4200
in.gov/dnr/parklake

Kentucky State Nature Preserves Commission
502-573-2886
naturepreserves.ky.gov

Kentucky State Parks
800-255-PARK (7275)
parks.ky.gov

Louisville Metro Parks
502-456-8100
louisvilleky.gov/metroparks

The Nature Conservancy
800-628-6860
nature.org

21st Century Parks
502-584-0350
21cparks.org

Index

About the Author

Photo: Emma Askren

After having spent more than 20 years as a university researcher and professor, **Valerie Askren** traded the ivory towers of academia for the hardwood forests and sandstone arches of Kentucky. The proverbial outdoorswoman, she has swum in Africa's Lake Malawi, climbed China's Mount Tai, sailed the coast of southern France, biked Nova Scotia, backpacked across Canada, and survived the biting cold of farm life in the Ukraine. She spent her honeymoon kayaking the Grand Canyon with her husband, Ben.

Valerie's background in natural-resource economics and her love of the outdoors have translated into a second career in writing hiking guides. Her busy life—she's not only a writer and adventurer but a mother of four—inspired her personal manifesto: "Think global, hike local." Valerie lives in Lexington, Kentucky, where a peaceful wooded path, beautiful public garden, or historical walking trail is always close at hand.

DEAR CUSTOMERS AND FRIENDS,

SUPPORTING YOUR INTEREST IN OUTDOOR ADVENTURE, travel, and an active lifestyle is central to our operations, from the authors we choose to the locations we detail to the way we design our books. Menasha Ridge Press was incorporated in 1982 by a group of veteran outdoorsmen and professional outfitters. For many years now, we've specialized in creating books that benefit the outdoors enthusiast.

Almost immediately, Menasha Ridge Press earned a reputation for revolutionizing outdoors- and travel-guidebook publishing. For such activities as canoeing, kayaking, hiking, backpacking, and mountain biking, we established new standards of quality that transformed the whole genre, resulting in outdoor-recreation guides of great sophistication and solid content. Menasha Ridge continues to be outdoor publishing's greatest innovator.

The folks at Menasha Ridge Press are as at home on a white-water river or mountain trail as they are editing a manuscript. The books we build for you are the best they can be, because we're responding to your needs. Plus, we use and depend on them ourselves.

We look forward to seeing you on the river or the trail. If you'd like to contact us directly, join in at www.trekalong.com or visit us at www.menasharidge.com. We thank you for your interest in our books and the natural world around us all.

SAFE TRAVELS,

Bob Sehlinger

BOB SEHLINGER
PUBLISHER